Activities
for
Personal Growth

*A Comprehensive Handbook of Activities
for Therapists*

Sheelagh Leary

MACLENNAN + PETTY
SYDNEY • PHILADELPHIA • LONDON

First published 1994

MacLennan & Petty Pty Limited
80 Reserve Road, Artarmon NSW 2064 Australia

© 1994 MacLennan & Petty Pty Limited

National Library of Australia
Cataloguing-in-Publication data:
Leary, Sheelagh
Activities for Personal Growth
Bibliography
Includes index
ISBN 0 86433 076 6
1. Occupational therapy.
2. Self-actualization (Psychology) — Study and teaching.
3. Interpersonal communication — Study and teaching.
4. Relaxation — Study and teaching.
5. Arts — Therapeutic use.   I. Title.
615.8515

Printed and bound in Australia

Dedication

Dedicated to my colleagues at the New Zealand School of Occupational Therapy. Thank you for your generous help and for your friendship, support and stimulation over many years.

Thank you

It is a pleasure to acknowledge the financial support given to me by the New Zealand Accident Compensation Corporation and the MacKenzie Educational Foundation to begin this book. Their support gave me the time to write and their confidence in the project was invaluable in the early stages of defining the book.

Contents

Introduction

Personal growth depends on life skills; understanding oneself, being able to communicate with others and being able to cope with stress. This practical book about generating life skills describes self-awareness activities, using the creative arts for self-expression, communication skills and relaxation. It offers abundant activities that can be used within the constraints of therapeutic sessions.

The first part of the book gives the activities. Each chapter describes a different kind of activity; what it has to offer, the demands it makes, its natural and therapeutic limitations and the skills it can be used to develop.

It begins with self-awareness activities. Self-awareness is a starting platform, a means of developing a sense of direction and increasing motivation. Self-awareness activities focus on self-image. They prompt people to examine their values and the choices open to them. They can sharpen and shape people's perceptions more effectively than talking and thinking.

The creative arts — drama, art, music, dance, creative writing and verbal activities — offer ways of expressing oneself. Values are examined and feelings and ideas grappled with.

Communication skills is divided into social skills and assertiveness skills. Social skills courses teach people what to say and how to say it. This chapter describes what to include and offers activities to make the learning effective and pleasurable. Assertiveness courses are more advanced than social skills. They focus on clear, direct communication and respect for others' feelings.

The final chapter in this section is on relaxation. This chapter discusses managing stress using stress management techniques, mental techniques and physical techniques, including massage.

Together these arts and life skills can be a route to personal growth and development. As well, they are fun, sociable and enriching.

The second part of the book describes how to manage and lead groups, how to create and use therapeutic opportunities, and how to teach effectively and get the most out of activities. It also covers the practical aspects of organizing a group session. These chapters are a good reference source for students seeking to understand the use of activities as therapy.

The activities and therapeutic rationale in *Activities for Personal Growth* are relevant to settings in which people are establishing or reestablishing their identities, getting to grips with, or rebuilding their lives.

The straightforward text makes it easy for therapists to explain both the activities and their values to people.

Many of the activities here are old favourites, some were shown to me by my students and others are new. The instructions are comprehensive without being rigid. Use them as starting points to create programmes for the people you work with.

PART I
The Activities

1 | *Activities as Therapy*

Activities   Activities are the essence of human existence. Through activity people establish their values and goals. Activity-based programmes have a role in all levels of health care; promoting wellness and personal growth, preventing health problems, meeting health needs, in rehabilitation, and in maintaining abilities and management. At most levels they can play a part in helping people find new directions for their lives.

Activities used to promote insight, personal growth, stress management and communication skills are planned with the patient/client if at all possible. When this is unrealistic, what is known of their values, interests and abilities are the basis of the therapist's planning. The activities must fit who the person was and is. They must involve the person and be accurately pitched at a level of challenge that extends them without being discouraging. Ideally, they should generate a sense of control and competence. And they should be enjoyable and interesting. Their relevance should be made obvious.

Social values govern people's perceptions of activities and what they see as worthwhile. The activities used in therapeutic settings should be versatile enough to appeal to a range of people and they should be easy to adapt to meet a range of needs.

Activities should be offered in a setting where people feel safe to try new things, where there is protection from failure and the support of others.

Accomplishment and the experience of empathy with others build self-esteem, the foundation needed for growth and the possibility of making the most of skills and opportunities.

In addition, activities are valuable in assessment of people's problems, needs and resources. They can provide concrete evidence of therapeutic progress and outcomes.

People   Occupational therapists are concerned with the way people function. What do they want, and need, to be able to do? People have the right to make their own decisions and to be responsible for their lives. Most are able to change. Therapists support people's strengths, value their experiences and beliefs and respect their choices. Increasing people's autonomy is nearly always a goal of therapy. Most problems cause some dependence, at least initially, but dependence, as a stage of acute health care, should be as brief as possible.

Inevitably, the decisions people make are influenced by age, gender, culture or disability. To change, they need information about their choices, resources for learning new skills, a supportive environment in the widest sense and sometimes a catalyst to start the process.

Healthy people lead balanced lives. Levels of work, rest and recreation are in harmony. When there is no balance in someone's life, or it is disrupted, the therapist works with the person to help restore or establish it. Every part of human function is connected, and problems or gains in one area will always have some impact on other areas.

Therapists Therapists should go beyond the treatment of immediate health problems and aim for as high a quality of wellbeing as possible. Health is both the absence of dysfunction and a positive state of wellbeing. Therapists must understand people and how they function. Knowledge of medical conditions and the problems that are likely to result from them is part of this. The social pressures and problems associated with disability, illness, loss and the effects of stress and the relationship of dysfunction to age, cultural expectations, personal values, emotional state and so on are significant. These factors will be the constraints, limitations and assets in the therapeutic situation, the things that reduce or maintain motivation.

Therapists are teachers, consultants and role models. As teachers they explain concepts, coach people in the skills they need, encourage them through effective praise and feedback and make use of group processes. As consultants they help others make their plans work. As role models they have a responsibility to show acceptable social attitudes, sound work skills, appropriate behaviour, good time management and a willingness to share themselves with others. At each stage they encourage the smallest glimmer of motivation as a starting point for change.

Therapists need to be able to use themselves in relationships as part of managing the treatment environment. Using oneself includes knowing when to be directive in the hope that information, activities and support will generate a response in people; when to be supportive; when to back away and let people try something on their own; and how to be a sounding board for people to discuss their concerns, abilities and goals. The relationship may be directive, supportive, didactic or one of a number of other possibilities. Skill in observation will guide the therapist's approach.

As people, therapists need to be interested in others and empathetic, but unpossessive. They must be aware of their own strengths and limitations. The capacity to be outward looking and sensibly optimistic is important. Valuing practical action and understanding the potential of activity and creativity in health care is central. They must feel that their goals in therapy are worthwhile and achievable.

In a treatment relationship the therapist attempts to interrupt cycles of negative reaction, build up self-esteem through successful experiences and build on existing values and goals or develop new ones. He or she works to motivate people to make adaptive, positive responses.

Motivation   Motivation is the set of impulses, based on innate tendencies and developed values and goals, that leads people to action. Essentially, it is the decision to act.

Motivation depends on feeling able to succeed — on having a positive self-image. If someone's self-image is poor, their willingness to try new activities will be low. When people's lives are disrupted their self-image often changes. Valued goals are no longer realistic and habit patterns are upset.

Motivation is not fixed. It is in continual flux between hope and reality. It is affected by the ups and downs of life. People are affected by disruption in different ways — they may feel challenged or helpless to influence what happens to them. Secondary gains from a problem, such as sympathy and assistance, may interfere with motivation too. Depression, a feature of many illnesses, also leads to reduced motivation.

Other things which reduce motivation are denial of problems, pain or fear of pain and negative defence mechanisms. Extraneous factors may play a part. People may be inhibited by their perception of what activities are appropriate for them, cost, transport, others' comments and so on.

For some, the task is to develop goals. Others need to explore their values and get a better perspective on their choices. The therapist offers such people activities which will help them to clarify their goals, give them practice in making choices and add to their skills. In adulthood, values, goals and interests do change and develop but the process is usually gradual.

At one extreme are people who are very dependent and must be directed every step of the way if they are to do anything. The therapist will reinforce any appropriate goals people have. Extrinsic factors like praise, clear feedback, novelty, others' expectations, persuasion, reward, confrontation and competition all have a place. Therapists manipulate the environment, in the widest sense, to increase people's motivation.

Some people are already self-directed and can plan their own activities. They use the therapist as a resource and a sounding board. The therapist helps them to identify the barriers between themselves and their goals, and to work out how these barriers can be overcome.

Motivation is the key to therapy; without it nothing happens. In practical terms, people's motivation is seen in the choices they make. Nearly all activities involve choices, and this can be used by the therapist. Motivation leads to creativity, thus allowing new insights and new ideas to occur.

When people feel secure and respected, they are able to look at a wide range of elements in a situation and use them to solve problems in a creative way.

The creative process The creative process begins with awareness of a problem or dilemma, or a sense of lacking direction. During this phase people alternately concentrate on the problem and give up. When a solution is found there is a sense of insight and relief, and work on the task, mental and physical, continues with relaxed concentration. The person knows what they want and how to go about getting it. The process of testing and evaluating solutions continues throughout life. If people fail to reach this point of solution and give up, they are left in a state of tension or apathy.

Sometimes the creative process is very quick. At other times the process is more prolonged and obvious. The creative process generates new ways of thinking and acting. Wellness and autonomy are its products.

2 | *Self-awareness Activities*

Self-awareness activities focus on self-image, that is, the inner concept people have of who they are. On the basis of self-image people decide what to do and say — and everything they do gives them some information, or confirmation, about who they are. The effect is cyclic: self-image influences behaviour which alters self-image and so on. Usually, self-image alters only very gradually. Exceptions to this are in childhood, when it is being established, and at times of life changes, such as starting a career, marriage or major illness.

The Theory

People's self-image is often inaccurate, unrealistically negative or out-of-date. Sometimes, for example, abilities develop but the image of self as a fumbling beginner is retained. To solve their problems people need an up-to-date, positive self-image. Working from the basis of who you were rather than who you are limits development but it is often difficult to leave behind a crippling self-image and build one which is realistic and positive.

Self-awareness activities are designed to help people understand themselves and how they think about themselves. With a new perspective people can explain themselves more easily to others and see their choices in life more clearly. In the long term, greater self-knowledge can lead to improved performance and increased competence in a variety of life skills. When people know what they need to change and are motivated to make the changes progress will be more rapid. However, self-awareness is insufficient as a goal in itself. It is only a means or tool for developing a sense of direction and increasing motivation.

Some people use thinking and talking as a way of avoiding painful feelings, griefs or weaknesses. Thinking and talking act as a protective denial. This denial can be gently confronted through activities. For others, 'doing and sharing' are easier than talking. This usually applies to people who lack confidence in their verbal skills, are depressed or have difficulty thinking clearly.

Activities from the creative therapies can sharpen and shape people's perceptions more effectively than thinking and talking. They make self-

7

image more visible, pushing people to examine issues that are important to them. Discussion as a way of increasing self-awareness is the main technique used by health professionals such as psychologists and counsellors. In occupational therapy, the emphasis is on self-awareness through concrete activity.

Self-awareness activities also offer people opportunities to use communication skills, take a leadership role, make decisions, use memory, be a member of a cohesive group and be creative. Some activities call for quick thinking, others for touch — acceptable physical contact — between people.

What kinds of activities are used?   Activities designed to heighten self-awareness should be pleasurable in themselves, companionable and fun. They should make no demands to do or perform something to a certain standard. Generally, they will answer a question such as, 'Who am I?' or 'Where is my life going?' (This question may only be implied.) In common with games, such activities should encourage spontaneity and active engagement with other people. They should recognize and emphasize positive feelings and strengths and build on them. It often seems easier to see problems and overlook the positive, but people's strengths and positive feelings are the starting point for growth.

As well as specially designed activities, many activities such as household management tasks or craft activities can be used to increase insight. People always project something of themselves into what they do, and a therapist can, and often should, make use of this. For example, the therapist could discuss the way a task is done (neatness, ability to follow instructions) and what it indicates about the person's values, skills and valuation of themselves. (See *ART, The pragmatic approach: art as an analogy* p. 83 and *Art and assessment* p. 84 for more detailed discussion of this concept.)

The emphasis should be on practical one-off activities which show people aspects of themselves in a concrete way. This gives a starting point for problem solving.

Group work   Although self-awareness activities can be done on a one-to-one basis, it is more common to work in groups. The people most likely to benefit from awareness activities often have difficulty with interpersonal relationships, so a group provides just what is needed — a setting for practice and experiment in relating to others. A group also provides a varied pool of opinions and often the support of others with similar problems. A good level of trust within the group is important, as are back-up and support services.

In group work there is potential for fun and laughter — activities that are fun help people learn concepts and they are more likely to accept ideas from experiences they enjoy.

Levels of awareness activities   Awareness activities can be divided into three levels. At their most superficial level, they are 'games', which help people get to know each other and themselves. Many aim at building self-esteem.

Middle level activities show people their options in life or build self-esteem. They are insight-oriented and valuable when people are learning social skills or coping with a crisis in their lives. Middle level activities aim to be gentle, however the process may still be uncomfortable.

At the third level activities are in-depth and use more interpretation and direct confrontation. People are pushed to face the issues affecting them. A sensitive attitude of caring is essential or confrontation can lead to distress rather than growth. Overwhelming pain and grief will stall positive adjustment. As a general rule, if you think a person can do little about an issue avoid confrontation.

With in-depth activities, as well as seeing their situation more clearly, people need to recognize the skills they require to make changes in their lives or the circumstances they have to accept and live with.

In-depth activities often look back into people's lives for causes of problems; this is an analytical approach.

Therapists should plan the level they intend to use, although there will always be occasions when people sabotage the soundest planning and keep a group superficial or make it confrontative.

The level of a session will depend more on the way the therapist presents and uses the activities than on intrinsic characteristics of the activities themselves. (See *WORKING IN GROUPS*, *Emotional issues* p. 218 and *Depth of topics* p. 219. See *DRAMA*, *Confrontation* p. 39.)

Therapeutic Application

Awareness activities are most useful with people who are motivated to work on self growth and relationships. In general, they are useful with people who have emotional problems. Awareness activities are a means of finding new directions.

People with mild to moderate anxiety or depression Anxiety and depression, no matter what their cause, blinker perception and limit ideas about what is possible and realistic. At times of stress it is especially important for people to see all the possibilities, as well as the constraints, in their situation.

Age groups Adolescents and young adults are more likely to find awareness activities useful because their identity is still being formed.

People coping with life changes Awareness activities can be valuable when people are coping with a crisis or significant change in their lives. A person who is in a new life role, whether at work, as a family member, as the result of a disability or problem, needs to alter his or her self-image. Role changes can involve grieving for the loss of old roles and fear of facing new ones. When the qualities people value, such as physical attractiveness, strength and ability, are limited or gone, an important step towards making the most of existing capacities is to accept a new self-image. Self-image will change with both sudden and gradual increases in disability. Ideally, self-image remains realistic and positive but in reality adjustment to loss and grief is rarely a smooth journey. The aim is to help people recognize and accept situations of loss and become better able to use their remaining potential.

Alcohol and drug dependence   Awareness activities can help people confront the problems that initiated or maintain their dependence. Generally, a strong system of personal support needs to be built up in groups where substance abuse disorders are treated. Confrontation is actively used to start a process of change and growth in a supportive emotional environment. Part of the occupational therapist's role as a team member is to use activities as a means of increasing insight.

A change of attitude, a change of behaviour   Self-awareness activities will be of most benefit when they are used as a basis for change. The kinds of changes therapists look for are changes in both the attitudes which underpin people's behaviour and in the behaviours themselves, that is, the things people learn to say and do more comfortably or effectively.

As a starting point for learning practical skills, such as budgeting, for example, people first need to recognize that they have to learn new skills. An activity examining the practical, emotional and value-based reasons why a person spends money, gives the information required for working out a budget based on real needs.

Contraindications, Precautions and Limitations

Sometimes awareness activities do more harm than good. They are contraindicated in the following cases.

People who have difficulty thinking clearly   To profit from activities which focus on emotional insights, the nuances of relationships or identifying values, people must be able to think clearly.

Difficulties in thinking can be caused by:

- Delusional thinking, paranoid suspiciousness or grandiose ideas. (Thinking is very unrealistic.)
- Brain damage. Brain damage, from whatever cause, leads to confusion and a shortened concentration span. An awareness of what has been lost can be acute in spite of the brain damage.
- Certain medications. Medication can cause marked drowsiness or lack of concentration. Blurred vision and tremor induced by medication will affect some art and written activities.
- Hyperactiveness. People who are hyperactive cannot concentrate long enough to benefit from self-awareness activities.

- Depression or anxiety. When moderate to severe, depression or anxiety can slow thought processes down to the extent that activities requiring clear thinking are unrealistic.

Note that although higher level awareness activities are not recommended, all these groups of people may benefit from, and enjoy, the lightweight or esteem-building level of awareness activities.

People will sometimes be inappropriately referred to an awareness group. In such cases make something of their unrealistic ideas if possible, or thank them for their contribution and move on.

People who find close relationships threatening   This is often the case with people who have schizophrenia. When a therapist uses awareness activities that these people perceive as threatening, they may side-step the activity and work in a way that defeats the therapist's purpose. For example, they may give concrete information when an emotional response was asked for or they may become distressed.

Close relationships can also be threatening to people who have had painful relationships.

People with severe emotional problems   The treatment of an emotional problem may be beyond the skills of the therapist or the scope of the group session.

People with severe physical problems   Other treatments may take priority.

People who are terminally ill   Awareness activities are generally inappropriate for people who are terminally ill but activities with an esteem-building or reminiscence/life review perspective may be useful. Such activities may also help people plan how to use the time they have. People who are terminally ill should be offered support to find their own way of dealing with their situation.

People who are very young or elderly   Awareness activities are unsuitable for children because their values and concept of self are only partially formed. Some of the activities may appeal as games, and others can be useful to children facing emotional problems such as family breakdown or hospitalization. They can also be appropriately used to generate tolerance of others and to raise self-esteem. In general, however, children are better learning about themselves in the traditional way, through play and education. Awareness activities may thrust a child too rapidly towards concerns which belong to adolescence and young adulthood.

At the other end of life, in old age, awareness activities are again of limited value because self-concept is well established, consciously or unconsciously, and people are reluctant to alter their perceptions and develop new interpersonal skills. An example of a realistic goal for awareness activities in old age would be helping individuals or groups to adjust to changes in their lives such as health problems or bereavement. However, by the end of a lifetime most people have well established patterns of coping with stresses.

People who become addicted to awareness activities The pursuit of self-knowledge can become a goal in itself, rather than a means to an end. The person may become too introspective and find it difficult to move on and make use of the insight they have gained. They may not develop new skills or take on new roles. Help the person recognize what is happening, get them to set very small, manageable goals and give them as much support as possible to reach these goals.

Precaution Self-awareness activities can make people more aware of their weaknesses without providing support. They can remove coping mechanisms which, although limited, at least helped people manage their lives.

Avoid scheduling emotionally demanding activities when there is no time or staff available to follow up problems. If possible, use a co-leader.

It is important to consciously focus on building up people's self-esteem and making them aware of their choices, as well as on increasing insight. Provide opportunities to learn skills linked to the insights gained.

The Therapist's Role

If possible the therapist should take part in each activity in order to appreciate the group's experience.

To help people who are floundering you might say, 'I'll give you a hand to get started,' 'OK what are your choices?', 'That will be fine as a starting point.'

Practical Organization

The value of awareness activities depends very much on how they are organized and presented. The starting point is assessment.

Assessment In relation to awareness activities key questions for assessment are: In what ways are people's perceptions of themselves limited? What social/emotional needs do group members have in common? What are their common abilities? Can they share information about themselves? Think clearly? Read and write? Will they be comfortable speaking in a group? How much can they work on and at what level?

Practical matters Some of these activities can take as little as five minutes and others can be extended over several sessions. Most typically they will take fifteen to thirty minutes. The environment should be private. Art materials, pencils and paper, clay and musical instruments are needed for some activities.

While the ideal group size is small, it is possible to have groups of up to twenty. In larger groups you will only be able to have limited contact with some group members. However, activities will benefit people anyway if the concepts they are examining are relevant to their needs. Use pairs and small group activities to counteract the disadvantages of larger numbers.

Participation   Ideally, in awareness-oriented activities everyone should participate. If some people are passive observers, others will feel less happy about sharing their thoughts and feelings.

Sharing cannot be forced but ways to make it easier for people, and more likely to happen, can be built into managing the group. Groups should have four to eight members. Too few, and people are likely to feel threatened by having to take a major role; too many and some will not participate. If possible, make a rule that people stay for the whole session. The more in-depth the activity, the more important this is to the emotional security and morale of the group. Each person must be willing to share and listen, to give and receive support and to respect what other people say as confidential. (See *WORKING IN GROUPS* p. 203.)

Choosing activities   Which activities will people enjoy and find socially acceptable? What basic capacities do people need to participate?

Involve the group in the choice of topic and outline how each activity relates to it before describing the activity itself and how to do it.

Sometimes an activity can be done first and discussed later, at other times it can be left to speak for itself. This should be a deliberate choice; not just something that happens.

The chain of decisions starts with selecting the topic and the specific concepts or teaching points to be covered, then choosing a medium and the way it is to be presented and used.

Plan variety and balance into the programme. Mix doing and talking, energetic and quiet, lightweight and in-depth, whole group, pairs and individual activities. Consider how much choice you will give people in the media used and how structured to make the activity. Build time into the session for reflection. (See *WORKING IN GROUPS, The stages of a group session* p. 212.)

Medium and method choices   Drawing, painting, collage, clay and sculpture can be used (see *ART* p. 77).

Mime, drama, role play and dance can all be used to explore ideas and feelings (see *DRAMA* p. 36 and *DANCE* p. 100).

Creative writing takes many forms: free verse, letters, checklists, questionnaires (see *CREATIVE WRITING* p. 111).

Music can act as a memory trigger for past associations or be used to represent moods, things or people (see *MUSIC* p. 92).

Objects can be used in the same way as sounds — for their associations. They can stand symbolically for people or feelings and thus be used as a starting point for examining values, feelings and ideas.

Topic choices Many topics can also be themes that carry on over a number of sessions, the theme giving cohesion to a series of sessions. Once a theme has been chosen the next step is to find or adapt activities to suit it.

Some of the topics have a 'gimmick' approach to make them more interesting. Present them as novel ways of tackling a serious subject.

Most awareness topics examine identity or relationships. The focus may be on:

- A situation: 'At work', 'On holiday', 'At parties'.
- Time: 'When I was ten years old', 'Six months ago', 'Every Christmas', 'A time of choice — a life crossroad'.
- An emotion: coping with anger, grief, worry, loneliness, hope, a sense of loss.
- A role or relationship: marriage, being a boss, being a daughter-in-law, being a member of a religious or racial minority, friendship, being a workmate.

The Structure of a Session

Warm up Focus initially on helping people get to know one another on a conventional social level. Choose warm up activities that encourage conversation. Discussing everyday events is less threatening than discussing emotions and problems and it is surprising how quickly a group will move from this level of interaction to reaching out to help or be helped when they are in need and the group climate is right.

Warm up is particularly important in activities where people will look to each other for support (see *DRAMA, Warm-up activities* p. 54).

Presentation People's perceptions of an activity need to be considered when an activity is presented. It may be something 'normally' done by women, children or some other subgroup in society. When this is so, either acknowledge this probable view of the activity when it is introduced and ask people to be tolerant of the activity for its potential benefits — stress the value of expressing ideas, through concrete, visual methods. Or be matter-of-fact. Ignore the possible negative connotations of the activity. Begin with a definite instruction and a manner that shows you expect people to get on with it. For example, with art or written activities say, 'Show how you feel about . . .', 'Put down your ideas about . . .' Avoid the words 'draw' or 'write' which may inhibit people who feel they have few skills in these areas.

The end product is unimportant. The only thing that matters is that the person can understand what he or she has written, drawn and so on.

Introducing topics and activities Either describe the activity in simple steps or show how it is done with some explanation and tell people how long they have for the task. The introduction should be brief; it is important to get on with the activities themselves.

Present topics in a positive way. Emphasize finding ways forward and problem solving. When people are asked to put down negative feelings and problems avoid dwelling on them. Instead, start work on solutions, look at the positive balance, what people are managing. Find things to laugh about, admire and enjoy.

Use visual presentations as much as possible. Even if the visual material adds little information it is a focus for discussion and explanation. For example, if the topic choice is 'Handling anger', an illustration showing an angry person enlivens the words of the topic.

Discussion Each activity is usually rounded off with discussion in pairs, in small groups or with the whole group together. People may speak in turn or be encouraged to speak up, comment and question as they wish. Each choice has different implications from a therapeutic point of view. For example, if people are to speak in turn there is pressure on each to respond; it is difficult to 'pass'.

Seating arrangements also influence or dictate the style of the discussion; closeness, comfort and privacy are the main considerations here. Sometimes unusual arrangements can be tried — for example, everyone lying on their backs, heads in the centre, or sitting in pairs, back to back, eyes closed, holding hands.

Discussion can cover the usefulness, limitations and personal application of the activity. What information has been acquired? How will it be used? How might it be relevant to an individual's life? These questions can be used as starting points for discussion. Encourage people to stay for this part of the session because it is during this stage that ideas are put in perspective, problems resolved and insights shared.

Leading questions for discussions 'How does this activity relate to your life?', 'What does it say about your life?', 'Were you able to . . . ?', 'Was it important to . . . ?', 'What skills were you using?', 'Did you enjoy it?', 'What is your opinion now?', 'What did you observe in others?', 'What worried you?', 'Hardest?', 'Easiest?', 'How important is it to share information about yourself?', 'What did you learn about others in the group?', 'What did you have to be sensitive about?' (See *WORKING IN GROUPS, Emotional issues* p. 218).

Ending the session Warm up and ending activities help everyone move from, and return to, their everyday routines. Get the whole group together and choose an activity that is lightweight, fun and sociable. There should be a clear link between the activity and the concepts examined by the main activities of the session. At the end of the session you may want to praise people for their courage in sharing, for their willingness to listen to others or for their support of each other. Affirm positive steps towards change.

Activities

The activities described here are unlikely to be perfect in every respect for the individuals or groups you work with; expect to tailor them to suit specific needs and abilities.

1. 'Who am I?' topics

'How I see myself and what has contributed to my self-concept.'

Symbols Get people to make a collage, drawing, logo, painting, clay model, a symbolic coat of arms or compose a tune, that answers 'Who am I?'

Symbols for self Provide art and collage materials.
• Ask, 'What is your favourite . . . ?', and when people have drawn favourites ask, 'Do these drawings represent who you are?', 'In what ways?'
• Ask, 'What flower (make of car, piece of clothing, book, song, type of music . . .) represents you best?'
• Get people to sort through pictures from magazines to find ones that answer, 'What am I like?' or 'Where do I belong?'.
• 'What colour (temperature, taste, shape, texture . . .) describes you best?' 'Now?', 'Five years ago?'
• Give one topic and suggest people make an elaborate symbolic picture or get people to respond rapidly to several topics.

Signatures Say, 'Sign your name'. Ask, 'What does your signature say about you?' Then get people to sign lovingly, angrily, joyfully, very, very slowly, in a place on the paper that seems right and so on.

Two ways People write the letters of their name down one side of a page, then put a word or picture starting with each of the letters across the page. The words or pictures can be cut out of magazines. 'Choose words/ pictures which you think sum up who you are.'

Nicknames and labels People paint, draw in clay, compose a chord or melody, show in a sculpture, act:
• ' "Labels" I was given as a child', '. . . as a teenager', '. . . as an adult', 'The best was . . .', 'The worst was . . .', 'The effect on me was . . .'
• 'Labels I give myself'.
• 'Words and phrases that describe me . . .' (allow only one negative to every two positive words).
• 'The roles I fill . . .', 'My favourite is . . .', 'The one I wish I didn't have is . . .'

Name tags   Each person makes a large name tag (say 10 cm by 15 cm). On it they write their name and put words or small pictures round the edge to tell everyone something about themselves. It can be something they are interested in, something they like or the way they feel.

What kind of person am I?   Begin by making a list of opposite emotional characteristics on opposite sides of a page with a line ruled between them, like this:

warm	cold
nervous	confident
quiet	talkative
competitive	co-operative
trusting	suspicious

(Other possibilities are gullible/astute, even tempered/bad tempered, optimistic/pessimistic, enthusiastic/apathetic . . .).

People then make a copy of the group list (or lists can be individual) and place a cross at the point between each pair of characteristics where they think they fit. For example, on the list above people must first decide if they think of themselves as predominantly 'warm' or 'cold'.

Next get people to put a circle on the point where they would like to be. Ask, 'Which line would you like to alter most?' 'What would be the first step to making a change?' 'How would change show in your life day by day?'

Finally, people think of a specific relationship or situation, and choose the most significant pair of characteristics in that relationship. They mark

Variation on What kind of person am I?

the two points on the line then discuss with a partner the changes needed to bring the two points closer.

Time line   Each person makes a 'Time line' across a long sheet of paper. They mark in the most significant points in their life, the points of change or crisis and write a brief statement explaining each.

eg 5 __ 10 __15 __ 20 __ 25 __30 __ 35 __ 40 __ 50

0 _____ 90

The intervals and start and end points can be on whatever scale suit the person.

Road of life   Get each person to draw (or model in clay) his or her life's road; the potholes, crossroads, straight stretches, hitchhikers, detours, hills, bridges, narrow and wide sections and junctions. Use the result as a basis for discussion — or let the activity speak for itself.

My personal shield   People draw a large shield shape on both sides of a piece of paper or card, choosing one side as the outside and the other as the inside.

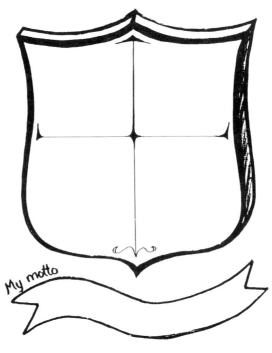

My personal shield

On the outside people put the things they can do and their abilities and on the inside they put things that are (or have been) important to them: failures, weaknesses, secret hopes, griefs. These are the things about the inner self that the shield protects or hides from the world.

Both sides of the shield can have a motto, slogan or logo. To make sure of a balance between positive and negative statements, get people to write one positive statement on the outside before each statement on the inside.

Masks In this activity people draw and write, or glue, pictures and words onto the outside of a large paper bag or box. The pictures and words show the way they think they appear to the world. Pictures or words about things that represent them, but are hidden from the world, are put inside the mask-bag or box. At the end of the session people explain their choices. Sharing inside cards should be optional. This can be a single-session activity or done over a number of weeks as a much more elaborate project.

My feelings now
- People use any medium to describe: 'My feelings about myself', '... my parents', '... my childhood', '... my work', '... my most important possession'.
- Or they show how feelings look; they draw anger, concern, hope ... or make a sound or musical phrase, or model feelings in clay.
- Using the same medium they show their feelings about childhood, work, hospital ...

Myself in hospital On a piece of paper get people to draw a frame representing the walls of the hospital. The frame should be eight to ten centimetres in from the edge of the paper. Inside the frame people depict themselves and their feelings about hospital. Outside the frame-lines they draw the way they feel about things outside the hospital.

Lost and gained People make two vertical columns on paper. On one side they draw or write, 'What I have gained from my illness (being in hospital, coming to this course ...)' and on the other, 'What I have lost'. A third topic which can be covered is, 'What I plan to gain'.

Comic-strip time line People divide a sheet of paper into a number of squares and draw scenes from their life in the boxes. Each picture should have a caption or speech balloons with dialogue.

Things I've done Use these topics as subjects for self expression in any medium.
- 'Things I enjoy doing most'. Ask 'When ...?', 'Where ...?', 'How long is it since you did ...?'
- 'Things I'd like to do'. Suggest people think about hobbies, sports, types of work, holiday jobs, holidays, family arrangements ...

- 'A balanced life means . . .' 'My life balance'.
- 'How my time is spent'. People make a pie graph to show how they spend their time and another to show how they feel about the things they do. 'Things I do that I like', 'Don't like', 'Have to do because others want me to . . .'

Time pie graphs can show a typical day, the time balance for last month, over summer, 'When I was a teenager,' or they can show feelings: 'My feelings today . . .', 'My feelings over the last few days . . .' (See *RELAXATION, Stress management techniques and activities* p. 178.)

I value   Provide a list (or get the group to make one) of values. When people cannot think of any more (or about a third of the time available is over) get them to rate the list with pluses and minuses then put the values in order of importance. This can be done individually or as a group. Examples of values are kindness, a good home, serenity, health.

My valuables   Get people to make a list, draw, paint a set number (say six) under one of these headings:
- Possessions I value most.
- Things that answer 'Who am I?'
- People I love most.
- Things I enjoy doing most.
- The music I like best.

Number each item. Get them to imagine what life would be like without each item, one at a time, on the list.

And how would they feel if each was restored to them, one at a time, after a year?

What I carry round   Each person chooses two to four things from their purse, wallet or pockets to talk to the group about. Where did they get the thing? What does it mean to them?

Metaphors and proverbs   Write a list of metaphors and proverbs (or get the group to make the list). Get people to choose ones that seem to apply to them, say four or five, and write them down in order of priority. Why did people make the choices they did?

Messages I carry in my head   Ask, 'What "should" messages do you carry in your head?' A 'should' message is something people feel they ought to do. 'Take a hanky with you', 'Don't show it when you are hurt', 'Little girls should be seen and not heard'.

Get everyone to draw or write down as many as they can think of and to decide whether or not these 'shoulds' are still useful in their lives. People's 'should' messages are often out-of-date or unrealistic, yet continue to influence the decisions they make. (See *RELAXATION, Straight thinking* p. 182.)

Child, adult, parent   Say, 'The child part of us needs care and is trusting, naive and active. The adult part of us is logical, mature, sensible and responsible and the parent part nurturing. When do you use each part? Are they in balance in your life?' Get each person to divide a pie graph or create a column graph, showing where they think their balance is.

The dinner party   Get everyone to make invitations for two to six guests of honour at a dinner party. The guests of honour can be people the invitor knows, historical figures or famous people. The invitations should say why the person is being invited.

This activity can be extended as a dramatic event if people in the group take the roles of each other's guests. Discuss suitable menus, settings and entertainment for each group of guests.

Pawns or players?   Using any medium, get people to show how they feel about the following statements. Discuss both general and specific situations while people form their opinions.

'People are just pawns. We have no say in our fate.'

'We are the players. We choose our own destiny. We make ourselves the people we are.'

Musical puppet   Play music that was popular when the people in the group were adolescents or young adults, or use film themes — a variety of short excerpts. Get the group to move to it, dance to it, '. . . as your parents would have wanted you to, then as you want to'. (See *MUSIC* p. 92).

2. Relationships between people

Round my table   Each person shows the people who would have been at the table for a meal when they were five, ten, fifteen years old (people choose one or more times in their life). They can choose a typical meal, a birthday party or a family gathering. Get everyone to draw the people, the tablecloth and the plates of food in a way that expresses the emotional climate and the relationships between the people. (The way people remember these details may not be as they actually were. It is the nature of the memory that is the reality now).

People in music   Get people to pick songs or types of music that represent significant people in their life. (See *CREATIVE WRITING, Job Descriptions, Advertisement* p. 111.)

My family tree   As an art activity people draw their family or use shapes to represent the people in their family tree. They make a traditional family tree or draw the family as a tree with branches, using colours and sizes to suit the personalities of the people. Pictures of people from newspapers or magazines can be used.

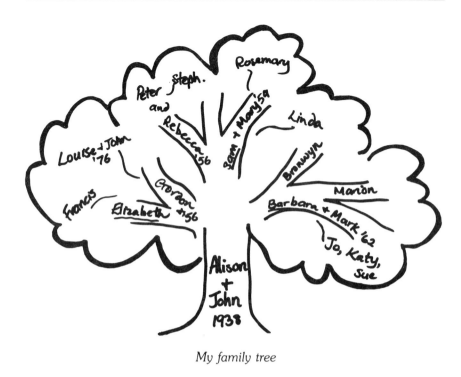

My family tree

Or they can model simple clay figures to represent the people (the size of chess pieces).

'How I see you' Work seated in a circle. Each person puts their name at the bottom of a sheet of paper. The papers are passed round the circle and each person writes their perceptions of the person whose name is at the bottom of the paper they have, folds it over, then passes it to the next person. In the discussion people share what surprised or puzzled them.

You may want to suggest suitable things for the group to comment on or set some limits on what can be expressed.

Creation in pairs In pairs, people work in silence to create a drawing, sculpture, collage or piece of music. They can either decide on a topic beforehand or just begin work and see what happens.

Who are you? This is a discussion activity for pairs. One person asks the other repeatedly, 'Who are you?' and when the other person has replied he or she says, 'Thank you. Who are you?' They go on until they are getting genuine replies with more depth. Other questions can be used such as, 'What do you pretend?' or 'What do you sabotage?'

Matrioshka dolls   Matrioshka dolls are wooden dolls made in two halves. In a set the dolls are graded in size so that they fit inside one another. They can be used to look at the defences people use to protect themselves.

Starting with the largest doll, describe each doll as protecting the smaller doll inside it. Ask, 'What is each doll hiding?' People can either take the set apart answering the question as they work or draw a set of doll-shapes and label them with answers to the question. For example, 'I show distance because I don't want to show fear, I show fear because I don't want to show grief, I show grief because I don't want to show guilt . . .' Do the activity a second time, describing each doll as a layer of support for the tiniest doll.

Going home   'When I go home it will be harder to . . .' This statement can be used as a discussion topic. Each person writes a statement which completes the sentence for them. All the completed sentences are put in a 'hat'. The 'hat' is passed around the circle and each person takes a sentence, checking to make sure they have not got their own before they pass the 'hat' on. Then, in turn, people read out the sentence they have and say how they would feel if they had written it, and what they might do about it.

3. Relationships in this group

Mural — 'This group'   Each person contributes to a mural about the group using whatever media are available.

Questions and answers   Each person takes it in turn to ask someone in the group a question. The person asked takes the next turn and can ask a question of anyone other than the person who questioned them.

Outline the type of questions which are appropriate at the beginning. Lightweight topics might be hobbies or favourite foods. More personal topics would be 'Your happiest moment', 'Something that bothers you', 'What is your most valued . . . ?'

Presents   For a group of up to eight — if the group is larger then divide it into two groups.

Each person puts their name at the bottom of a long sheet of paper and passes the paper to the person on their left. Everyone draws or writes down a gift for the person whose name is on the paper and folds the top over. They choose a gift they think the person would really enjoy or appreciate. Pass the papers on round the group adding gifts until everyone has their own paper back. The 'presents' can be abstract or concrete, for example, 'A job you will find satisfying', 'A scarf with a blue border', 'Peace of mind'.

The gifts can also be drawn and put in separate envelopes. The envelope can be decorated and a reason for giving the 'gift' written on the back.

People can choose a song they would like to 'give' each person in the group.

Gifts Say, 'If you could give three gifts to the group or members of the group, what would you give?'
'If you could take three things away, what would you take?' This can be something people in the group would be glad to lose, such as sadness, anxiety . . .

The group as a bouquet Ask people to draw (or write) the kind of flower (car, book, item of furniture and so on) each member of the group is like. Or people answer, 'If this person were a flower (animal, house) they would be a . . . ?

Where I am At the end of a session provide a large sheet of paper and ask each participant to write his or her name on it, choosing a place which represents where they feel they belong in relation to the group. This can be a regular activity at the end of group sessions.
Alternatively, divide a large piece of paper for each group member into as many segments as there will be sessions. Each person fills in one segment each session, showing how they felt about being part of the group that session.

How I look, how I feel Each person draws two or more faces, one to show how they try to appear in the group and the other to show how they really feel.

4. Responses and expectations

Poker face 'In a society which pits man against man, as in a poker game, people keep a poker face; they wear a mask and let no one know what they are up to.' Use this statement as the basis of an activity to bring out the things people hide and the things they show. After the activity, discuss whether hiding or showing feelings is desirable, when and in what circumstances.

Bits and pieces The equipment for this exercise is a selection of articles such as a rock, a pretty cup, a leaf. Each person selects something, and has a minute or so to think about it. Then, in turn, people describe the article they have chosen. What sort of characteristics does it have? If it were a person, what sort of person would it be?

5. Challenges, problems and opportunities

Goals 'My long term goals are . . .' On the far right of a piece of paper people draw something to represent their long-term goals. On the left they draw something to represent the steps towards this goal.

Discuss starting points, the size the steps should be, routes to goals and obstacles.

The contract   Each person needs a copy of a model contract. It should be well laid out and fill the whole page. It is probably best to hand-write the script and make photocopies so that the document does not look too legal, especially with people who are likely to be suspicious. Working in pairs or small groups, people decide what goals to put on their contract.

GOALS CONTRACT

I, _____, will by _____

achieve the goal _____

As a first step I will _____

The first step will be accomplished by _____

Contractee _____

Witness _____

Date _____

Adjusting   There are some things that cannot be changed, things that people must learn to live with. Each person identifies (draws, says, writes down) some things like this in their lives. Discuss ways of increasing acceptance of what cannot be changed.

Sentence completion — 'I just might...'   At the end of a session or course, people in the group take it in turns to complete the phrase, 'I just might...'

Right now   'The problem that is worrying (annoying, upsetting) me right now is...' Use this sentence as the basis for an art, discussion or writing session. (Avoid this activity with people who are delusional.) Allow at least half the time available to complete the activity with responses to, 'My choices in this situation are...'

Barriers and brick walls   'The things which will prevent me using the ideas I have learnt in treatment are...' (See *ASSERTIVENESS SKILLS, Personal barriers — the brick wall* p. 167.)

Diets   People plan a wholesome 'Needs' or 'Emotional needs' diet for themselves or someone emotionally close to them. Food stuffs in this diet might be love, fairness, recognition, exercise.

A barrier   With a group which has shared a number of sessions and is aware of the general purpose of the sessions, begin a session by saying that the topic for that day is barriers. And the barrier this session is that you have prepared nothing for this session, will not make suggestions about how the time is to be spent but expect the session to last about the usual length of time. (This is not an 'activity' to turn to when you have had no time to prepare but it can be an effective way of getting people to feel they could more actively use the group for their own needs or be assertive enough to take the lead.)

Decide whether to have art or other media materials available in the room.

6. Choices and decisions

My problem

a. First people write one problem at the top of a page.
b. Next, they write as many solutions to the problem as they can think of, likely or unlikely.
c. In pairs, people try to contribute further solutions to each other's list.
d. Working as individuals again, people put pluses and minuses beside each solution (up to three of either), rating them according to how effective they think the suggestion would be for solving the problem.
e. Finally, people look at one of the best solutions and list in two (or three) columns the advantages, disadvantages and perhaps neutral elements related to this solution. (These advantages and disadvantages can also be rated with a plus and minus system to indicate the strength of the advantage or disadvantage).
f. If the best solution still seems viable, people list the steps required to reach the goal by this solution. The steps should be broken down into the smallest possible units.

An alternative is to write a list of consequences opposite each solution. This helps to clarify the value of the idea.

Crossroads   As an art activity each person draws a crossroads and at the end of each road puts the different options facing them. In the spaces between the roads, they list (or draw) the people and factors involved in the choice. Relevant factors might be constraints related to the choice.

If this subject is used for a discussion the group can lie on the floor like the spokes of a wheel, heads in the centre, and take turns to relate the crossroads they are thinking about. The group can then choose one or more to discuss at length according to the time available.

Agony column   Get people to compose answers to agony column letters, working in small groups or pairs. Compare replies.

Choices   In any medium, 'Areas of my life in which I have choices and can make decisions.' 'Areas of my life in which I have no choice.'

7. Building esteem

A positive sense of self-esteem results in people thinking that their values matter. The activities in this section are mostly for groups but can be done by a therapist and one client. They can be done as a 'fun' way of giving people a boost, or as a serious project related to a significant need. When an activity is done to raise esteem this goal should be clearly stated rather than implied. Recognize esteem as a commodity or characteristic which people can work to increase.

Get people to think about situations or relationships in which they have little self-confidence and work on these first. Many people feel that their positive attributes are too slight to count for anything. They will reject the idea that they are 'kind' or 'tolerant' or 'truthful' because they can think of many instances when they were not. The way round this is to be specific and list instances and examples.

Many awareness activities help people to look at their values and see how they were established. (See *WORKING IN GROUPS, Feedback and praise* p. 218.)

My self-esteem now   Get people to divide a piece of paper into three sections (any way). In one section they list areas in which their sense of esteem is high, in the second section, areas in which it is low and in the third, reasons for their levels of esteem. They then add specific examples of positive actions or thoughts to both the first and second sections. As a group, discuss ways to build esteem.

Self-talk   Get people to make a list, written or pictorial, of the things they want to change about what they tell themselves.

Next, get them to make a postcard listing two or three of the messages they want to work on. The postcard can be carried in a handbag, or pinned up in a place where the person will see it often. (Work out a place where the list can be kept if the person does not want other people to see it.)

Caring about each other   Everyone in the group has two pieces of paper. On one they write down one thing they feel good about in themselves; on the other a concern or worry.

All the 'feel good' papers go in one 'hat' and all the 'concerns/worries' in another. Each person takes a paper from each hat, checking that they get someone else's paper and not their own.

In turn, people read out one of the papers they have as though it were about them. They discuss the effects they think this characteristic would have on their self-esteem and on their sense of control in life. Go round the group a second time for the second characteristic.

This activity can also be done with each person writing down a secret, a problem, an ambition, a characteristic they do not like, a hope, a concern, or something that irritates them. Maintain a balance between positive and negative topics.

Self-esteem — when and why Get people to think about situations or relationships in which they have little confidence and try to work out why. What part do people and place play? Self-talk? Be as specific as possible. How can the situation be changed?

Giving compliments Each person puts their name in a hat. The names are mixed up and everyone takes one, making sure they do not get their own. People must pay a compliment to the person whose name they have drawn. Get people to do this several times, taking a different name each time. Increase the difficulty of the task by specifying that the compliment has to be:
• Written and about appearance.
• Written and personal, that is, about a personality characteristic, action or effort that is admired.
• Verbal and about appearance.
• Verbal and personal.
People can use these levels of difficulty to give themselves compliments too.

Name compliments The name of one person in the group is written down the side of a chart or blackboard. (Sometimes it is a good idea to write the name as a heading too). Across from each letter a word is written (two or three if the name is short) which starts with the letter and fits the personality of the person. The person reads the list aloud, or someone else reads it to them, then it is rubbed off and it is the next person's turn.

For example, M A Y

        M Merry
        A Attractive, artistic,
        Y Youthful

Feathers in my cap Each person writes down some things they are proud of on feather-shaped pieces of paper. If people are stuck, others in the group can help them.

Esteem sentences 'The nicest thing that happened this week is . . .', 'A good (kind, helpful . . .) thing . . . did today is . . .'

'Successes' bulletin board Get people to write about things they notice others doing or saying. The items can be pinned up and changed at regular intervals. The board should be used to recognize all levels of contribution, effort or cause for celebration.

Talent scouts Select three people to be an interviewing panel of talent scouts. Each person in the group tells the panel of a particular talent or

Feathers in my cap

attribute that they possess. People can only give positive attributes. When they do, they get a cheer and clap, otherwise the panel says 'No, something else,' or 'Something more personal.'

A pat on the back   Each person has a card pinned to his or her back and a felt-tip pen to write with. The cards should be about half A4 size. Everyone writes one positive adjective on everyone else's card. At the end the cards are taken off and given to the people who were wearing them.

Columns   Each person makes three columns on a piece of paper and heads them Accomplishments, Skills/talents and Strengths. People list their attributes under each column.

Even partial skills or accomplishments count. People tend to take their accomplishments and skills for granted and not recognize their value. Making this list can be an ongoing project, with people adding to it as they develop more skills, or recognize the skills they have.

The cup   Photocopy or draw a prize cup so that it fills a whole page. Inscribe it with:

WINNER'S CUP

This cup was presented to _____

for _____

and _____

and _____

and _____

and _____

Date _____

Therapist's signature _____

The group works together to fill in each person's list. They can sign it instead of the therapist. A variation of this exercise is to make 'Accomplishment certificates' or 'Progress certificates'.

Validation scavenger hunt   On a walk get each person to collect two to five items which symbolize their strengths, talents or abilities.

Alternatively, get everyone to bring a set number of things which are important to them to the session, for example, a photograph or a gift they value.

In both these activities, invite people to talk about what they have found or brought to the group.

Photographer's model   In turn, each member of the group is 'posed' for an imaginary photograph. The photographers (the rest of the group) talk about how they would show the person's best characteristics, appearance and personal qualities.

Meeting needs   Each person in the group can ask to have one need met, for example, be listened to for five minutes, have a card written to them, have someone remind them about something each day, be given a cup of tea, be given a shoulder massage, have someone be their 'buddy' and partner them in giving up smoking . . .

Gossip   Each person chooses one person who they think likes them (for example, a teacher or workmate). They then write down, tell a partner, or tell the group what they think that person would say about them. Ask the group, 'What else might this person who likes . . . say?' (See *CREATIVE WRITING, Advertisement, An appreciation, A reference* p. 122.)

8. Sentence completion activities

Although 'sentence completion' suggests a discussion or writing session, the endings to these statements can also be shown through art, clay, drama or with a musical instrument. Each person in the group can respond to the same part sentence or people can work in pairs.

Working in pairs, people sit facing their partner, not too far apart. They are given a new sentence every two minutes, so that each person has a minute to speak, using the part sentence as a beginning. The speaker's partner must not interrupt during the minute.

Alternatively, give partners a different but similar sentence every minute. Use a selection of sentences, choosing ones which people are likely to be able to talk about for a minute.

The same part sentence can be repeated and completed several times in quick succession or new part sentences given in quick succession. Some part sentences can be the basis of a whole session.

Part sentences

Names

My name is . . .
My associations with my name . . .
I was given my name by . . . because . . .
I would like to have been called . . .
Nicknames I've had . . .
My favourite nickname . . .
My associations with my nickname . . .
The nickname I liked least is . . .
The colours I see my name(s) . . .

Discussions could focus on family trees, name associations, changing fashions in names, changing names through marriage or by deed poll.

Myself over time

At two I was . . .
At five I was . . .
Six months ago I was . . .
Now I am . . .
In six months time I will be . . .
(Select an appropriate time scale.)
The most important moment in my life was . . .

When I was a child

When I was a child my favourite game (friend, teacher, holiday) was . . .
When I was a child my father/mother was . . .

Favourites

My favourite food is . . .
My favourite kind of person (clothing, music) is . . .
Favourite things I like to do alone (with others, sometimes, often) are . . .
My favourite gift is . . .

I feel . . . when . . .

I feel angry (happy, relieved, supported, not alone, able to cope, stronger, anguished, ashamed, confused, like crying, lonely) when . . .

Values
I like (love, hate, admire, appreciate) . . .
I am proud of . . .
I feel concerned when . . .
Love is . . .
Happiness is . . .
Being a woman is . . .
Hospital . . .
Health is . . .
Death is . . .
Status means . . .
Money means . . .

Sabotage (If necessary, explain what sabotage means.)
I sabotage myself when . . .
I sabotage this group when . . .
I can help myself (this group) by . . .

My best friend's description Everyone has to fill in a card with the following headings, as though they were their own best friend.
Introducing . . .
His/her personal qualities are . . .
For a good time she/he likes . . .
His/her hates are . . .
His/her loves or likes are . . .
In the future he/she will . . .
She/he needs support for . . .

Changing the perspective Get people to complete these sentences. Do several of each.
I should . . .
I need . . .
I can't . . .
I could . . .

When people have completed these get them to change the perspective by changing the beginnings of the sentences to:
I will . . .
I want . . .
I won't . . .
I choose to . . .

Words about me
. . .able
. . .ful
. . .ist

Needs
I put myself first when . . .
When I put myself first . . .
I put . . . first when . . .
When others do not consider my needs I . . .
People don't agree with me when . . .

My dream
My dream house (job, family) . . .
The day (age) I'd most like to relive . . .

If's (Do a number of these in quick succession or do one in depth).
If someone said they would do anything to please me, I'd ask them
to . . .
If I were . . . (age) and . . . happened, I'd . . .
If I inherited a fortune . . .
If I was given six months (twenty-four hours) to live I'd . . .
If I was asked to give a speech to . . .
If I had $10 ($100, $1000, $10,000) I'd spend it on . . .
If I had to spend it on someone I like I'd . . .
If I were a man/woman I would . . .
If I was younger I would . . .
If I was stronger I would . . .
I've avoided facing . . .
I hope to . . .
In five years . . .
Next year . . .
By next Thursday . . .
Tomorrow I will . . .
Today . . .
The kind of help I could accept is . . .
If I could change one thing, I would . . .
The job I'd like is . . .
I need to work on . . .
If I could give three gifts to . . . I would . . .
Just for today I'll . . .
Things I'd give up television for are . . .
I'd like to be famous for . . .

What do I want to be? Get people to depict or rank, or ask them 'What
do you mean by':
being successful
enjoying life
being liked or popular
being friendly

having an easy job
being rich
serving
being the centre of attention

People can extend the list as the first part of the activity.

Topics   To draw or use in sentences, or speak about for two minutes:

love	hurt	boredom
loneliness	time	children
hospital	my face	yesterday
my hero/heroine	crucial decisions	

Choose topics according to the needs, interests and abilities of the group. They can be concrete, abstract, age-related, controversial and so on.

Admiration

Things I admire in people are . . .
Things I respect in people are . . .
The person I admire most is . . . because . . . One thing I have in common with that person is . . .

Relationships

People I'm close to . . .
I wish I was closer to . . .
I don't like . . . in relationships.
The things I give most in relationships are . . . at home (work).
The things I receive most in relationships are . . .
I feel confused (guilty, afraid, sorry, jealous) when someone . . .
In a group I am . . .
I am . . . when someone shows me affection.
I am . . . when someone is sexually attracted to me.
I am . . . when someone touches me.
I am . . . when someone is angry with me.
I am . . . when I am not sure what is going on.
I am . . . when people are indifferent to me.
(Each of these sentences can be reversed, thus inviting a longer answer. 'When someone shows me affection I . . .')

My mother . . .
My favourite Aunty . . .
My grandson . . .
A couple is . . .
Being a friend means . . .
Things I look for in friendship are . . .

Marriage . . .
Being wanted is . . .
Being left out is . . .
I miss . . .
Compromise/negotiation means . . .

Memories to share
My happiest day . . .
An embarrassing moment . . .
A mistake . . .
A surprise . . .
A turning point in my life was . . .
An opportunity I took (missed) was . . .
A kindness I received . . .

Who are you?   People complete these sentences about their partner or others in the group.
You seem like the kind of person who . . .
Your name should be . . .
Realistic goals for you would be . . .
I wish I could give you . . .
You deserve . . .
I can imagine you . . .
I admire the way you . . .
Your best points are . . .
If you were angry I would expect you to . . .
If you were happy I would expect you to . . .
What I like about you right now is . . .
If you were a flower you would be . . .
If you were an animal you would be . . .
If you were a colour you would be . . .

Sharing secrets, taking risks
What I'm not saying now is . . .
I'm pretending . . .
If I took a risk I'd tell you about . . .
I'm afraid . . .
I feel vulnerable when . . .
I try to give the impression that . . .
My secret fear is . . .
Excuses (rationalizations) I make when . . .

3 | *The Creative Arts*

DRAMA

Many people enjoy drama. They may enjoy acting impromptu scenes or whole plays or find role play a good way of learning. Drama mirrors life: its emotions, pleasures and griefs, its work, games and play. It can help people come to terms with a wide variety of problems.

For the therapist, drama provides a powerful tool for personal change and growth, as well as being fun. There are many kinds and levels of drama activities, which means that the activity can always be suited to the needs and abilities of the group. The nature of it allows you to stop and explore significant moments, redo the action or linger to reflect on what people have tried or learned.

Therapeutic Application

Drama activities take many forms. Some are brief, lightweight and fun, others require people to take risks and work hard. Through drama people experience the following.

Exploring roles A role is what people do because of who they are (mother, golfer, group member). Major roles are made up of sub roles (cook, snappy dresser, questioner). Through drama people can develop the skills needed for competent role performance in real life.

Major health problems usually lead to the loss of some roles so it is often relevant in therapeutic contexts to identify the roles which people must be able to take. Which do they need to develop, maintain or use less? Roles only exist in relation to other people so they must be considered in their social context.

All drama activities, from plays to psychodrama, explore roles in some way. In a play, the roles are largely defined by the author, although there is usually scope for the players to interpret the subtleties of the play. In psychodrama, people play out the roles they take in eveyday life. In an improvised puppet play, roles are assigned and developed on the spot. Each context provides suitable opportunities to investigate different roles.

The art of the therapist is to work out the roles people need to explore and provide them with opportunities to do so.

In drama, people try new roles and hear — and see — others' reactions to them. A frequent aim of therapy is to increase the number of roles people are able to take. 'Role flexibility' gives people more ways of being, for example, a mother or a workmate. Roles that fit a person's values will be added to their repertoire when they are at ease in them. Learning any new role is likely to change the way a person functions in other roles too.

In the therapeutic situation people rehearse and practise roles until they feel bold enough to use them in their everyday lives.

Opportunities for choice and decision Opportunities for choice are often very limited in treatment situations, especially in long-term care. There is a wealth of choice within drama activities and in most there are no right or wrong decisions. It is only in the more structured, performance-orientated activities, that there is success or failure, a product to be judged.

The process of making decisions is closely related to mental health. In long periods of hospitalization and many psychiatric conditions the ability to make decisions is likely to be reduced. The same can apply to any severe disruption in life. Making a reasoned decision, or a spontaneous one increases a person's courage and confidence. In other words, practice in choosing and deciding makes it easier to do.

This is the baiss of learning through drama; making decisions and experiencing the result. When people do not make choices they do not learn or develop skills, and are in danger of becoming dependent and institutionalized.

Spontaneity Spontaneity can be defined as doing what you feel like without holding back because the situation feels safe and your imagination is stimulated. People can take risks in a drama exercise. They can have a go at being affectionate, shouting, being a boss — many roles which for them may normally be socially unacceptable or difficult. It is like play in childhood — the rules are flexible, experimentation is allowed and much is learned. Over time it makes people more sure of themselves and less anxious about being surprised by their emotions. It has been said that all learning is based on spontaneity, or the ability to respond in a new way in a situation.

The more spontaneous people can be, the more life roles they can take. Spontaneity can be the catalyst needed to resolve a therapeutic stalemate.

The warm-up process at the beginning of a drama session helps people feel free to experiment. It should stimulate imagination and makes it easier to improvise.

Learning through doing In drama, people do, feel and think all at the same time. This gives them a more integrated understanding of what they are experiencing. It is a pragmatic approach on all three levels and this is often more effective than simply theorizing about a problem or responding to feelings. When people are anxious or depressed they are often only able to respond at one level.

Physical activity People are up and active in drama, stimulated in body as well as mind. They 'feel' the physical patterns of their own action and this reinforces what they are learning, whether it be social skills or assertiveness training.

The physical activity can include opportunities to practise gross or fine movements, co-ordination, balance and so on. It can also be energetic enough to stimulate the cardiovascular system with all the benefits this gives.

Relationship skills Caring and sharing, talking to people and emotionally identifying with them — these are all very much part of the experience of drama.

- There is physical contact with others. Touch is an accepted part of the activities and meets an important need when people are isolated from their friends and family for whatever reason. Many of the usual social rules about contact between people, and who may touch who, are changed and freer.
- Specific interpersonal skills such as eye contact, observation and turn taking can be incorporated.
- Verbal skills — drama activities give people opportunities to use and try out their voices in new ways.

And there is more Drama offers people opportunities to work on cognitive skills such as memory, problem solving and concentration:

- Relaxation is learned by 'being relaxed' as part of a role in drama. (See *RELAXATION, Positive imagination* p. 185 and *Drama* p. 187.)
- Educational skills — drama activities can involve the learning of skills such as reading, writing and maths.
- Life enrichment. This aspect of drama is especially valuable in institutional settings where people's life experiences are limited.
- Work skills. In a play or any other major production many skills may be required that do not relate to the drama itself. These may be therapeutically valuable, for example, punctuality and cooperation.
- Responsibility. Learning a part in a play, attending practices and so on, all require responsibility.
- Drama provides a bridge between past and present in role play, playback drama and psychodrama.

Contraindications, Precautions and Limitations

Some drama activities, especially those with little structure, are demanding. It is important to match activities to the group's abilities and your own skills. More structured activities are usually simpler.

Some people perceive drama activities as trivial, or think they lack the skills needed. Others feel it is simply not for them. The following are some of the problems you may have to deal with.

Aggressiveness Be cautious about situations that could encourage negative acting out. Drama activities can provide a safe setting for the release of negative feelings but the line between acceptable and unacceptable acting out can be a fine one.

Thought disorder People who have schizophrenia can be over stimulated or become confused with certain drama activities. Use activities which are straightforward and concrete, with a clearly defined structure. Give them the opportunity to try uncomplicated role plays and trust exercises which are low key and not too personal. Work in sub-groups of three or four. Activities involving eye contact and touch should be used with discretion.

Memory loss/short attention span People who are confused or who have a short memory span will need simple instructions repeated at intervals. Unambiguous, structured activities can be valuable in that they provide social contact, opportunity for reminiscence, exercise and general stimulation. If the activities match the group's interests and abilities they are also likely to be enjoyed.

Anxiety, emotional distress For these people it is necessary to plan safeguards into the activities you choose. Use activities that have a strong games element rather than an emphasis on personal insight. (See *WORKING IN GROUPS, Emotional issues* p. 218.)

Limited mobility Choose activities which require little movement or can be done seated.

Confrontation In some drama activities, psychodrama in particular, people can suddenly become aware of (that is, confronted by) conflicts or aspects of themselves they were previously unconscious of. When this occurs without safeguards, people may find they have 'exposed' inner feelings which they did not intend to. Drama can turn a spotlight on the self, leaving the player feeling naked in centre stage.

Safeguards to protect people from distress can be built into even the most confronting drama techniques if they are correctly structured. To increase the safeguards:
- Develop trust and cohesiveness in the group. Ensure that trust is made obvious in the warm up and restate your expectations about relationships in the group and confidentiality whenever this seems necessary. Adolescents are particularly likely to be self-conscious.
- Give reassurance; it is quite common for people to be distressed in some types of drama activities. Encourage them to see this distress as

part of the process of coming to terms with problems. The cathartic effect should be resolving and relieving.

• Have support people available, and make sure there is time to follow up problems.

• Plan sessions so that there is time for discussion and resolution of problems.

The impact of a drama activity can come from a number of factors, for example, people relating the drama to their own lives or perhaps to a comment from someone in the group. Despite this, people will usually set their own pace to control what, and how much, they are able to confront. Difficult insights can be dealt with at a gentle pace.

On the other hand, over-protecting people from their feelings can interfere with potential growth and is often based on sentimentality. Confrontation is a catalyst for change. Give people the support they need to accept feelings and insights which they find difficult, and support them through their grief, for what is or what might have been. In this way you help them to move on and face the challenges of their future. (See *WORKING IN GROUPS, Emotional issues* p. 218.)

The Therapist's Role

The principles involved in leading any therapeutic group apply:

• Plan a varied programme likely to interest the group.

• Focus on therapeutic goals. In each session define the goals for each person as well as the goals for the group.

• Encourage others to develop leadership skills.

• Participate if possible.

• Avoid focusing on one person for too long.

• Maintain an expectation of confidentiality.

• Set limits on disruptive behaviour.

• Work within your own strengths and limitations.

• Plan how you will stimulate involvement, imagination and energy.

• Ongoing evaluation of the group.

Leading and following In drama activities 'leading' a group should be done by 'following'. This means picking up cues from the people in the group about when to move on, slow down or ask leading questions. Be aware of your own feelings; constantly ask yourself, 'What am I seeing?', 'Where does this lead?' Aim for a relaxed, creative concentration and a depth of involvement. It will be stimulating and emotionally satisfying — and very tiring!

As well as being led by the group you need to be decisive and 'run' the show. Use short, directive statements. Instructions should be clear and simple. For example, point and say, 'Go to that side of the room' rather than, 'I'd like everone to go across to that side of the room, please'. Or,

'John, would you begin?' rather than, 'Would someone like to be the first to start?' Be definite in tone, without hesitancy, bossiness or ordering.

It is difficult to lead and be led at the same time, but it is possible. Give yourself time to think on your feet. The pace should be unhurried, without losing momentum.

In more formal drama, the leader will also be a teacher and coach.

Practical Organization

The practical requirements for drama are varied but there should always be enough privacy for people to feel free to act or express themselves. For some activities a large space may be needed.

Getting started Starting is probably the hardest part of any creative, action-oriented activity. Once an activity is under way and you are committed the impetus of the moment will keep it going.

Start with techniques and scenarios which are straightforward, such as theatre games, play readings and role plays aimed at training people for specific skills. Move on to new techniques when you feel comfortable. Find a way of experiencing drama methods first-hand if possible, or, ideally, assist someone else in organizing or leading a particular type of activity before you try it yourself. If it is difficult to get first-hand experience, it may be possible to see films of others' leadership techniques. Experience is particularly important when you are working with people who are potentially suicidal or psychotic.

Planning programmes and sessions How easy will it be to develop trust in relationships? How motivated are people to change? Are they limited by intellect, confusion or physical abilities? What will they enjoy?

Practical considerations are:

- A suitable place to work (atmosphere, facilities and so on).
- Informing those who need to know about your plans.
- A programme that will be varied yet cohesive. Have more ideas ready than you think you will need, especially with theatre games. Then there is no risk of running out of material. With experience, less planning will be needed in activities like role play because most of the material will come from the group.

Choosing an appropriate title for sessions is vital. It should be as accurate as possible so that people come with realistic expectations. Titles like 'Action methods group' and even 'The drama group' are too vague — add sub-titling or a brief, specific list of the group's activities. A title like 'Play reading group: two one act mysteries' is clearer.

Take photographs, video or camcorder films of productions or special events for a reminiscence session later or to advertise the group. Video can also be used to help coach people in particular skills.

The format of a session Drama sessions invariably begin with warm-up activities to create a sense of common purpose. A third of the time for each of the three areas — warm up, body of session, review/wind down — works well for less structured types of drama activity. In the more structured types of drama activity, the body of the session can be longer, especially when people know each other well and have been working together over a period of time. However, do not be too easily tempted to lengthen the central part of the session, even when it seems important to work on things that arise. People will continue to think about and work on events which are significant to them anyway.

There must be time at the end of the session for completing and reviewing what has been done. A review should include asking for people's reactions, getting them to think about what else they could have said, planning other ways they could have done things and so on. Limiting the consolidation and review time often leaves you with the feeling that the session is unfinished, that there were things people would have liked to ask or say. You need time to check people's feelings and reactions so be flexible about the content of each stage. When you plan the next session start where the previous one ended, and use the feelings and ideas that were being expressed then in the warm up to the new session.

Types of Drama

Describing the activities that come under the broad umbrella of drama clarifies their use in treatment, promoting health and maintaining skills.

Warm-up activities The warm-up time starts when people arrive. It includes the general greeting and chatting that occurs when people meet, a description of what is planned, its application to the group, and the methods that will be used. It orientates people and sets their expectations. It also facilitates spontaneity.

Warm-up activities should be short and simple. They should focus on the needs and abilities of the group, and the session to come. They often include gross motor activities to raise energy, diffuse tensions and get people out of their normal roles and in contact with each other. Other goals of the warm up include arousing curiosity, a creative readiness to see things in a new way and a feeling of support for each other. Sometimes the warm-up process is called 'framing the session' because it gives a framework or a skeleton to flesh out in the body of the session.

The activities should generate cohesion and mental and physical energy. They set the tone, and they warm you up too.

To involve everyone choose easy activities that are unlikely to make people self-conscious. Use simple game-type activities with no 'performance' role. This is especially important with adolescents who are often very self-conscious already.

Be sure to spend enough time on this part of the session; assuming everyone is on the same wavelength can be a serious mistake. People can quite easily be 'warmed up to confusion' (that is, they do not know what to expect), or 'warmed up to dependence' (they expect the therapist to make all the decisions). See what is happening in the group.

Avoid having a plan that is too definite for the warm up because part of the task is to be aware of what people are 'warmed up to', that is, what they are thinking and feeling. Avoid telling people what you think they may be concerned or pleased about, or that they are 'going to have a great time' or 'find the session worthwhile'. These are things which people will decide for themselves. Explain the format of the session and how the time will be used. Check people's understanding and reactions. They need to have enough trust to feel comfortable about taking risks and being spontaneous. Make a formal agreement about confidentiality.

Warm ups for a rehearsal or play can be a quick theatre game or a snack, drink and general discussion. Before a play-reading, discuss what the play is about, how it will be done, the parts and so on.

After a break part way through the session, remind people what they were involved in as a sort of secondary warm up. A break can provide a new starting point which allows you to make use of something that came out of the initial warm up.

Activities for ending drama sessions   Everyone should be involved in the ending. In some groups it is practical to have a regular routine at both the beginning and end, thus allowing a familiar pattern to be built up. This is particularly worthwhile with people who are confused or who have limited intellectual capacity.

Lightweight theatre games are often used at the end of a session to bring everyone together in an activity which is fun. This ends the session on a pleasant, sociable note, and reinforces positive relationships in the group.

Levels of spontaneity and structure in activities   The more structured the activity the simpler it is for an inexperienced person to lead. Structure means knowing what is going to happen next, having a 'plot'. Thus, a play with a script is at the most structured end of the continuum while psycho-drama, with no preplanned action at all, is at the least structured end. The following types of drama are described in order from most to least structured.

Formal theatre

Plays are stories told through action. The script of a play gives a set of roles, a scene and a plot. Unlike other drama activities there is an end product, the performance, and of course in this respect, unlike other types of drama, it is possible to succeed or fail.

The complex process of planning and producing a play, on whatever scale, offers many opportunities to a therapist. Each person must learn their lines, understand their character, practise, use their voice and body in new ways and have the confidence to perform. Within the structure of the words and the roles there is still considerable scope for personal interpretation. For any substantial production you must have a stable cast, so play production is most suited to situations where people are in long-term care or attend a community centre regularly.

Choosing a play What kind of play will meet the needs of the people in your group best? Period piece? Romance? Thriller? Theatre of the absurd? How will the choice of play be made — can a number of people contribute to the decision or is this impractical? However the choice is made, the play should extend people without over-taxing them. Be clear about your therapeutic goals and the specific ways in which they will be achieved. Of course, an enjoyable end product is also important!

Check the play:

- Does it have enough appeal to sustain the group through the various stages of production? Are the characters interesting? And the plot and story line? Is it worth people's time and attention? Can you find enough substance in this play to hold your interest too?
- Is it suitable in length and complexity, or can it be easily adapted? Is the number of characters right, or can more be added or subtracted? Can everyone be involved in ways they will enjoy or will some of the cast spend a lot of time doing nothing?
- Will the play involve personal growth for all the cast, or will it only develop individual talents? Is there scope for developing people's skills?
- Does the commitment to performance and the anxieties this entails, limit the fun or therapeutic value? How about the amount of work involved?

The performance Once a play is chosen there is scope for trying, discussing, discarding, modifying and compromising so that the final interpretation of the play is created by the cast. All kinds of decisions need to be made, about where and when to practise, stage management, programmes, advertising, when to present the play, props and costumes. Props stimulate the imagination of both actors and audience. If your budget is small make simple costumes which can be used again for other roles without too much alteration. They should be as easy to take on and off as possible. If they are made of good quality fabrics and are well designed they will add to the sense of occasion and complement the part and the player. They help turn a play into an event.

Each rehearsal should give some scope for improvisation and everyone should see that progress is made. In a therapeutic context the rehearsals are as important as the final production.

Remember to take photographs of the production to share and enjoy later.

Play readings

Play reading is the simplest use of a play. It is better to have a rehearsed play reading than produce a play for performance which is beyond a group's abilities. A play reading can be a step towards the challenge of public performance. It is also a good way of choosing a play to produce and finding roles that suit people. Some narrative poems and short stories lend themselves to reading aloud.

With no audience, a play reading can be done with the group sitting in a circle or round a table. When there is an audience, have the cast move on and off the stage as they would in a play production so that no one is confused about who is 'there' or 'not there' at any point. It is generally too difficult for people to act unless they have practised beforehand, so it is better to simply make a good job of the reading. If possible, the cast should have an opportunity to read the play through before reading it in front of an audience.

The choice of length of play can be difficult; one act plays are often too brief and full length plays will be over-long unless people are good readers. Possibilities are summarizing the first act and starting at the second or giving people a chance to read the first act before the session. For almost any group, choose plays with parts for as many people as possible even if the ages and sex of the characters have to be changed. Encourage poor readers to take at least a small part even if they need a little prompting. The support of the group for its less able members can be very positive for both givers and receiver.

Sets of plays can be requested through libraries or obtained by joining a drama society. Describe your group so that the librarian can suggest titles.

Other types of performance-oriented drama

Variety shows and talent quests are comparatively easy to organize because they are made up of sub-items which can be planned and rehearsed separately. Arrange the items in order of greatest contrast and encourage people to keep their contributions brief. Such shows can include all the types of drama listed below. When elderly people are encouraged to put on their own performance, it is most likely to be a variety show.

Mime   Mime highlights body language and can be done with or without a narrator, to a tape, record or reading. It is a good way of encouraging people to develop acting skills. Charades is a simple mime game.

Miscellaneous   Ideas include: pantomimes, plays with audience participation, poetry readings, story readings, joke telling, skits, musicals, parades with an acting component, dramatized songs, action songs, Punch and Judy and puppet shows, festivals, pageants, dances, conjuring and magic, stilt dramas, play back, mask and head-dress work, charades, making videos.

'Living history theatre'   This combines reminiscence and drama. People act out or relate incidents from their past, coopting group members as new characters are needed. The therapist's role may be to encourage them to elaborate or take a particular focus, for example, music, working years, courtship.

Playback drama   In playback drama one person relates an incident that was important to them and a number of people in the group act it out, each representing a part of the story. Two people might play the opening of the story, another represent 'feeling excited', another 'anxiety', another the final action. They can either show what happened or what the person felt. Stories can be acted through sequentially or all the facets of the story shown at the same time.

Instant replay   'Instant replay' is similar to playback drama but briefer and more superficial. Everyone can be involved. One person in the group tells an incident or scene and everyone acts it out. (See *VERBAL ACTIVITIES, Reminiscence* p. 140.)

Group play writing   A group can plan and write its own play as a shared creative writing project.

First decide on the content: the story (usually a problem or conflict to resolve, involving either one person or a small group struggling towards a goal), the characters, the emotions involved, the setting, the time and so on. When the ingredients are established make full use of them. It is difficult to make progress if people keep changing the ground rules or basic scenario. The play can be refined as it is acted out.

Theatre games

These are also called 'Theatre sports'. The term covers all the many kinds of drama activities which involve make-believe, are action-oriented and take between five and twenty minutes. Theatre games can be simple or complex, long or short. They are easily graded so sessions can be planned at different levels. The range of themes is limitless.

Many theatre games can be abbreviated as warm ups or a cluster can be used to explore a particular theme. They are useful for generating trust, eye contact and spontaneity, and they provide a way of looking at relationships. While the emphasis is usually on fun rather than personal meaning and problem solving, this can be changed by the way the activity is run. For example, in 'Trust walks', where one person leads a blindfolded partner, the interpretation and analysis afterwards can focus on insight. When insight is a goal, discuss what people found hard, easy, worthwhile and so on. However, most often the emphasis will simply be on social interaction and fun, learning through doing.

An important feature of games is that they have rules. People know what is being asked of them from the beginning. In this sense theatre games are quite structured — but there is no 'right' or 'wrong' way of playing them.

Within the basic rules of a game the degree of structure can be varied, giving either much or little opportunity for improvisation. For people who can only make very limited decisions in their personal lives, theatre games provide an opportunity to see their ideas being used.

Drama Skills   In using theatre games to teach people basic drama skills, the following points are important:

- 'Show' rather than 'tell' a story (speak gibberish, or get the audience to put their hands over their ears to emphasize the 'show' aspect). Encourage people to share what they are doing with the audience, to focus on 'communicating' with them, to play to them.
- Each person needs a clear, detailed picture of their character, rather than a generalized concept. They need to create a mental picture of their immediate and wider environment, their age, their cultural background, where they are, and where they are going to and coming from.
- Focus on the reason for each action.
- In theatre games, there is usually no audience, but when there is the audience is part of the drama, and players must recognize the roles the audience play as observers, admirers, critics and so on.
- Players need to be sensitive to the roles of other actors — theatre games are team games. They must 'use' what other players offer rather than 'block' (that is, stop or hinder) a direction another actor leads towards.
- Avoid mechanical acting out of a role. This is more likely to happen when people rote learn parts and then try to act them in a preconceived way. They should respond spontaneously in the situation.

Stimulate ideas for theatre games by using:
- Music. Live music of any kind is likely to have more effect than recorded music.
- The first words of a story line. 'What if . . .', 'Can you explain . . .' or suggest a trigger word.
- Objects which evoke feelings and ideas: a hat, a magazine, a piece of furniture. Choose things which are beautiful, intriguing or likely to have interesting associations.
- Stimulation of any of the senses: a smell, a sound, a texture.
- A photograph, an idea, a theme, a topic.

Many traditional and 'new' games can be used in the context of a drama session (see *Theatre Games* p. 46).

Mask work

Masks can be made as part of the session, hired or bought. Alison Lee (*A Handbook of Creative Dance and Drama*) makes the following points concerning masks:

- Masks transform the wearer into another person, animal, emotion or attitude. The identity and meaning come from the mask's expression and size.
- Masks invite the wearer to see the world through the 'eyes' of the mask.

Masks are powerful; do not underestimate the strong, unfamiliar feelings they stimulate.

• Masks should be put on and taken off with a clear briefing/debriefing statement about the roles being put on or taken off with the mask.
• Masks need to be treated with respect.
• Masks lessen people's inhibitions about performance. Encourage wearers to share what they are doing and thinking with an audience.
• Mask work should be larger than life and calls for big shapes, and moments of stillness and stylisation.

Precaution If the people you are working with currently experience hallucinations or delusions, or are seriously confused, be cautious about using masks.

Role play

Role play is acting 'as if' a particular set of conditions were the case, for example, 'as a friendly person', 'as if I were overjoyed', 'as the boss'. It means considering the world from someone else's point of view to see how it feels and fits.

Role play is derived from psychodrama but it is faster, more superficial and problem-orientated. The goal is to help people find alternative, and more effective, ways of interacting with others in situations such as job interviews or conflicts. In a therapeutic situation the roles played are usually ones people are likely to take or meet in their everyday lives. Although the aim is to develop roles, role plays should also be fun.

All roles involve certain sets of actions and feelings. They also carry particular responsibilities or privileges. Role play allows people to explore all these aspects of being someone else.

Role play is an effective problem-solving process. It enables people to see that there are several ways of coping with particular circumstances. A specific situation can be played out many times in different ways in a supportive atmosphere. Recognizing the best approach may only come after the event, along with recognizing what was astray before. Role play shows people their choices in relationships.

Specifically, role play may be used to:

• Find new ways of handling common situations. (What roles do I want to be able to take?)
• Help people see themselves in a detached, objective fashion, and see how others see them. (How do I look in the role of employee?)
• Work through and, if possible, resolve problems from the past. (Why am I shy?)
• Rehearse new ways of doing things, practise social interactions. (What do other roles feel like? Can I do this or that a different way?)
• Learn from others, develop an appreciation of their needs and problems, and their strategies for handling them.
• Identify and reinforce productive behaviour.

In role play, it is often the unasked questions which are answered through the experience.

Contraindications

Role play is a poor choice when people are confused. Simple, pre-structured role training (see p. 52) is more likely to be suitable.

Procedure for a role play

Although the process as described here seems detailed, it is actually quite fast in practice.

A role play should only involve two or three people.

Choose the situation to role play

Problem-solving role play Ask people to think of situations they have experienced which they would have liked to handle better or which they anticipate experiencing in the future. The group should agree on the situation they want to explore. Write the suggestions on a blackboard or white board or verbally summarize them for the group to consider. The situation chosen should be one that can be acted out in two to five minutes, can be described in specific, concrete terms and is on a small scale. Sometimes you will need to devise a problem which is relevant to the group.

Fantasy role play This uses a 'game' approach (for example, 'off on a magic carpet to the land of dreams'). Note that even 'fantasy' roles will reflect people's real feelings and values, because people can only act on the basis of who they are and what they know. As a therapist, be aware that people may be surprised by the depth of their emotions and their degree of involvement. When appropriate, ask questions afterwards, like 'What part of yourself did you use?' Choose ideas which will stimulate the imagination, and structure the activity so that people feel secure to experiment.

Briefly discuss the chosen situation What is the aim of the role play in this situation? It may be useful to prepare brief script outlines on cards, giving a description of each person and an outline of events. Or work out each character role in brief discussion.

The group as a whole should be able to gain by identifying with the people in the main roles.

Tell, or remind people, of the ground rules of role play:
- Confidentiality. People must feel secure that whatever they do or say will not be shared beyond the group. A sense of security can be achieved by discussing the purpose and methods of role play and gaining a commitment to confidentiality from every group member at the beginning.

- Co-operation. People should be supportive of others and expect to help them. They should plan to co-operate rather than compete.
- Everyone participates. The group should be small enough for most people to join in the action, and for everyone to join in the discussion.
- No advice giving. People can say what they would have done — or liked to do in the role play — in the sharing at the end.
- Focus on the present. This is not the time for wishing things were different, grieving for the past, or planning revenge. The purpose of role play is to look at alternative ways of responding in situations. Encourage a commitment to apply what is learnt to real life.
- Show ideas. Role play is about showing ideas and feelings rather than talking about them.

Select the participants Choose the main person (the protagonist) first. This person goes to the front and helps choose the others (auxiliaries) needed in the role play. When role play is based on a situation the protagonist has experienced, it is important for that person to choose the auxiliaries so that the role play is as close to the original scene as possible, given the people in the group. (This does not apply to acting out an anticipated situation or a fantasy role play.)

In problem-solving role play, the protagonist also selects the starting point and what he or she specifically wants to explore. The protagonist then directs the auxiliaries so that the scene reflects their memory as accurately as possible. Keep role plays brief. They should be a kernel of an interaction that can be replayed several times in quick succession.

Scene setting Ask the protagonist about the setting. Where is this incident happening? Who is in it? What is the mood? This scene setting helps everyone visualize the situation.

'Interview' type questions can be asked at other stages of the role play, but only with the aim of clarifying a situation rather than analyzing it.

Prepare the group to observe Let everyone know that they are expected to share their perceptions of what happened, at the end. They should focus on what is happening in the role play rather than think about past or future possibilities or the rights and wrongs of the situation.

Start promptly Begin without too much discussion. Get people to just do it and act as well as possible. Stop once the problem is in the open. Everyone should then stay out the front, in their roles, for a period of discussion.

Discussion Was it real? Why not? If necessary, re-enact the role play.

A scene can be done several times, with the actors being changed for all or part of the role play.

Debriefing   When an actor leaves the role he or she should be 'debriefed'. This means restating who people are as themselves, as opposed to who they were in the role play. Say, for example, to John, 'Now you're back to being John'. This is important in order to clearly demarcate acting from real life, and to remind people that they are now responding and speaking as themselves, not as their character.

Sharing   At the end everyone should say how they feel about the role play. First, ask people in turn for comments on the parts that worked well, then go round the group again and discuss what could be changed. People can say what they would have liked to say or do in another role or as director. Each person should be allowed to speak without interruption or comment from others, and everyone should contribute. Make the tone positive rather than focusing on what the protagonist should have said or done. No analysis of the protagonist is allowed.

The effect of role play can be cathartic, allowing the release and resolution of feelings. It allows people opportunities to express themselves in new ways.

In role play the therapist:
- Supervises the steps of role play.
- Suggests roles or incidents which most of the group can identify with.
- Ensures that people are clear about the goal and procedure.
- Checks people's feelings about the role play and their part in it.
- Keeps therapeutic goals in view and supports people in their growth.
- Observes which roles are absent, adequate, over or under developed in each person, so that opportunities can be made for that person to try new roles or give up roles which are unproductive or harmful.
- Works to create clarity for the person so that he or she can make choices.

Role reversal

Role reversal is a technique from psychodrama which can be used in role play. The director of the role play 'freezes' the action and the main person (the protagonist) and the person he or she is interacting with (the auxiliary) change roles and redo a unit of interaction.

Role reversal is only possible when the auxiliary has seen and experienced enough of the protagonist's role to understand and reproduce it. The technique enables both to see the other's role more clearly. The protagonist, particularly, hears how he or she sounds to the auxiliary because the auxiliary tries to faithfully reproduce the role of the protagonist.

Role taking

Use this handy technique in the middle of any activity where you see a therapeutic opportunity. You might say to someone, 'Try making that a question', 'How would an assertive person do that?' People will find it easier to take a risk in small-scale interpersonal encounters initially.

Role training

In role training people work to improve their skill and competence in specific roles. The emphasis is on training or rehearsal rather than analysis. Rehearsals prepare people for using the role in real life. Before someone can take a role they must 'play' it (for example, a student nurse 'plays' the role of 'nurse').

Role training is useful in assertiveness courses, before an interview or in any new social interaction. It is best done on a one-to-one basis or in a very small group. Sometimes it helps to learn small sections of a dialogue by heart, for example, the opening statement in a particular situation.

People can also work on a specific kind of role. For example, a role that is used in group interaction (harmonizer, questioner), in a work situation (efficient person) or in a situation where roles conflict. Coach people in their roles by using numerous mini role plays of different but similar situations, until they master the role and are comfortable with it. The importance of role playing lies not so much in learning the right way to do something, as in developing the ability to be flexible, choose, compromise, negotiate, listen and so on.

Warn people that when their ability to take roles expands others may feel threatened. Where roles overlap, negotiate. The result of one person becoming more capable is usually a gain for others — but the benefits may need to be pointed out.

If a group is new to role play, or shy, it may be best to start with simple role training exercises, such as 'Making a request', 'Leaving a social event' or 'Meeting and parting in a brief encounter'.

Techniques from psychodrama used in role play

- Mirroring. In mirroring another person takes the role of protagonist so that the protagonist has the opportunity to see him or herself as if in a mirror.
- Empty chair. This powerful technique is useful when people are shy or embarrassed about role play or psychodrama. The protagonist can:
  a. Speak to an empty chair, pretending that a particular person is sitting in it.
  b. Sit in the chair and speak from it in the way someone spoke to them, then stand to reply.
  c. Use several empty chairs so that they can speak from, and to, a number of people who are not present.

  It is important for the director to keep the pace slow enough to avoid confusion about who the protagonist is speaking to. Clarify by restating who is who at each change if necessary. For example, 'Now sit in the chair and be your dad'.
- Concretizing. Concretizing can be used as a general approach but it is

also a technique in its own right. As a general approach, the director encourages the protagonist to speak in concrete, specific terms, as though the events were happening now. As a technique, chairs, cushions or objects of some kind are used to represent people and settings. The person constructs a picture of a situation talking about it as they work. For example, the protagonist might say, 'This seat is Joe, and this one is my daughter', as they move the seats to show the relationship between Joe and the daughter.

This technique is particularly useful in one-to-one work, when the protagonist is describing a situation involving a large number of people. Using symbols is less threatening than acting and helps both therapist and protagonist visualize the situation and the relationships.

* Doubling. An auxiliary (often the therapist) speaks as the protagonist's 'double' when the protagonist becomes tongue-tied. The double says what he or she thinks the protagonist is trying to say, using the same manner and tone. Advise a double to get into the same body position as the protagonist first, and to try to use the same speech and mannerisms. The double 'shows' the protagonist what they have been saying in order to help them to go on. The protagonist can, of course, either accept or disagree with what the auxiliary offers.

Psychodrama

Psychodrama aims at an in-depth understanding of self. As a therapist it is wise to learn about the powers and safe use of psychodrama firsthand through being part of a group doing psychodrama.

Briefly, psychodrama is a form of group therapy based on the psychoanalytic perspective. Problems in relationships between people are clarified by re-enacting part of a situation in the life of one person (the protagonist). People act themselves in a scene they experienced in the past and, usually, they react in the same way that they did then. It is very hard not to 'act' as oneself because this is the way of responding that comes naturally. The scene is acted in the present and action is more important than dialogue.

This experience of reliving the past is usually intense because the psychodrama accentuates and exaggerates the incident being worked on. All the people involved concentrate on the story and the feelings of the protagonist, trying to understand them and to play a part in the drama. Feelings that cannot be adequately described are acted and the psychodrama shines a spotlight on aspects of the past, present and future. It often shows people the roots of their problems and enables them to make choices for the future based on fuller self knowledge. Therapeutic 'acting out' may remove the need for destructive behaviour in everyday life.

Although the situation that is relived is part of the life of one person in the group, others often become aware of parallels and contrasts in their own life and feel a heightened empathy for the protagonist. The closer the problem is to the problems of others in the group, the more involved they will feel and the more they will learn from each other. This is an important consideration in the warm up, and in the process of selecting a problem to work on.

When the incident has been played out the rest of the group share their experiences with the protagonist, and reassure him or her of their support. The protagonist must never be left feeling he or she is alone facing their problem. It is a positive experience to help someone else and feel empathy with them.

In full psychodrama there is always a trained director. The director and protagonist work as a pair with the pace set by the protagonist. The director's expertise lies in making the techniques work for the protagonist and group, and in coping with issues as they arise. (See *Confrontation* p. 39 and *WORKING IN GROUPS, Emotional issues* p. 218.)

Activities

Warm-up and ending activities

Warm-up activities should be short, five to ten minutes, and simple. In summary they:

- Require only minimal equipment and instructions.
- Involve physical activity to stimulate energy.
- Are purposeful. They focus on the needs of the group.
- Help people get to know one another.
- Introduce the session.
- Reduce anxiety and increase trust and cohesion.
- Are fun and lightweight.
- Are done by everyone in the group, usually including the therapist.

Choose activities which will reinforce the main activity of the session and present them so that they have a task or conflict element. This gives people something to work on. (See *SELF AWARENESS, Activities* p. 16, for more warm-up activities.)

After a break in a session Have a mini warm up to reorientate people and revive their energy levels.

Ending activities Ending activities should be brief. They are to help people integrate the experiences of the session. They should emphasize success and draw the group together.

Warm-up activities and greeting games

Medleys

- Get people to walk about the room and greet each person they meet non-verbally; greet them verbally; shake hands; greet with their shoulders.
- In pairs, one person moulds the other into a shape, then the sculptor becomes a mirror image of his or her partner.

- In pairs, one person rolls a 'floppy doll' partner across the floor, or gently unfolds them from a tightly curled-up ball. Say hello.

Introductions
- People walk round, shake hands and say, 'Hi, I'm . . .'(use your name!) to each person in the group.
- This can be an individual or group activity. People make quick collages of a pre-decided topic and then talk about what they have chosen to include. As a warm up the topic should relate to the theme of the session. Set a time limit and use small sheets of paper.
- People list four to ten words that describe them. They share their list with the group.
- The group sits in a circle. Everyone gives one word describing how they feel right now or one word describing how they felt on the way to the group. (Inviting people to give just one word avoids long contributions, yet gives you some idea of their mood).
- 'My favourite window' — each person describes the view from a favourite window.
- 'An advertisement for me would say . . .' In turn, people complete the sentence including at least three different things about themselves.
- The group passes a handshake round the circle and back. Each person gives their name each time, so that people hear all the names twice.

Mime introduction Each person chooses one to three things they do, or would like to do, at some time in their lives. They mime their choices and then tell the group what they were doing. 'I'm Susan, and I showed cooking, shopping and netball.'

Share a feast In turn, each person announces the dish they have brought to an imaginary banquet. People circulate and 'share' the feast. (This is not such a good activity if everyone is hungry!)

Five-minute debate This is run like a debate, with people assigned to teams of three. Allow teams one or two minutes to decide on a speaking order and division of ideas. The aim is to raise a few ideas quickly rather than explore issues thoroughly. The audience can think about what they would expect to be covered and thus be ready with prompting or challenging questions. (See *VERBAL ACTIVITIES, Debating* p. 141.)

Colour introductions 'Describe your favourite colour and something you like in that colour' or 'Describe an imaginary walk round your garden' (house, favourite place) or 'Describe a favourite day'.

My name is . . . Go once round the group, getting each person to say their name in an ordinary way, then go round again asking them to say it in a different way — softly, angrily, playfully — and finally the way they would like others to say it. What do people say about themselves when they say their own names? There is scope here for coaching people to be more definite, energetic, gentle and so on in the way they say their name.

Throw a cushion, ask a question   When you explain this activity, give examples of the types of questions that can be used. Tailor the questions to the degree of knowledge the group has about each other already and the type of relationship you want to develop.

Examples of lightweight questions are, 'What did you watch on TV last night?', 'What did you do over the weekend?', 'Do you like skating?'

More personal questions are, 'What would you like to get out of this session?', 'What topics do you find it most difficult to share your feelings about?', 'Tell us one thing that makes you angry'.

Spin a yarn   Prepare a ball of wool by making knots in it at intervals. The group stands in a circle and one person begins by throwing the ball to someone else. The catcher talks and unwinds the wool until they come to a knot. They then throw the ball to someone else, holding onto the wool where the knot is with their other hand.

As an introductory activity, people can talk about themselves. At other times this activity can be used to discuss any topic. It is a good way of ensuring that no one person dominates the conversation and that everyone has a turn.

Word stories   Each person is given a word.

Nouns: Everyone is given a word to act out in a little story. People either say what their work is as they start or it is a guessing game and the group works out the word each person was given. Suggestions: holiday, storm, grapes, snake, horse, door, snowflake, dolphin, ruby, fear, pride.

Verb suggestions: sailing, lassoing, batting, teaching.

Adverbs: Each person acts in the manner of their adverb, for example, ponderously, wildly, demurely and so on.

On the map   Have a large map of your country and another of the world. Each person takes it in turn to put a large-head pin or a little flag on a pin in the place where they were born. As a second round people put pins in a place that is significant to them — it might be somewhere they enjoyed living, where their forebears came from, where they had a holiday, or somewhere they have always fancied going. Each person acts out something related to their choice.

Progressive introductions   Going around the group, each person introduces themselves giving their full name (including middle names) and their main life roles, for example, Simon Alexander Leary, plumber's apprentice, skier, brother, flatmate and so on. On the second round they give only the main points, for example, Simon, plumber's apprentice. On the third round they give just the name they like to be called, Simon.

Silent greeting Everyone moves about the room greeting others non-verbally. Suggest different ways of doing this, for example, 'Make eye contact with people and smile', 'Nod to people', 'Wave', 'Shake hands with as many people as possible', 'Share a quick hug'.

People can then link arms with a partner and go about greeting other pairs.

Interview introduction Getting people to interview their neighbour and introduce them to the group is a good way of starting a session when people do not know each other well. Interview topics can be general or relate to the purpose of the group. Topics: Discuss one of your favourite experiences, share your earliest memory, discuss your favourite book (poem, television programme), describe your family (dream house, holiday, beginnings, hobbies). Say who you'd like to be. Who your hero is.

Each person then finishes sentences aloud as a way of introducing their partner to the group. The sentences can be presented in a number of ways, for example, on a blackboard or on individual cards. Sentence ideas: 'For a good time my partner likes to . . .', 'The things my partner hates/loves most are . . .', 'In five years' time my partner hopes to . . .', 'Two things I have in common with my partner are . . .'

Fit the label Each person is given a card with a heading at the top. Heading ideas are: 'Likes pavlova?', 'Has blue eyes?', 'Takes size five shoes?'. Players circulate and ask as many people as possible if they 'Like pavlova?' and so on. Players write each other's names and 'Yes' or 'No' after them. After five to seven minutes people take turns to read out what they have discovered about one another.

Alternatively, the questions could ask for individual details. For example, 'Favourite pudding?' 'Main hobby?'

Give me a clue This game was designed for the elderly. The group forms a circle with one person in the centre. They address anyone in the circle with a guess. 'I think you once worked as a waiter.' If they are right the person tells a little about their experiences as a waiter, and if they are wrong the person asked might reply, 'No, but I've done some barbecue cooking.' (If possible the person asked must pick something related to the question to share with the group and 'show' how they did it).

Change turns after each person in the middle has asked, say, three questions. Questions might cover family size, places lived or travelled to, birthday month, hobbies, likes. If necessary, help people with ideas about how they could respond.

Spot the lie   Each person gives a brief resume of their life (set a time limit) but includes one major lie. At the end of each story the group has to guess which bit was untrue. Encourage people to include unusual things they have done so that the 'lie' is less obvious.

Who am I?   Each person writes their own name (or the name of a famous person), or draws a sketch of something (a flower, an animal . . .) on a piece of paper, and the papers are pinned to their backs. People then try to collect a list of who everyone else is, or what is on their label, at the same time as trying to prevent others from seeing their label.

Come into the circle   The group forms a circle with people spaced at arm's length from each other. Each person says their name and how they are feeling at that moment. Alternatively, people jump into the circle in a way that shows their mood.

Act your name   As a means of introducing people, each person acts their name, either letter by letter, in syllables or through a book or song title that has their name in it. Discuss how people feel about their names and nicknames and how they came to get them.
   In another activity, the group renames each person in turn, with names that seem to fit. (Keep the tone of the group fun and supportive).

If I was someone else I would like to be . . .   Each person completes this phrase with the name of someone they would like to be. People can add 'because . . .' after the name. Answers can be funny or serious. They then pretend to be the person.

Physical warm ups   Use tag games, stretch and flop rhythms. Or get people to, 'Move like a kite', 'a cloud', 'a gust of wind', or any way they like. At intervals call out, 'Try another way.' People must use different ideas each time.

Follow the leader   Each person leads the group in turn for one physical activity, so that everyone contributes to the warm-up exercises.

Move to a spot   Each person looks round the room and picks a spot. Suggest ways for people to move to the place they have chosen. Ideas are: take a route that includes three right angles, walk backwards, stomp crossly, do a funny walk.

Jackson's shake   People start by wriggling and shaking just one finger, then one hand, the other hand, forearms and so on. Gradually they include more of the body until their whole body is shaking and jumping. Then they go through all the stages in reverse, back to stillness — and relaxation.

Body contact hellos Call out body parts at regular intervals and people move about the room greeting each other by touching the relevant body part: shoulders, thumbs, toes, backs, elbows and so on.

Throw an imaginary ball Say to the group, 'Say someone's name and throw the ball to them.' People can say what kind of ball it is too, 'Jane, here's a ping pong ball . . .'

Pairs challenges
Finger fight In pairs, people start with their right fore fingers crossed like swords and on the signal 'go', they race round their partner and try to tag them on the back.
Push In pairs, people face each other with their palms flat against the other person's. Each tries to push the other person back. Alternatively, people link arms, back to back, and push their partner backwards. Winners push winners. (Discussion topic — do you let yourself get pushed round in other areas of life?)

Yuk This activity is good for generating energy when people are reluctant to get started or complain of listlessness. Tell them that they are all weighed down with 'yuk', and it has to come off before any work can be done. Get them to stand in a circle and, gently at first, shake up and down to jiggle the 'yuk' off. Gradually, they get more vigorous and fling their limbs about, scraping the 'yuk' off their bodies, making any sound effects they feel like at the same time. End with some light dancing movements so that people can show how free they feel now. Finally, people gently flick and polish each other with imaginary dusters.

Simon says Use this game as a way of doing a range of warm-up exercises. 'Simon says stretch . . . bend . . . do a knees up'. Or, 'Simon says be naughty children at a party', 'pretend you are watching marvellous fireworks' and so on.

Funny floors People walk about the room as though the floor is made of: mud, quicksand, slippery ice, rubber, or covered in two feet of water, three feet of water, water deep enough to swim in and so on.
Alternatively, say to people, 'There's a funny wall beside you, it's made of rubber (it's prickly, sticky and so on). Reach out and feel it, push it, prod it.'

The circle Get the group to form a circle for a variety of action, sound and contact activities. The group can:
• Join hands, go into the centre, raise their hands, say 'Hello', return to their place, circle to the left and so on.
• Do some swinging, stretching movements.
• Greet each person by chanting their name.

People turn to a partner and do a neck massage, rub backs, pat each other's backs all over, blow a 'hot potato' (a hot potato is air blown through cupped hands onto the middle of the person's back through their clothes).

A puppet This is a movement warm up in which people imagine that strings are attached to them, pulling them in different ways. Call out the body parts that are being pulled: 'left knee up', 'right shoulder up', 'move to the back of the stage', 'right arm out'.

Theatre games

Theatre games are designed to be sociable and fun. They can be linked to people's life attitudes and values and they provide opportunities for people to be the centre of attention, make decisions and so on. The can also be used for specific purposes such as to reinforce aspects of everyday activities, provide social contact, develop imagination or encourage self-expression. Start with concrete activities and images and move to more abstract ones as the group becomes experienced.

Encourage people to show whatever they are portraying as vividly as possible, in order to sharpen drama skills. They should have a clear, detailed idea of who they are, and of all the whens, wheres, whys and hows of the situation. Get people to exaggerate the action and take plenty of time. People can act or mime a situation, then do it again changing one aspect, such as the emotional content. Many theatre games work well when a large group breaks into groups of three to five and prepares skits to show each other.

Let's pretend This type of activity can be used as a guessing game or as an exercise to portray something vividly.

If members of the audience put their hands over their ears, it will encourage the actors to concentrate more on 'showing' than 'telling'. People can also talk to each other using nonsense words. Gibberish helps people 'show' what they want to convey. This exercise is valuable for developing vocal skills. Work in pairs initially. Topic ideas include: 'Your last visit to the dentist', 'A pretend phone call'.

You can also get people to argue or talk to each other using numbers instead of words.

Ideas for 'Let's pretend' include:

- *In the kitchen* Make a dinner, stir in this and that, shake a bottle, take off the top, pour some in, sniff and taste some of your brew from a spoon, lay the table, light the candles . . .
- *In the work shop* Measure, cut, check, nail together, sand paper, get the paint . . .

  Use all kinds of settings — each room of a house, a garden, a sports ground — and all the everyday and unusual activities which happen at the places you think of.

- *Combine setting and age group*   Be a particular age: a five-year-old starting school, ten-year-olds playing with a ball, a teenager out on the town with friends and so on.
- *History, books*   What or who have people always wanted to be? A disc jockey? An interpreter? A robot? . . .
- *Visits*   Visit an imaginary museum, art gallery, eastern market . . .
- *A journey*   Act out the events of a journey by train, bus or plane. Act out incidents that occur along the way. Each person could be responsible for one stop. Where is everyone going?
- *Explanation*   Begin by setting up something 'odd' that must be explained. A window that is wide open, a pair of shoes on a table, a shirt hoisted as a flag on a building . . .
- *A day in the life of . . .*   An old house, Santa Claus, a member of the royal family, Dr X on the ward, a coin, a taxi . . .
- *Picked categories*   The categories are place, people, object. People choose one of each then plan a scene using all three.

Mime   All the topics above can be mimed, with or without a narrator. Some ideas work best done individually, others are better in a group.
Ideas for mime are:
- Change a bicycle tyre. Discover the flat tyre, collect spoons or levers and patches. Finish by pumping the tyre up, putting things away and riding off.
- Give a speech on how to cook spaghetti (curl your hair, peel a banana, eat with chopsticks, run the country).
- Act a sound, for example, a gargle, a sigh, a shriek, gasp, gulp.
- Act a word called out by a leader: 'soft', 'spring bulbs', 'a pencil writing', 'a prehistoric monster', 'a school of fish'.
- Act a comic strip.
- Walk another person's walk. One person can lead the whole group or people can work in pairs.
- Act a situation called out by a leader: 'Nervous person meets ghost', 'My first parachute jump'.
- The mood or story of some music. Play the music then ask, 'What do you see?', 'Show us what is going to happen'. Poems can be done the same way.
- Be a famous couple: Romeo and Juliet, Jack and Jill, Bonnie and Clyde . . .
- Act out what you would do in a fantasy place: the beach, an airport, the snow.
- Solve a problem: moving a piano, trying to catch a mouse, being late, coping with an accident, fixing a broken zip.
- Act out a nursery rhyme.
- As a group, co-operate to act as tins on the supermarket shelf, peas in a packet, parked cars, a bouquet.
- Act to a recording. This can be done as a skit, using a prerecorded

voice which is in complete contrast to the person doing the acting.
• Using the script of a play, act to it without saying anything.
• Do a chain mime. Three or four people leave the room while those left
behind plan something for one person to mime. Without being told
what they are trying to mime, each person is called back into the room
one by one, watches the mime, and then does it for the next person
until all the group have tried to repeat what they have been shown.

A melodrama Make up a melodrama. First work out some characters
together, so that the group has a selection of the classic characters of
melodrama to build into the story. Candidates might be:
• The tall, dark, handsome hero, or a macho one who is blond, blue-eyed
and tanned (a prince?).
• The sweet, innocent heroine,
• The mustachioed villain (with cigar and Alfa Romeo . . .)
• The heartless landlord.
• A wicked witch (with cat, bats and broom).
• The heroine's anxious parents.
• A bronco, stage coach or Mercedes.
• A king, queen and their daughters: Fat, Thin, and Beautiful.
   Once the characters are established, the group works out a rough plot
scene by scene, then acts each scene fleshing it out as they go.
   The story can be told through the action alone or through a narrator. If
there are more people than roles, a separate group can make sound
effects. For sound effects each of the characters is associated with a sound,
so a story about a witch and a beautiful heroine might begin like this,
'Once upon a time, a wicked witch (shriek, cackle, cackle) needed the hair
of a beautiful maiden (ahhh) for . . .'
   Many children's stories can be adapted and used in this way, as can short
romance stories from magazines.
   People can try writing their own episode of a popular television series.

Mock event Hold a mock wedding, circus, banquet, auction, television
quiz show or product investigation programme. Attention to detail is
important — the banquet, for example, should be complete with splendid
decor, footmen and butlers.

The hat Have a selection of hats: top hat, school cap, balaclava, helmet,
sombrero . . . or a more everyday selection. Talk about the role that
goes with each hat. If you do not have enough real hats, make some out of
newspaper, sticky tape and pins. People take it in turns to choose a hat and
play the role. The rest of the group can observe, or join in and relate to the
'hat' role.

Slow motion People act a fight, a tennis match or a race in slow motion.
Or get each person to use their chair (jacket, cup) as though it were

The hat

'something else'. The chair might be a wheelbarrow, a beehive, a music stand. The jacket might be a dancer's cape, a baby's bedcover and so on. This activity is good as a guessing game.

People use a chair in different ways: as a two-year-old would, or a businessman asserting his authority or an elderly person with osteoarthritis. How many ways can people sit down?

The visitor The group sits in a circle and each person in turn has 'a visitor' on their chair. They get up, greet the visitor, exchange questions, respond to their imaginary replies, say goodbye and sit down again. Encourage people to be imaginative about who the visitors are. Once people have chosen their visitor, get them to build up a clear picture of how the person walks and talks — as much detail as possible. Where has this person been and where are they going?

The whopper One person tells a story while the others help to elaborate it by exaggerating their belief in its truth.

Behind the scenes People act out, 'Behind the scenes at a coronation', '. . . television production', '. . . with an Olympic games rowing eight before the race'.

A letter to guess   Each person (or small group) chooses a letter and acts it out silently while the rest of the group guesses what it is.

Alternatively, act out colours, musical instruments, a character from television, an animal, an orchestra, the life of a flower (coin, newspaper).

Pairs of words to act and guess   People take it in turns to act out a pair of words. The rest of the group tries to guess what they are doing. Ideas: play poker, eat eclairs, dry dishes, bounce balls, run races.

You can also do pairs that go together, for example cup and saucer, chalk and cheese, or pairs of opposites, for example, black and white, up and down.

More 'guess' starting points
* Who am I?
* Where am I? Where am I going?
* What am I buying (doing, eating, playing)?
* I'm making a . . . ?
* My sport (hobby) is . . . ?
* What animal am I?
Or use proverbs.

-INGS to act and guess   Skating, leaping, hang gliding, icing a cake, purring.

Passing things   Each person opens an imaginary parcel and describes what is inside. Alternatively, allow the group to ask three questions and make one guess before they are told what is in the parcel.

Free association ball pass   People pass a large ball round at random. As each person catches the ball they say the first word that comes into their minds. This can be done with a theme.

Pass an imaginary object   People take turns to be the leader in this activity for small groups. Each leader chooses an imaginary object to pass round the group with suitable sound effects and actions. Possibilities are: a curled-up hedgehog, an electric shock, a brimming bucket, a newborn baby.

Pass the parcel   A parcel is passed round the group while music is played. When the music stops the person with the parcel takes off one layer of paper. Each layer of paper has an activity instruction written on it, so the unwrapping is a lucky dip of activities. For example, 'Sing a nursery rhyme', 'Shake hands with everyone in the circle', 'Ask everyone to pay you a compliment', 'Pass the parcel to someone wearing red.'

The instructions can be for the person who unwraps the layer or the whole group. The list can be made up by the group beforehand, with each person writing on one of the wrapping paper layers. People will then only write things they are prepared to do themselves.

As a bonus, the parcel could contain something nice for the group to share at the end.

Body language People say with their feet, 'I'm nervous', 'I'm waiting', 'My shoes are too tight', 'What a lovely carpet', 'Mud!'. You can also make a paperbag foot puppet for this activity. Get the group to sit in a circle on the floor or on low chairs.

People say with their shoulders (or hands, head, mouth), 'I'm on holiday!', 'I don't understand', 'I'm surprised', 'I'm worried', 'It's itchy', 'I'm upset'.

People lie on the floor in pairs, their hands above their heads in their partner's line of vision and have a 'hand conversation'. Any of the topics above can be used.

Come over the fence There is an imaginary fence stretched across the room. One person is on one side of the fence and the rest of the group is on the other side. The person on his or her own must silently beckon and persuade people to come across. People in the group are doubtful but one by one they cross, then help with the coaxing.

Puzzled pair Set up a story, preferably a transaction of some sort, in which people either do not, or will not, understand each other. One of the two characters can be changed at intervals but the story is continuous.

Story ideas: One person wants to buy something but the other does not want to sell; one person wants to go to a dance, the other does not; one person tries to persuade the conservative members of a board that they should change policy. Use any situation in which one person is required to be persuasive.

Ask a group 'How many ways can you make a circle or line?'

'Hello' People say 'hello' as though they have not met for a year (ten years, since yesterday, since one of them became famous), as though they are about to go on a long holiday together, gleefully, sorrowfully.

They can then say 'goodbye' as though one person is emigrating, going on holiday, going shopping.

Copying Everyone moves round the room in different ways, walking, hopping and so on. Periodically, people change the way they move. The therapist can also tag people on the shoulder at intervals, and from then on that person must copy someone else until about half the group are copying others. At the end, ask if people could see themselves being copied.

A gag Have a 'World's worst...' contest (driver, spaghetti cook, film censor, dictator).

Two feelings   People work in small groups planning, then acting out, a scene which concerns two feeling words.

People sculpture activities

Sculpting is a creative relationship. Use it as a self-awareness activity, for fun and to develop group cohesiveness.

In pairs

• People take turns to mould each other as though the person being moulded is made of clay, wire, flexible plastic or is filled with water or sawdust.
• People make each other into figures showing particular emotions. They speak for their sculpture, 'This is Paul, he's feeling . . .'

As a group

• One person sculpts the group into a scene. It could be a tableau of a wedding, a group at the beach, a group round a dinner table.
• One person sculpts the group into something: a plane, a building, something at a fair ground.
• One person sculpts the group as their own family and shows the relationships between family members. They either work silently or talk about what they are doing as they go.

Chain sculpting   Two people begin work in front of the group. One is the 'clay' and the other the 'sculptor'. The 'sculptor' continues to arrange the 'clay' until the group calls 'freeze', when the 'clay' must hold the position they have been moulded into.

'People sculpture; The bird feeder'

Now a new 'sculptor' is chosen to work on the first 'sculptor' who is now 'clay', until they in turn are 'frozen'.

Continue until the whole group are involved. The activity can be done to a theme, for example, 'Trees in the wind', 'God making the animals', 'A machine with moving parts'. With mechanical images it is good to work to a steady rhythm which sets the pace. People can use furniture and props to add to their sculpture — whatever is available.

Blindfold sculpting in groups   Divide the group into two. One group, with their eyes open, are the sculptors and the other group, with their eyes shut, are the clay. It is a good idea for the sculptors to have a brief meeting beforehand to decide what they are going to do. The sculpting can be done through spoken directions to 'the clay' or the sculptors can physically mould their 'clay' people. When everybody has appreciated the creation, the groups swap over.

Self-sculpting   In this activity all the members of the group agree on what they will be and then they work together to make themselves into whatever they have chosen. Try this activity without verbal communication.

Blindfold sculpting   Working in pairs, one person is a blindfold sculptor and the other makes themselves into a strangely shaped statue. The sightless sculptor must get into the same position as the sculpture by feeling where the limbs are. Begin this activity using arms only, then move on to all kinds of starting positions — lying, sitting down and so on.

This activity is more complex if two pairs work together, one pair 'sighted', the other pair copying them.

Decide on the rules at the beginning — can the sculpture give verbal clues? Can the sculptor recheck? How much time do they have?

Face sculpting   In pairs, or standing in a circle, one person moulds others' faces. They can make everyone look sad, joyful, scowling and so on.

Relationships

Picture people   Cut out a selection of pictures of people from magazines or newspapers. Include the rich and famous, screen personalities and a variety of 'ordinary people' — builders, traffic officers, mischievous children and so on. The pictures can be chosen at the time by the group or, better still, prepared ahead.

Each person selects a picture of someone they would like to be and pins the picture of that person to their chest. Everyone moves about greeting and talking to one another as though they were the person pinned to their chest. People respond in kind.

Choose a setting for the meeting: on a train, in a restaurant or in a shopping mall.

Chess   If some people are not familiar with chess the director will need to describe the moves of the different pieces before starting. In a kind of role play, one person is chosen to be the King of a chess board. The King assigns roles to everyone else, 'black knight', 'white queen', 'white pawn' and so on. Everyone is placed in relation to each other as they might be at some stage of a chess game.

The director moves his or her pieces, defending or attacking for either side alternately. After every few moves, stop the action and discuss how each piece feels in their role. Are there any life parallels?

Awareness activities with an action focus

Coaching   The group selects one or more characters — for example, an aggressive salesman, bossy teacher, kind granny and little child at the zoo, then coaches people in the roles, suggesting things they might do or say in that role. Do it again, exaggerating the roles. If possible, go on to look at the roles people really want to develop in their lives.

The mirror   People stand face to face in pairs and, taking it in turns, one person copies the other person's every action. The movements can be very subtle, unexpected or vigorous.

The leading person can use these variations:

* Create a dance with the other person.
* Have a tune in mind and see if the other person can work out what it is (Blue Danube waltz, Jingle Bells) from the movements.
* Do the activity to music.
* Begin only with one hand and work up slowly to using the whole body.
* Start some distance apart and finish with palms touching.
* Limit the action to the upper body only.
* Choose everyday actions like cleaning teeth, brushing hair, sweeping. Or people can choose any type of role to act.
* Use emotions and facial expression: fear, joy, rage.
* Try to trick and surprise the other person, or create a particular kind of mood.

After each person has had a turn as leader, have a few minutes where neither person is the leader but the pair must move so that they are always in the same position as each other. Each pair should keep moving so that the leadership can alternate, with either person deliberately leading. Discuss the kinds of relationships that resulted.

These activities can also be done in a group, with one person leading. People stand in two lines with each person copying the person diagonally opposite them. The movements zigzag along the line from the leader.

Blindfold messages   People say, 'Goodbye', 'I'm scared', 'I'm thrilled', with their eyes closed. Try this with and without sound. The idea is to communicate with other people despite being unable to see.

Trust and touch games

Two and two make one   In pairs, with one person as the supporter, the other person sees how far they can lean in different directions without falling. Get people to try this back to back while moving their feet forward, with their hands on each other's shoulders and palm to palm. The supporter should only need to give gentle support.

Head rock   People work in pairs, with one person lying on the ground with their eyes shut. The other person cradles the first person's head in their hands and gently rocks it and moves it up and down and round. The pace should be caring, indulgent and gentle.

Trust rock   Three people work together in this trust exercise. They get in a line with the two on the outside both facing the person in the middle and standing close enough to rock them backwards and forwards. The person being rocked must keep their back, hips and knees straight, and use their feet as the fulcrum they sway from. The people doing the rocking should have their feet apart so that they have a good base of support to work from. (Take care if one person is especially tall or heavy.)

Trust circle   Work in groups of no less than six and no more than nine. If you divide into more than one group, make sure that all the taller people are in one group and the shorter in the other. In each group each person has a turn in the middle. The person in the middle stands with their eyes closed and lets their body fall and be caught, pivoting on their feet with their legs straight. The group must stand shoulder to shoulder with their hands out ready to support and guide the person who is falling. They can gently pass the person from one side of the group to the other, making sure that more than one person is doing the catching each time. If people are passed too fast they will feel insecure or disorientated.

Blind walk   This well-known trust exercise can be done in a number of ways. People work in pairs with one person wearing a blindfold or shutting their eyes and the other leading them on a walk. The person leading can hold their partner's hand, guide them with arms linked or direct them verbally without any physical contact.

As a variation, change partners part way through, so that the blindfolded person does not know who their second partner is until the end. Do it with a line of blindfolded people, each person holding on to the shoulders of the one in front.

This activity can be done in a limited space or outdoors in a large area. The leader can take their partner round to meet others or introduce them to a variety of sensory experiences, such as feeling and smelling a shrub, the rough bark of a tree, a car and so on.

Discuss and set limits beforehand.

Which hand? (Note: This activity may seem threatening to some people). Everyone closes their eyes and finds a partner. In turn, they feel each other's hands so that they will recognize them later. They then move about again and when everyone is well mixed, they open their eyes and hunt for their partner. Decide if feeling cuffs will be allowed or not.

They can also feel each other's hair, face and clothes, then separate, open their eyes and find their partner.

Spiral Everyone walks round the room in the same direction, gradually spiralling in towards the centre until they are all in a tight milling bunch. Then the direction is reversed and the spiral grows bigger and bigger until everyone is out at the edges of the room again.

Tangles Everyone stands in a cluster, closes their eyes and reaches out to find two free hands to hold. Then people open their eyes and try to untangle themselves into one or more circles.

Wind in The group holds hands in a circle and chooses one person to be the centre of a spiral. This person lets go one hand and the rest of the group spiral in round and round them to make a tight human coil. They then unwind again.

Blind circle Get people to take off their shoes and stand in a circle with their eyes shut. They then walk straight ahead to the opposite wall. When they reach the wall they turn round and walk back. Take it slowly and carefully!

They can also walk across the circle and reform as a circle.

The knot Divide the group into two. The members of one group hold hands in a circle and form themselves into a tangled knot by ducking under and over each other's arms. The other group does not watch. When the tangled group are ready the other group tries to untangle them.

Electrons The group forms a circle holding hands and everyone makes a mental note of who is on either side of them. Then people move round being 'electrons', the leader instructing them to go backwards, sideways and so on. On the call, 'Huddle', everyone rushes to form a tight cluster in the centre. Each person reaches out for the two hands they held before, then the group tries to expand into a circle again.

Activities to focus on voice

Verbal exercises For work on pace, volume, intonation and so on, use choral reading, whispered scenes, singing, chanting, action songs, plays, poems or prose — whatever appeals to the group.

Sound fling   Form a circle with a leader in the centre. The leader makes a soft sound and a small movement and the group copies them. The leader gradually makes the movement larger and the sound louder until they are ready to 'fling' it to someone else who changes places with them and starts a new movement and sound.

In the mood   This activity can be done by one person in front of the group or the whole group together. Begin by choosing a mood. Recite a poem, read a passage or sing a song using the mood. For example, sing or recite 'Mary Had a Little Lamb' or 'Little Miss Muffet' as though it were the saddest thing that ever happened, or as though it were funny, worrying, a cause for hope, astonishing, frightening and so on.

Alternatively, get people to take turns reading a piece from the newspaper as though it were in a particular emotional vein. Select passages which in fact have little emotional tone, such as a gardening column. The whole group can respond with the reader. People can also read in the manner of a politician, a kindergarten teacher, a cricket commentator or a cross mother.

Read descriptive poetry aloud together   Some narrative poems lend themselves to being divided into parts or to being acted out as they are read.

Converting   Tell the group, 'I'll make a sound, you turn it into a picture with your bodies, hold the pose for a few moments then turn it into a movement.' When the first sound has been thoroughly explored someone else can be the leader.

Television   Divide the group into two. One group 'switches on' the other, talking about the programme they expect to see. The group that is switched on tries to give what has been asked for.

Another option is to get people to plan and mime a comic strip as a series of tableaux.

Storytelling   Like all good stories, the ones you use in drama should progress from an intriguing beginning which sets the scene, through the substance of the story, to an ending which ties up loose ends and completes things. The ending can also raise a number of questions or take people back to the beginning again.

Group stories   The group seats itself in a circle and one person begins a story. At whatever point they choose, they hand the story over to someone else in the circle. It is best to make the turns random, rather than go round the group in order. This kind of story works best if people make an effort to stick to the theme given by the first storyteller rather than change the tale radically. One way to maintain continuity is to have a main storyteller who takes every second turn.

With small groups, say two to four, the members can all make up the story and act it out at the same time. Ideas for starting points are: a television commercial, a scene from a doctor's waiting room, a school class with a new teacher. Each person announces who they are at the beginning and one is chosen to start the action. The others respond with each person trying to relate to everyone else in the scene.

Arguments Give a small group (say three to five) something to quarrel about. Each person has a role: placating father, dominating older sister, blaming mother and so on.

Pairs stories In pairs, people make up a story by taking turns on every second word. Again, people should make use of what has been said already rather than going in a completely different direction.

Unfortunately, fortunately In this two-person dialogue one person starts what they say with, 'Unfortunately . . .' and the other with, 'Fortunately . . .'

Forward reminiscing People act out 'the first thing you plan to do when you leave hospital'.

Good news, bad news In pairs, people take turns telling each other imaginary pieces of news.

Two at a time Each person in the group chooses a role. Two go to the front and interact using the roles they have chosen. Another person comes up to join them and one of the first people must find a reason to leave. Another joins the pair and the other person from the first pair must leave and so on. Each person comes and goes from the action as naturally as they can. For example, the first two people could be a lion tamer and a shop assistant. The shop assistant sells the lion tamer some meat. As the transaction ends, a nurse joins them, and starts to talk about safety to the lion tamer . . . the shopkeeper leaves . . .

Liar's tag Form a circle and choose a person to take the first turn. They start on an action and someone asks them what they are doing. They must say something *different* from what they are actually doing. Now the asker does what the first person said and gives the next wrong answer when they are asked what they are doing. For example, person one is sawing a plank, they say they are knitting a jersey, person two knits and says they are playing with a kitten and so on . . .

Colouring in Sentence by sentence one person tells a story and the other person 'colours it in', that is, fills it out with adjectives and adverbs.

The magic shop   This is a drama game about the cost of things such as life skills and personal qualities. The goal is to clarify people's goals and the costs and consequences of them. In the 'magic shop', all kinds of qualities are for sale: humour, placidity, optimism, justice, courage, energy. One person is chosen as the shopkeeper and all the others are customers. Payment can be made with characteristics which people have but don't want, for example, intolerance or greed. The shopkeeper decides how much intolerance or selfishness must be given for a bag of hope or six kilos of love, for example. He or she can also offer bargain lines or compromise deals. Shoppers have to decide whether they really want to part with the characteristic or whether it does serve a purpose in their lives.

Alternatively, people can give good qualities they have or ones that will lead to what they are asking for. ('I'll give love for love', 'But you've already got it', 'But you can't have it unless you give it'.) Tolerance can be given for respect, energy for skills and so on. The shopkeeper can decide what the quality will buy, and can ask for suggestions from other shoppers if they are short of ideas. Shoppers can also ask the group for ideas. The shopkeeper can dress as a magician and use a wand and trinkets to represent goods.

Try changing the role of shopkeeper to auctioneer. The 'lots' to be auctioned can be printed on cards or a blackboard or chart. There may be several lots of certain items while others are grouped together. The auctioneer can put a 'reserve' on some items (that is, set a minimum price). Ideas for lots are: a sack of honesty, bags of love, tons of enthusiasm, boxes of kindness, bottles of thoughtfulness and packages of commonsense (optimism, sympathy, strength). The first step of the activity could be to make up a list of the items for auction. The auctioneer puts the items up like so: 'Now we come to lot five, a big sack of honesty. Who'll give me ten tokens for this lot? Eight tokens?' Buyers can pool their money and share a lot or do some bartering among themselves at the end.

Relive a day of your choice   Each person takes it in turns to mime the day they have chosen, then to describe it to the group. Do they regret it? Miss it? Hope for more like that? Or just relive and enjoy it?

Controlled conversations   Two people, A and B, play out this activity in front of the group. The conversation topic is one of the participants, A, and the rules are:
- The conversation must follow a normal pattern of turns.
- No questions are allowed.
- The subject cannot be changed. After about a minute B becomes the topic of conversation.

Fantasy journeys   'Design a costume, find a chariot . . . off you go to the land you choose.' You can make detailed suggestions or get the group to decide on the content of a shared fantasy. Once the place is chosen, ask

the group to contribute ideas about what everyone sees and does there.
Ideas include:

> At the sea . . .
> In the snow . . .
> At the circus . . .
> On a tropical island . . .
> Diving on a coral reef . . .
> An action packed adventure — a shipwreck, a struggle through a
> blizzard, with Captain Cook on his travels.

Babysitter   One person is chosen to be the babysitter for the group, who
then decide what age they are and their circumstances. They might be
toddlers at bedtime in need of a story, seven-year-olds being served a
dinner they dislike, pre-teens with the music up too loud, a mixed group
being supervised while they play a game of French cricket.

Change the babysitter when the first one is worn out!

A story in two circles   Divide your group in half and get them to stand in
two circles, one inside the other, with the inner circle facing the outer. Each
inner circle person will have an outer circle partner.

Each of the circles is given a concept to act, for example:

- The outer circle is a bubbling sauce and the inner circle spaghetti. The
  spaghetti is served, the sauce is poured over it.
- The outer circle is a group of gardeners and the inner is a row of plants
  quite overgrown by weeds.
- The outer circle consists of teachers and the inner of pupils in a reading
  lesson.

Make sure that the circles have equal time in the more dominant roles.
People can stay with the same partner or the circles can join hands and
move round in opposite directions at intervals.

Drop dead   Everyone moves about the room, perhaps to music. When
the music stops or you call 'stop' the person nearest to a particular point
must 'drop dead', but the manner of their death must be different from the
'deaths' of each of the people before them.

Have a number of spots in the room ready to call so that no one knows
who is likely to be the next 'victim'. (If you are working in a unit where
there is a history of suicide leave this activity out — there are plenty of
other activities. It is also a poor choice as the last activity in a session.)

Consequence scene setting   Each person writes down *a location, a
character, a circumstance* and *an aim* on separate slips of paper. Collect all
the slips of paper in four separate containers, one to match each heading.
The group (or each group) needs one slip from each of the containers, and
each person needs a character slip. The group(s) weaves a story from their
collection of slips and acts them out in turn.

The sultan and the slaves People take it in turns to play the role of the sultan, directing everyone else as their slaves. The slaves must do whatever they are told for a set length of time, say five minutes. If there is not time in one session for each person to have a satisfying turn, continue another time!

The scene can be varied by each person when it is their turn — they don't all have to be sultans. Other possibilities are: the captain of a spaceship, a bad, bold pirate, a headmistress.

The new world Each person has three imaginary pieces of paper. They decide on the size of paper they want, but the bigger the better. People put their first imaginary piece of paper on an imaginary easel and draw themselves a new world. In order the papers are: a. all the vital things, b. the fairly important things and c. the trimmings or luxury things. Everyone shares their 'pictures' when they have finished.

This chair is empty Everyone sits in a circle with one vacant seat. The person to the right of the empty seat says, 'This seat is empty, I'd like King Kong (Elvis Presley, Good King Wenceslas . . .) to come and sit next to me.' Each person has to accept one invitation during the game. The person to accept the seat then moves to their new seat in the manner of the character. Continue until everyone has had a turn.

Mystery envelope Each person gets an envelope containing a blank piece of paper. They open the envelopes and read the blank papers aloud with great ceremony. Another version is to have a magic newspaper which gives any news people want. Pass the newspaper from person to person for each to read in turn.

In the paper People describe an incident from the newspaper as though they were an eyewitness to the event they have chosen. This can be prepared ahead. Ask people to look out for articles which interest them.

Sociodramas

Improvisations on conflicts and values Divide the group into pairs and give each pair a scene to act out, including a description of the characters, their values and relationship. Brief the pair separately so that each knows the scene and their role — but each brings a new factor to the situation.

Scenes could go like this: 'One person has lost their job, the other is the person's spouse . . .' or 'One person has damaged the family car, the other is a parent (sister, traffic officer) . . .'

Topic ideas include:
- Just failing an exam.
- Not getting a promotion previously boasted about.
- Being an outsider.

- Discovering a 'past'.
- Coming home late.
- Life with teenagers.
- Financial problems.
- Marital problems.
- Traffic offence.
- Wife employed, husband unemployed.
- Door to door salesman.
- Receiving a complaint (of any kind).
- Replying to a person who talks about the 'loony bin' or 'nut house'.

Instead of pairs, groups can be large with people having a variety of relationships: husband, wife, child, mother-in-law, boss, bank manager, teacher and so on.

Endings

The activities at the end of a session bring the group back together as a unit. Avoid challenging or disturbing activities; this is a time for reaffirming the group's support for one another, for tying up loose ends and reviewing what has been accomplished. Many of the activities already described are suitable. Keep them short.

Three of the activities given here involve acting out an ending. In psychiatric settings topics like suicide or violent death may come up. However, these topics are best avoided at the end of a session, when there is no time for follow-up. If necessary cut the topic short with a comment like, 'That's not suitable because the session ends in five minutes.'

Departures   Each person departs, in turn, from inside a circle of people holding hands. They must each find a significant, non-verbal way of leaving the group. For example, make eye contact with each person, shake hands, give an imaginary gift to each person or a shoulder hug.

Each person returns for the others' departures.

Mime an ending   Everyone mimes a goodbye. It could be immigrants departing on a boat or plane, the final speeches and bouquets at the end of a big conference, parents seeing their children off to school for the first time, a retirement speech and party . . .

A melodramatic ending   Act the final scene of a melodrama. The villain comes to his deserved end, the hero gets his bride.

Sculpture a finale   One person is given the opportunity to sculpt the rest of the group into a final tableau.

Finishing sentence   Each person must act the end of this sentence, 'What I'll remember from this session is . . .'

Brett's handshake   Each person in turn puts their hand in the centre of the table, one on top of the other. The bottom hand is pulled out and put on top, then the next and so on. Start slowly and get faster.

A R T

Art is a very personal experience which can have therapeutic value well beyond distracting people from emotional or physical problems.

Therapeutic Application

Art is a form of self-expression which can be used to help people understand themselves. With art, people attempt to create order and meaning out of the complexities and contradictions of their ideas. Art allows people to see themselves 'from a distance'. They get an objective view. Often there is recognition of self or a problem. Art is a visual aid to understanding and highlighting personality problems because there is an end product which can be examined, re-examined and compared as changes occur. It gives people an opportunity to comment on self or ability. It is a direct route to insight.

Art activities also provide a means of communicating when language has been lost through disease or illness. It is socially useful when people have poor verbal skills or difficulty expressing themselves. Many art activities make good warm-up activities or provide useful variety in a mixed session of activities.

Those who are likely to benefit most from art are people in the age range from late adolescence to middle age. They should not be currently psychotic or severely anxious or depressed, and they should want to work on personal growth and insight. In adolescence, especially, art amplifies and reinforces identity. (See *SELF-AWARENESS ACTIVITIES, Therapeutic application* p. 9.)

The Theory

Art therapy or using art as therapy?   There is debate, as there is in the other creative therapies, about the relative merits of art therapy and the therapeutic aspects of art in a more general sense.

Art therapy   In art therapy the focus is on therapy; art is a means to an end. People work at their own pace. Spontaneity and self-expression are more important than technique, the end product or accurate representation. The relationship between the therapist and the client is just as important as the activity.

Art therapists undertake a specific course of training. However, people who understand the concepts of therapy can also use art as a therapeutic medium in a more limited but still valuable way.

Using art as therapy When art skills and the quality of the end product are the focus, the therapeutic aspects of art become the creativity and discovery that art stimulates, and the thought needed to produce a good result. Art brings satisfaction, discipline, skill, a sense of healing and the opportunity to resolve and sort through feelings and ideas. In this case, technique and the quality of the end product are both valued.

Distinguishing between art therapy and using art as therapy could imply that there is a sharp division between the two. In fact, they are end points on a continuum. Therapists can operate within and at either end of this continuum. In this chapter the focus is on the art therapy end of the continuum.

Contraindications, Precautions and Limitations

Accidents are less likely if commonsense precautions are taken:
- Wipe spills up promptly and clear away scraps of card or paper on the floor.
- Ensure that people have room to work and circulate without disturbing others.
- Teach people to use sharp implements such as trimming blades or lino tools correctly.
- Table easels designed to hold projects upright or semi-upright may be useful.

Physical limitations
- If people have visual limitations offer bold colours, large paper and paint brushes, sponges and thick soft pencils.
- People with joint or muscular problems, hand tremor or poor co-ordination may need a stabilized working surface and built-up handles on paint brushes and other implements. Tape paper down, use a vice to hold pieces of card or board firm and build up and/or increase the weight of the handle of the brush or implement used. Paint with non-traditional 'brushes' such as a sponge or a square of cardboard.
- Skin problems can be aggravated by paints, dyes and continual washing. Use coloured pencils or felt-tip pens. People with respiratory difficulties may be adversely affected by powder dyes and paints or strong-smelling solvents. Make sure the area is well ventilated.
- Drug side effects may alter vision, co-ordination and fine movements or cause nausea. If drugs make people prone to nausea avoid paints, glues or dyes with strong-smelling solvents.

Other limitations
- Thought and perceptual disorders: people preoccupied with delusions and hallucinations are better off doing structured art activities than

exploring delusional ideas through art (unless the team approach for the patient is psychoanalytic or the project being used is part of an assessment process).

- Isolation: solitary art activities isolate people. This may be just what the person needs, or it may make the activity a poor choice. Base your decision on an assessment of the person's needs.

- Social perception of activities: some people will view art as an unsuitable kind of activity for them — they may feel it is childish or messy. Activities that could seem childish must be presented with sensitivity. It is important for people to perceive the activities being offered as appropriate to their age and skills. (See SELF-AWARENESS ACTIVITIES, Presentation p. 14.)

- People who doubt their artistic ability cause another type of problem. The 'I can't draw' syndrome is common and inhibits people's interest in any form of art work. Try well structured, one-off activities and plan the presentation carefully.

- Other sources of reluctance are the self-revealing nature of art, the impossibility of achieving a 'correct' result and impatience for a quick result.

- Note that artistic people can find it harder to just draw or paint a feeling or idea freely if the creative/artistic aspect of the work is important to them.

- Age and cultural considerations: injunctions to children to 'keep themselves clean' may inhibit them from trying activities they might enjoy. The elderly present other problems: they are likely to have fixed ideas about what is appropriate. Similarly, different cultural groups will identify more positively with some types of art than others.

The Therapist's Role

The therapist plans both the art activity itself and the things which support it: appropriate stimulation and themes, the amount of structure, how the dynamics of the group will be used and an environment that will suit the group.

In warm up for group or individual art sessions discuss the goals of the session and the way art is to be used. Explain the range of tools and materials available and how to use them.

As therapist, aim for a level of personal self-awareness which enables you to share in an open, undefensive way what you are experiencing. Aim to role model learning through art — both enjoying it and taking it seriously.

Try the activity   Ideally, try an activity out so you know in advance how successful it will be and which parts of it are likely to be tricky. Trying it out also provides you with some examples to show.

Discussion   People stimulate each other by talking about what they are doing. A regular time for looking at finished work and discussing it gives people an opportunity to learn from each other. The topic might be: 'Similarities/differences', 'What I liked/did not like', 'What was clear/ unclear'.

Some people may feel uncomfortable about others looking at their work. They may also be unwilling to talk about it. If discussion and sharing are expected in a group activity, make sure this is clear from the beginning.

Generate individual discussion by asking questions based on careful observation. The therapist has an enquirer role. Typically, he or she might ask, 'You seem to be . . . ?', 'This looks as though . . . ?' State what you see, phrasing it as a question. The idea is to make use of opportunities which arise as people work. Working this way is called using the 'objectives of opportunity'. Does the person's interpretation coincide with what they have done? Encourage people to explain their ideas aloud to others. The therapist tries to help people in a process of discovery rather than provide answers. Even when someone is silent they may still be working their way through a problem.

Practical Organization

While the session is in progress, expect only to guide behaviour and work habits rather than demand tidiness or particular results. It is important not to inhibit free expression. A session of one to two hours can realistically be divided into five to ten minutes of warm up and discussion, twenty to forty minutes of silent individual work, followed by sharing and discussion with the whole group together. If there are more than ten people, divide the group into pairs or small groups but recognize that the group will need some time all together to maintain cohesiveness. The pattern is contact, then withdrawal into personal ideas, then back to the group to share ideas and feelings. People need time to draw into themselves and recognize their own experience before returning to the group.

A break between completing work and discussion is often a good idea. Cleaning up or getting a drink make good natural breaks.

Structured and unstructured sessions   The choice of type of session — structured or unstructured or somewhere between — depends on the group and the situation.

In unstructured sessions people use whatever style and materials they like and select their own topics. They understand the purpose of the session and expect to discuss their work and its meanings with the therapist or group afterwards. Many art therapists see this as a dynamic and beneficial approach because it imposes no constraints on people and they are likely to produce work that is significant to them.

In structured sessions a theme and medium are chosen by the therapist or group. This helps people get started and overcomes the hurdle of a blank piece of paper. The structure also provides a common focus for the group.

Themes can be open-ended, 'Show something significant to you', 'How are you feeling now?' or more specific 'Anger', My future', 'Loneliness'. The theme can be chosen specifically to facilitate group dynamics or development of relationships within the group.

If time is limited it is simpler for everyone to use the same medium — otherwise offer a choice. Discussion at the end of the session enables people to explain their feelings, fantasies and ideas and to experience the group's reactions.

Most of the suggestions which follow focus on group work but the ideas can be used in structured one-to-one work as well.

The work area   Art calls for a well-organized work area, good lighting, a stable surface to work on and materials of reasonable quality. Storage and display areas should be available.

Where to work   A group working round a large table forms a circle looking inwards. This creates a good work atmosphere. It gives a sense of purpose, and tools and materials can be shared across the table. On the other hand, insight-oriented groups may work better with clipboards, seated on the floor, so that tables and easels do not form a barrier between people. In some cases people will work best on their own, only coming together for the beginning and end of the session.

Materials   Use paints that are non-toxic and be familiar with the properties of any dyes, inks and solvents you have. Store them with safety in mind and keep track of them when they are in use.

Equipment and materials should be easily accessible and well displayed. Although it is not necessary to have expensive materials, people do respond well to good quality materials. If you let people choose which materials to use and how messy they can be, they will usually be more willing to help clean up.

Vary the art activities you use — both in method and materials. The choice of colour of paper, whether to use coloured pencils, charcoal pencils, paints, inks, dyes or crayons, will all affect the associations people make.

Have cover-alls or smocks available to protect people's clothing.

Displaying work   Mounting and displaying work to its best advantage is a way of valuing the artist.

Theoretical Perspectives

There are three main theoretical perspectives on using art for insight and personal growth: gestalt, pragmatic and psychoanalytic. Within each it

Displaying work

is usual to choose media which produce quick results, so felt-tip pens, pastels, crayons, poster paint and clay are used more than oils or water-colour paint.

The gestalt approach

In the gestalt approach current reactions, thoughts, feelings and relation-ships are explored. The aim of this 'here and now' approach is to complete or resolve troubling experiences.

Compared with verbal psychotherapies, 'now' — the immediate ex-perience of the task at hand — is much more important. Even though people will use their perceptions of the past or future in their work, they are encouraged to focus on the present, to express and explore their feelings of the moment. In the artistic creation hidden thoughts and feelings reveal themselves and clamour for acknowledgement. The process of creation provides a bridge between inner and outer realities, and a basis for personal growth. It enables people to explain their fears and fantasies and reconsider their values.

The gestalt approach recognizes that the process of art, like active involvement with any creative project, is healing in itself. It gives people a sense of resolution.

Therapists using this approach help people accept their experiences as valid and as having a significance and usefulness worth exploring. In the gestalt approach the therapist should:

- Encourage people to 'watch themselves' and notice the thoughts which arise as they work. Ask questions to help people do this, 'How does what your art shows fit in with your life now?', 'How important is . . . to you?'
- Stimulate spontaneity, playfulness and fantasy as routes to insight. Encourage people to 'let themselves go' — there is a lot to be learned, seemingly by chance, when people 'play'. Some useful starting phrases are 'Try . . .', 'Have a go at . . .', 'Let's picture . . .', 'What if . . .'
- Help people recognize what they are seeing. Often, consciously or unconsciously, feelings and thoughts are disguised in symbols. However, beware of projecting your own meaning onto a person's art or reactions.
- Help people use what they learn. What are their options? How can they act on them? What would they like to change?

Examples of topic choices in this approach are: 'Myself now', 'My fears', 'Myself as a tree', 'My goals', 'Myself in relation to . . .'

The pragmatic approach — art as an analogy

This approach is closely linked to the gestalt approach but has a more matter-of-fact, performance orientation rather than an insight focus. As in life, order must be created out of chaos, fantasy translated into reality, materials handled so they work. This approach fits in well with product-oriented art and craft activities.

The choices people make build up a picture of the way they function. A person's approach can be diffident, expansive, half-hearted, sloppy, compulsive, carefree, persistent — the way a project is carried out is likely to say something about their general skills and approach to life. In a therapeutic relationship the therapist makes use of the opportunities which arise as people work. They can use a session to develop personal qualities such as persistence, neatness, organization or communication skills. Almost any topic will serve in this approach.

The psychoanalytic approach

The psychoanalytic approach looks primarily at the influence of the past on the way people function in the present. In art, people 'project' or show things which are significant to them, and this can provide a shortcut to information about feelings. The theory is that insight into the causes of feelings and problems will enable people to leave the problems behind and grow emotionally.

This approach can only be used with some knowledge of the person's history and with their willing participation. It also requires an understanding of psychoanalytic theories. Full use of the psychoanalytic approach requires comprehensive training. Its use in occupational therapy should be limited because art is only used in it as a means to an end. The activity or occupation itself, is secondary. It has a place when the therapist is a member of a team whose overall approach is psychoanalytic.

The aim is to help people verbalize their feelings. Content, colour, symbolism and method of working are all seen as significant. It is usual with the psychoanalytic approach to allow about twice as long for discussion as for painting or drawing, for example thirty minutes of painting/drawing time and sixty minutes of discussion.

Some studies have suggested that projective art accurately reveals information about personality, mood and mental state, thus making it useful in assessment. Others have found it no better than other assessment techniques. It can be regarded as a useful adjunct in a battery of psychotherapeutic possibilities.

Common topic choices are: 'My family', 'My childhood', 'Close relationships', 'Caring and neglect', 'My moods', 'Aspects of my parents I see in myself'.

Art and assessment

Much has been made of the projective aspect of art activities. Subject, symbolism, colour, design, techniques used and the person's approach have all been used to assess state of mind. With colour, for example, large amounts of red in a painting are said to be associated with anger and aggression, and smaller amounts with warmth and positive feelings, while black is said to represent fear and depression. Although some of these assumptions may be valid, there have been no consistent findings about the meaning of colour in art. In general terms, there are no reliable ways of judging state of mind from art work, except in the case of certain types of organic brain damage.

Any interpretation of a piece of art should be made or confirmed with the artist. It is only through the artist's comments that the meaning of an image or choice of colour can be understood. For instance, an artist may see blue as cold and remote or cool and soothing — either view, at least superficially, fits in with commonly accepted interpretations of the significance of blue. Ask neutral questions like, 'Are the colours significant to you?' Or give your impressions to prompt a reaction, 'I see . . . in this. Is that accurate?'

What do you look for as a therapist? The subject matter of a painting often has an association with current mood and concerns but it can also reflect people's perceptions of the past or future. Some symbolism is common to many people, a snake or cross, for example, can signify the same thing to a number of people. Other ideas are individual. Again, any interpretive assumptions, even when the therapist knows something of the person's life, experiences and current ideas, can only have doubtful validity. Interpretations based on one session or a single piece of work are likely to be particularly inconclusive.

The construction of a piece of work is relevant to assessment. Is it full of intricate, busy detail? Or is it flowing (sharp, painstakingly meticulous, bizarre, full of symbolism)? The practical choices people make concerning size of paper, the way the work fills the space, and the style of applying paint also give information about the way they are thinking and feeling. The difficulty comes in knowing where the boundaries of 'normal' lie. What is 'normal' for this person? What is part of their creativity?

Confusion (from whatever cause), brain damage, obsession, anxiety, mania, depression and schizophrenia, in their extreme forms, can all be recognized in art. People with brain damage may show signs of perceptual problems in their art work.

With any interpretive approach, it is sometimes helpful to keep work as a basis for comparison later on. A series of drawings over time may vividly show changes in the way a person is thinking. When work is kept as a record (and this should only be done with the person's permission) make sure the person's name, the date and any comments are put on the work, preferably in a consistent manner, and that it is stored in a way that makes it easy to find again. A signed release statement from the artist must be obtained before art work is reproduced or used for display or educational purposes.

Activities

'Who am I?' Get people to paint or draw colours and patterns that answer the question, 'Who am I?'

Memories People make a picture of a memory; their happiest, saddest, earliest . . .

Goals People make a picture or construction in any medium to represent their goals in life.

Where I come from, and where I'm going With this topic as a heading, people divide a page in half and fill one half with things that symbolize their past and one with things that symbolize their future.

Life scroll Each person chooses a length of paper to suit them and draws a scroll of their life story. This activity can be done in one session or carried on over several sessions.

Half and half   People divide a piece of paper in half and on one side draw something they like about themselves and on the other half something they want to change. Work to a time limit of five minutes.

Focus on associations   People put a word in the centre of a page, inside a small circle. They make spokes out from the circle and on each draw something they associate with the word. They can use a word which seems important to them (for example, hope, anger) or the name of a significant person in their lives.

Scribble pattern   The instructions for this are, 'send a line anywhere like a scribble, to make a very complex pattern, then colour parts in. Draw yourself somewhere in the picture and perhaps other people as well. Give a name to the pattern that results.'

Shared valuables   Tell people to draw something they value. After two minutes ask them to pass the picture to the person on their left. They must carry on with it as though it were theirs. This activity can be done with everyone having access to a range of colours of paint, crayon or pastels or each person having their own colour. This last approach means that each contribution can be identified afterwards.

Shapes, colours, lines   Any art medium is suitable for this activity, including collage. Instruct people to, 'Use coloured shapes to represent on paper people who are important to you. Include yourself as a colour shape too.' People then connect the shapes with lines which reflect the relationships they have with those people—strong lines, dotted lines and so on. People can use definite shapes like squares or triangles or abstract shapes and splodges.

My family as animals   People draw their family as a group of animals. What qualities does each person have in common with the animal that represents them?

Thumb prints   Thumb prints are a type of block printing, the ball of a thumb or finger being the block. Prints can be made on coloured card, using ink from a stamp pad. A home-made stamp pad can be constructed from cotton wool or a piece of sponge soaked in ink or paint. Use fine felt-tip pens to draw features on the prints and turn them into people, animals and so on.

Pavement art   Chalk can be used for a quick picture or crayon for a slightly more enduring effect. The work can be done on an outside wall — concrete blocks, fibrolite or paint — or on a pavement. (The owner of the wall needs to be happy about this of course!)

Thumb prints

Design a personal flag Flags can be designed in any medium. For an indoor wall or ceiling hanging, they can be made in almost any fabric — although flags made of fabrics of different weights are likely to hang less well than those made of fabrics of the same weight. Outdoor flags can be made of anorak (parka) nylon or shower curtain fabric. As well as the traditional shape, they can be wind-sock shaped or like Chinese fish kites.

Meaning shapes People draw or paint words to look like their meanings. 'Fog' would be wispy, 'sad' droopy and so on. Each word can be repeated several times or people can use a number of related words. They can create a background to suit the word or words.

Drip patterns A blob of paint is dripped onto paper and tilted so that it runs, then re-tilted several times to form a pattern. When the first blob of paint will go no further, more blobs are added. This works best on glossy paper. Try wet paper too.

Blown blobs Blobs of runny paint or ink can be blown to create patterns. This can be done with a straw, or people can just get close to the paint and blow. Experiment with matt, glossy and wet papers.

Blob doodles Get people to make blobs or drips on a page and turn and tilt the paper to make the blob run one way then another. Next, get them to add to the pattern and images suggested by the blob shapes using a pen or pencil.

Doodle and discuss   While a discussion is in progress give everyone paper and pencils or crayons and encourage them to doodle as they talk. Compare results.

Texture   People create a pattern of texture using any medium (pencil, pen and ink, clay, collage), on a choice of type, size and colour of paper. They can use texture to show a relationship, event, place or person.

Multi outline picture   Trace round a cut-out cardboard template, or any flat shape, numerous times, moving the template unit only a little for each new image. Build up flowing or symmetrical designs with the outlines.

Three colours   People can paint what they like but must limit themselves to three colours.

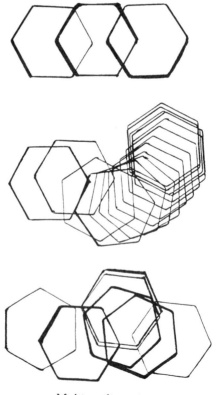

Multi outline picture

Bits and pieces sculpture   These are constructions made out of paperclips, straws, sticky putty (Blu-tack), toothpicks, plasticine, plastic bag ties, match boxes, corks, bottle tops and any other handy, everyday materials. Sculptures made with cheese cubes and toothpicks can be used to decorate the lunch table then eaten!

Lines in a mood   People let their pencil travel fast, slow, hard, lightly, waveringly, gently. They make lines that bristle or rage, are full of hope, fun or sorrow. How does a sound look?

Transformation   People draw a familiar object on paper first as though they like it, then dislike it. They show it in curves, straight lines, as a solid, as something ephemeral . . .

Silhouettes   Pin up a large sheet of white paper where there is a good source of light — a desk or standard lamp usually works well (or put tinfoil round a light shade to direct the light where it is wanted. Check the shade regularly for overheating). The person whose silhouette is to be drawn sits so that they cast a strong shadow on the paper and keeps perfectly still while someone else traces carefully round their silhouette. The silhouette can be cut out and mounted on a black or coloured background, or the pattern traced onto black card, cut out and mounted on a white or pastel background.

Paper twin   People work in pairs and draw life-sized silhouettes of each other. First one person, then the other, lies on a very large piece of paper and their partner draws round them (use bold pen or dark crayon). People can complete their silhouettes on their own or together, adding clothing, hair, features and comments round the edge. The comments could be on likes, dislikes, beliefs, feelings, accomplishments, significant events or people in the person's life.
   A smaller scale version of this activity involves tracing round hands or feet and decorating them with rings, freckles, hairs, nails and perhaps tattoos.

Graffiti   Provide art materials, wall or poster space and specify that the graffiti must have some symbolic significance. People may wish to sign their contribution. Another approach is to get everyone to work on a separate sheet and combine them afterwards.
   Decide whether to work to a topic or theme.

Partners   (Pragmatic approach) Partners share a piece of paper and make a doodle together without talking. A discussion question afterwards could be, 'Are there any parallels in this interaction with other relationships you have?'

A visit   Partners talk about a particular place they would like to visit (beach, city, tropical reef). Each draws or paints the place for the other.

Introduction   After talking to a partner, people make a collage or painting to represent that partner. The discussion can go on as people work but once painting has started no one is allowed to make specific suggestions about what their partner is painting. The picture can be used as a basis for discussion or as a way of introducing people to the group.

Shared pictures   Work in any medium. Themes or subjects can be chosen by the group or individuals. Each person begins a drawing then after a predetermined time, say one or two minutes, hands their drawing to the person on their left, who carries on with the work trying to be sympathetic to the first person's intentions. The group can work in silence or with ongoing discussion. People go on having turns until everyone is satisfied with the result.
   Alternatively, use a large sheet of paper that several people can work on at once. Put it on a table or the floor, or pin it to a wall. Turn the sheet round at intervals.
   As a variation, let each person use only one colour and pass papers on until there is some of each colour on all of them.

Symmetrical patterns   In groups of two or four, people take turns to lead the work or copy. Divide a paper in half or quadrants. The leader makes some marks in their segment and the others copy. Working clockwise, the next person takes the lead and again the others copy. Finish when each person has had a turn.
   Alternatively, people work in two groups. The paper is divided vertically into thirds and each group has one of the side thirds as their own while the centre third is shared with the other group. There should be negotiation over the themes and colour used in the centre third so that there is some link to the outer thirds. However, each group should do their initial planning independently.

'Create an island where you can live'   This can be a group or individual activity. People represent their ideal world in any medium: clay, paint, pencil, pastels, papier mâché. It could be a desert island, a hidden valley or even a private planet. Or it could simply represent their present world.
   As a group project everyone must negotiate what will be included and where it will be placed. Who adds what? How will the group work together? What are their concerns, how do they plan to have fun? Stay safe? Feed themselves? Care for each other? What community facilities do they plan: library, sports stadium, park, pool?
   A simple variation is for people to draw themselves and five things that are important to them on a desert island.

Arriving As an ending activity draw, paint or model 'The new self that is emerging'.

Murals

Choose a theme or a topic and decide as a group how to work on it together. Some ways of making murals are:

- Map out a rough outline of the mural beforehand then plan who will do which part. (If detailed drawings are made the actual creating of the mural becomes a mechanical, rather than creative exercise).
- Everyone chooses a sub-topic that fits the theme and the group decides where each person will work.
- Each person makes a picture and these are combined afterwards as a mural. Themes with scope for individuals to 'do their own thing' in a group are a zoo, jungle scene, cityscape. It may be important to create a background or to link the parts in some way.
- Each person is given just one colour and the group must negotiate the content of the mural and the division of work.
- The group works on sheet plastic with felt-tip pen. The mural can be put up over a window to give a stained-glass effect.
- Working on one long piece of paper, people choose their own topic but, by negotiating with their immediate neighbours only, try to create a cohesive result.
- Two or more people take turns drawing or painting a mural but without any conversation or planning. They try to develop some unity in their work.
- Symmetrical murals: two, three or four people work at opposite ends of a mural, copying what each other does and taking turns to lead.

Finger painting This is an activity in which mess is expected and acceptable. Some people enjoy the cool slippery feeling of finger paint, others may find it messy or unpleasant. Provide aprons and good cleaning facilities.

With many finger paint recipes the mixture must be made ahead of time so that the thickening medium reaches its natural consistency and is cool enough to use when needed.

Some people find it easier to start with wet hands and warm finger paint. Finger paint can be coloured with generous amounts of tempera colour or any other colouring medium that will not stain hands but will give a good, intense colour. Make bright colours or deliberate pastels. Wishy-washy or dull colours give very disappointing results. Only two or three colours are needed because too many colours will mix and look muddy.

Note that this activity is unsuitable for people who have had recent surgery on their hands, wounds or skin conditions. Have hand cream available for people to put on after washing up.

Finger paint recipes There are two main ways of making finger paint. The first is:

- Dissolve half to one cup of cornflour or flour in a cup of cold water in a saucepan.
- Add three cups of boiling water.
- Bring to the boil stirring briskly to avoid lumps.
- Stand the pan in cold water to cool if the mixture is needed quickly.
- Divide the paste into separate bowls and add a generous amount of tempera paint to each.

The second is:

- Dissolve wallpaper paste or soapflakes in warm water.
- Cool to give a jelly-like base.
- Add colour as above.

Method: Work directly onto a table top or firm paper. The table should be one that is easily cleaned and white or light enough to see the patterns that are made. Put about a tablespoonful of paint onto the table or paper and swirl patterns in it with the fingertips, knuckles or palms. Specially cut cardboard 'combs', stiff bristle paint brushes, lids, corks, pieces of wood and other implements can also be used to make patterns (check that these will not scratch the surface people are working on).

Make patterns to music or a theme word or phrase or make a pictorial scene.

Prints can be taken from the table by lying paper over the pattern and rubbing it gently on the back. Firm, rough-surfaced paper or cartridge paper work best (newsprint and other lightweight papers are unsatisfactory because they become very wrinkled when they dry).

MUSIC

'Why is music of such value to me . . . ? Simply, music lifts me: my feelings, thinking and spirit are extended beyond the strictures of ordinariness.'
E. Gaston, *Music in Therapy*

Therapists use music to generate discussion and reminiscence, stimulate movement, inspire patterns and pictures or set a mood. At times, music will 'reach' people when nothing else does.

The Theory

Music and music therapy   Music as therapy or musical education as a therapy? The focus a therapist takes depends on the way they perceive themselves; primarily as a musician/teacher of musical skills or primarily as a therapist. 'The main difference lies in the use of music itself. While music education is concerned with perfecting musical endeavour and music as a product, music therapy is concerned with eliciting changes in behaviour via music.' (C.H. Schulberg, *The Music Therapy Source Book*.)

For musicians/teachers, therapeutic changes occur in the course of musical education; the music serves both therapeutic and musical goals. Musical education, in all its forms, adds to people's skills, is often sociable, organizes behaviour and changes attitudes. Lessons can be structured to meet these kinds of goals.

Music therapists, on the other hand, are musicians who have done additional training to add therapeutic skills to their musical skills. They choose how they will use music from a broad spectrum of possibilities. They may focus on musical skills or on appreciation. Or they may use music to create a social occasion which helps people link with each other and reminisce. They help people experience, express and work through their feelings, using musical activities. Gains in musical skill are secondary.

If the roles are clearly defined, a therapist with limited musical expertise can often work with a music therapist in a complementary relationship.

Therapeutic Application

Rhythm is a key element in making music work as therapy. It carries people along and energizes or soothes them. It persuades them to be involved. In a general sense, the pleasure, diversion and stimulation of music make it therapeutic.

The values of musical activities are not always obvious and someone who appears uninvolved may still benefit because much of the value depends on the feelings it engenders.

Social value There is communication in music making and companionship in experiences shared. Some people find it easier to express themselves through singing or with instruments than through speech. People with intellectual disability for example, may have few other means of communicating.

Social skills training can be enhanced. Through musical activities people learn to use voice qualities such as appropriate volume and variety of tone. They can learn the rules of conversation, how to share time with others, take turns, follow and lead. (See *Voice exercises and singing* p. 95.)

Music can be a recreation that enriches people's lives. An expanded repertoire of leisure activities brings potential benefits such as increased self-esteem and social contacts. It can be a lifelong interest and passport to friendships. When people work in a group the expectations of the group can help each person to rise to their potential.

Music plays a role in socializing people to their culture because one way cultures are perpetuated and reaffirmed is through festivals and musical customs. It is important to recognize that music and sounds can have quite different meanings for different cultural groups.

Music is valuable when people's sensory experiences are limited.

Emotional value States of emotional distress can be calmed by music. Its use has been advocated for extreme anxiety, restlessness, respiratory dis-

order, fear, insomnia, withdrawal and anger. It is also soothing to people who are bereaved, or isolated through illness, loss of speech or retirement.
Music can help people with memory loss retain links with their lives. Confusion may be diminished and reminiscence readily triggered by music.
Music counteracts apathy and depression. It is involving, and allows feelings and ideas to flow. This flow can initiate a process of grieving, and allow people to express anxieties or acknowledge and work through problems. When people 'lose themselves' in music they find a way of retreating for a while. Music is more likely to arouse positive feelings than negative ones like anger or fear.

Physical value   In dance, there is opportunity for appropriate physical contact and exercise. Music helps people persist — even extend themselves — in exercise or work.
A more specific use of music is with people who have had head injuries. At an early stage after a head injury, when someone is unconscious or semiconscious, music can be used to help the person remain aware of their surroundings. Choose music and songs which the person is known to have liked, or songs from when they were adolescents/young adults.

Contraindications, Precautions and Limitations

Music has great therapeutic potential but there are drawbacks. Possible problems are deafness, over-sensitivity to sound, epileptic seizures and negative psychological associations with specific music.
If someone in a group is partially deaf make sure they are placed in the best possible position to hear. They are likely to respond better to low-pitched tones than high ones. A person who has had a stroke should be placed with their unaffected side nearest to the source of the music.
Over-sensitivity to noise can result from conditioning or brain damage. Sometimes noise tolerance can be built up gradually. Rarely, epileptic seizures are triggered by sounds, usually ones with a high pitch. It is important to know what kinds of sounds need to be avoided for people with this problem.
Occasionally, psychological problems like depression, psychosis, confusion or anxiety are reinforced or worsened by some types of music (for example, the harshness of heavy metal or discordant music, or the sadness of country and western). Any music can have strong personal associations for people which may be pleasant or unpleasant.
Ask people about their likes and dislikes. Personal taste and associations should be acknowledged and catered for. Most people dislike some types of music because it is foreign to their musical background. Others have negative associations as a result of school music lessons or being made to practise an instrument. A minority will be unwilling to participate because of religious beliefs.
Musical ability is often judged by ability to sing. Poor singing, in children

especially, can wrongly lead people to doubt their capacity to enjoy music and join in other kinds of musical activities. They may be deprived of opportunities to participate.

Sometimes people are reluctant to take part in activities because they feel they have no musical skills. Even if this is true — and it is often simply that they have been discouraged by earlier experiences — there are activities in which limited skill is no barrier to participation or pleasure.

A few people are tone deaf. Usually their speaking voice is flat because they cannot hear differences in tone and pitch as most of us do. It is difficult to deal with this but, again, it is possible to underestimate abilities or capacity for pleasure. Fortunately, severe tone deafness is rare.

Practical Organization

Equipment Make sure that the music equipment you plan to use has sufficient volume for the venue. An alternative to recorded music, and one which may give you more control of the result, is to get the group to sing, chant or clap to provide a rhythm for an exercise, drama or art activity.

Headphone sets will be needed for individual programmes.

Preparation From the therapist's point of view some musical activities take time to prepare, others require musical skills, and for some a good range of resources is needed.

The setting should be free of extraneous noise but people should feel free to make a noise. Acoustics can be important.

Activities

Voice exercises and singing

Voice exercises and singing can be used as part of social skills courses to work on voice volume, pitch and pace. They can also be useful for some physical conditions which involve difficulties with articulation and speech such as cerebral palsy or Parkinson's disease. For people with cerebral palsy, music can enhance physical control in areas other than just voice.

Matching voice and instrument Working in pairs, one person tries to match their partner's voice in volume, pitch, pace or feeling, on an instrument. Voice or instrument can take it in turns to lead, giving different types of practice in recognizing and using aspects of voice. When the voice leads any brief statements can be used; when the instrument leads the voice says or makes any sounds that fit in with the instrument. For example, if the voice makes a long 'ahhh', the player might play long 'A' on the recorder.

Volumes People lie on the floor (or sit with their eyes closed) and make a sound that only they can hear, then one that only the people nearest to them can hear, then half the people, then the whole room. Everyone keeps their own sound going while they listen to see how many other sounds they can pick up.

The sound machine A group becomes a 'sound machine'. Each person chooses a sound they can make quietly, loudly, high, low, with different intonations. One person acts as the conductor, using hand signals to bring in different sounds and to raise and lower volumes. People can make sounds to a theme: sounds can be flowing, jarring, staccato, angry, soothing and so on. Or they can tell a story in sound: The river to the sea; The return of the swallows; A journey through life; Lost and lonely, found and loved.

Sing-a-longs Some people are happy to sing anytime, anywhere. Some will join in a group singsong when they can hide in the group's exuberance. Others are strictly listeners. For some musical harmony is essential while for others a sing-a-long is primarily an occasion for socializing and nostalgia.

Describe the session you have prepared and invite people to participate, recognizing that it may be impossible to suit everyone's tastes. Lead with warmth and enthusiasm — but without overdoing it. At the end of the session ask people their likes and dislikes in songs, accompaniment and presentation and try to accommodate their ideas in future sessions.

The easiest songs to use are those which have a reasonably definite, simple rhythm and are pitched neither too high nor too low.

Aim for a mixture of familiar and new songs. Songs which are overused, or a repertoire that never changes, will make people lose interest quickly. On the other hand, it is important to retain a proportion of familiar material.

Other considerations when choosing songs are age appropriateness, cultural origins and sociocultural connotations (religious songs, wartime songs). Hymns and other religious songs can be useful in orienting people to a particular season but the words may reinforce negative ideas or delusions.

You will get a better result if people stand tall, shoulders back, or sit up straight before you begin. Try some deep slow breathing and shoulder and arm exercises first — indicate that you anticipate involvement and a good quality of effort.

Words can be written on flip charts, overhead transparencies or printed sheets. Large print books or reprints of old song selections can be useful or teach people songs by rote, one or two lines at a time. Check that everyone can see the words and the leader before you begin.

Piano, guitar and fiddle are the instruments most often used for accompaniment, but others can be used: harmonica, recorder, lyre, auto harp or melodica. With live accompaniment the player can respond to the needs of the group. Pre-recorded accompaniments and some records of the sing-a-long type can be useful but check the songs and their clarity and pace beforehand.

It is better to have sessions which are short and snappy rather than go on until people's enthusiasm dwindles. The tempo of a session is important too. Too fast and people will feel confused, too slow and they will be bored.

Following a theme makes it easier to choose a range of songs for a session and leads easily to reminiscence. Ideas for themes include:

- Selections from shows (*Oklahoma, My Fair Lady, Hair, Cats . . .*).
- A composer (Irving Berlin, Gilbert and Sullivan).
- A singer (Bing Crosbie, Burl Ives, Elvis Presley, Rod Stewart).
- A type of song (folk, country and western).
- Music of a particular culture (Irish folk songs, Jamaican calypso, Indian).
- An emotion or relationship (loss and grieving, marriage, lullabies).
- Choral music.
- Festival music (Christmas, St Patrick's Day).

Music and movement

Action songs   Use action songs to encourage general activation, a wider range of movement, improve body image and increase concentration span.

Mirrors   In pairs, first one person then the other takes the lead in movements and the partner copies them as though they are a mirror image. The leader can move backwards or forwards, use vigorous or gentle actions, stand or sit. Many types of music can be used.

Music and relaxation

Music is good for relaxation, but note that just because a piece of music is slow and dreamy, does not mean it will soothe or relax. It is the way a person feels about a piece of music that makes it relaxing or not. Instrumental music is usually more relaxing than vocal; cello, lute and classical guitar music are especially soothing and steady. Baroque music, even when it is lively, is usually serene. And of course lullabies are designed to be relaxing.

Music is more relaxing, the more it involves people. People who are fully involved in listening forget their worries and become less tense.

Music and art

Emotive, pictorial or strongly rhythmic music can be used as a stimulus for art, creative writing or drama. However, people can feel confused if a definite approach is not chosen at the beginning an of 'art to music' session. Suggest one of the following approaches:

- Make the patterns of the rhythm on paper.
- Depict something concrete or abstract suggested by the music.
- Draw a continuous line showing what the music is doing now.
- Draw the story the music tells across a page.

Mood setting

Use music in warm up to create a particular atmosphere for the activity which follows. Tell people what you are aiming for: 'I've chosen this because it makes me feel energetic (relaxed, clears my mind . . .) and I hope it will make you feel that way for this session.' After the music ask for people's comments — but be careful to avoid telling them what they feel! Of course music can be used to influence mood at other times too.

Music and drama
Music can be used to help create a setting or introduce or end a drama activity.

Musical quizzes
Musical quizzes have great social potential. Compile a quiz on tape. Possible themes are: a country or city, foods, colours, an era. Excerpts should be between a half and two minutes long and the full tape not more than fifteen to twenty minutes. Judge how long a group's interest will be held, noting that it is better to leave people wanting more than glad to get to the end at last.

   Questions might be: 'What is this piece from?', 'Who wrote (sang, played) it?', 'Where did you first hear it?', 'What instruments could you pick out?', 'Did you see that film?'

Music and self-awareness
People music   Get people to compose signature tunes for each member of the group, or choose existing songs that fit people's personalities. People can do this for their own group, a staff group, or public figures.

Two piano conversation   One person tells a story or asks something and as they talk they play on a piano. The other person responds only on the piano. It is not necessary to be able to play the piano for this activity; people simply press high or low notes and make patterns of rhythm, pace and loudness.

Play feelings   Using the technique in the previous activity, people 'play' feelings: 'Anger', 'Excitement', 'Loss', 'A bargain!', 'I'm relaxed', 'Tomorrow . . .', 'I'm listening', 'I'm curious'. (See *SELF-AWARENESS ACTIVITIES*, *Part sentences* p. 31.)

Music and identity   Ask people, 'What songs or music would tell people who you are now or who you were as a child? What music would you like to be like? What music has happy associations? What has sad ones? What song or music would you like to give to . . . ?' People can give their answers to a partner or the group.

Musical autobiography   Get people to sing or hum tunes which represent who they were as a child, adolescent, young adult and so on.

The meaning of music

Play some music and get people to write six adjectives to describe the piece. Ask, 'What would you call it?', 'What does it seem to be about?' Share and discuss people's responses at the end of the session.

Musical activities for specific age groups

Young children Most small children will make spontaneous rhythmic sounds with their voices, bodies or things they pick up, and this can be used to develop a sense of rhythm. Join in and copy the sounds back to them. Then encourage them to repeat their 'tune' so that you play the same sounds alternately. If the child varies the pattern, change yours to match. If they do not, try varying the pattern yourself and see if they copy you. Vary the objects you use.

Songs and finger plays Songs and finger plays should be about things children are familiar with or currently learning: body parts, animal names, foods, colours. Felt board illustrations can be used to complement songs. Gradually build up a basic repertoire of songs, introducing only one or two new songs each session. Check that the children understand the words and that the pitch and range of the music are suited to their voices. A good way of teaching songs to small children is to let them join in with an adult singing and gradually learn the words. Keep the material simple but try to use all their abilities, energy and interest in sounds.

Music to move to Use songs which tell stories or action songs, or use an instrument to make sounds which fit particular images. Giants call for low, loud, slow notes while fairies tiptoe to pairs of high notes played in rhythm.

Adolescents A therapist can help a disabled adolescent by making the music and 'in' things of youth more easily available to them. Adolescents need to be involved in the choice of musical programmes and activities. Shared television watching, jam sessions, discos, creative dance, break dancing, whatever is in vogue, can be used.

Themes likely to be relevant to this age group will involve developing identity and interacting with others. Some self-expression topics are: 'Who am I?', 'Sabotage', 'Imagination', 'Life roles — what are my choices?'

The elderly Music is a good starting point for reminiscence because it awakens memories of the past. It establishes a relaxed non-threatening atmosphere conducive to thinking through life events, changes and dilemmas. Collect songs and music from different phases of people's lives; school and Sunday school songs, animal songs, courting and wedding songs and so on. Seasonal and festival music can help orient people to the time of year and festival activities. Use the associative quality of music to stimulate discussion.

Accompany exercise sessions with music that appeals in style and pace.

Music with distinctive lyrics relating to past and present attitudes works well.

Some groups may enjoy studying or sharing a particular type of musical interest.

DANCE

Dancing is a form of exercise, a means of releasing tension and a way of making social contact with others. It is also a way of expressing thoughts and feelings — for every idea and thought there is a dance that will do the talking. There are social expectations associated with dancing. And of course there is the possibility of performance and the complexity and fun of costuming and staging. For some people dance is a hobby or art form, for a few it is a profession.

Folk dances help a culture maintain its traditions and identity. Many kinds of dance can be used in therapeutic situations: folk dances, ballroom dance, creative dance and so on. Popular dancing has high appeal for some groups.

As dance skills improve, so too do co-ordination, reaction time, strength and stamina.

The Theory

Dancing/expressive movement as a skill or dance as therapy? When dance is used as therapy the primary aim is to provide a healthy leisure activity and/or work on actual or potential problems through dance. When dancing or expressive movement is sought as a skill the main goal is to improve the quality of the dancing. However, the goals of dance as therapy and dancing as a skill can overlap.

What role does a focus on dancing skills have in therapy? Some therapists feel that developing dance skills can be as effective as focusing more directly on therapeutic goals. Their view is that dancing is naturally therapeutic. They also say that working on an identifiable dance skill or towards a performance motivates people to work harder.

Therapeutic Application

The type of dance used most in therapy is expressive movement. It is extremely adaptable and allows people to respond to music in whatever way they want. Because there is no need to learn complex steps or have high levels of fitness anyone can participate and, within the bounds of commonsense and medical contraindications, there are no right or wrong ways of doing it. Expressive movement helps people relax. It can be done simply for pleasure and exercise or, if desired, there is scope for learning movement routines and creating something new.

The usual therapeutic aims in expressive movement are social interaction, encouraging self-expression and improving physical wellbeing. Socially expressive movement is a type of dance that is suitable for any age group, for all-female groups and, with thoughtful presentation, for all-male groups. Physically it can be gentle or vigorous, depending on the type of music played.

Heightened self-awareness is very much a part of this activity. The way people move is connected to their thoughts and feelings. Through expressive movement people explore their feelings, fears, hopes and values and the insights from this exploration may change their perception of themselves.

Expressive movement can be a way of adjusting to changes and problems and of coming to terms with them. As a process it involves retreating into self and using movement to give form and expression to feelings and this can be strengthening and clarifying. The heightened sense of self may be accentuated and built on if the session is followed by discussion or role play.

Another common therapeutic aim in dance is to control emotion through action. People learn to stand or move in a serene or a lively manner, whatever is appropriate, as a way of breaking a cycle of negative feelings, tensions and stiffness. Feelings change to match the movement change.

For elderly people with poor mobility, movement will involve mainly the torso and upper limbs, and the focus will be more on fun, sociability and fitness than on emotional insight. In the introductory part of a session outline the goals, and at the end congratulate people on what they learned and what they worked on.

Contraindications, Precautions and Limitations

Some people may see expressive dance as childish, feel self-conscious, be disturbed by moving in an uninhibited way, or be upset about being watched or about physical contact with others. Sometimes self-consciousness is the result of disability or poor body image. Occasionally competitiveness can be a problem. Adolescents, particularly, may be self-conscious.

In a physical sense, dance in some form is nearly always possible. Some dances will be too strenuous for some people and occasionally dance will be a poor choice for people who experience delusions (sexual fantasies, paranoid misinterpretations of others' intentions). Fast movements and sudden changes are contraindicated for people with hypertension. People who are deaf will be unable to hear the rhythm of music for dance.

Usually, however, the potential drawbacks can be minimized through the way a session is introduced and organized. The name you give to an activity can make a difference. 'Creative dance' may put people off whereas 'Movement to music' or 'Expressive movement' could tempt them to try it out. Emphasize the therapeutic values ('It's relaxing', 'It keeps you fit and supple') and have a matter-of-fact expectation that everyone will join in, without over-persuading anyone who is really reluctant. One useful idea is to work in a circle. This has a number of advantages: everyone can see everyone else and no one is wondering who is looking at them; people can appreciate others' choice of movement; there is a feeling of equality and a circle readily allows for both contact and distance between people. Another idea is to have people stay in one spot and dance with their eyes closed.

Make people's first experience of expressive movement a brief part of an exercise or dance session and structure the session by telling people what feelings and ideas will be the basis of the activity and perhaps what parts of the body will be used. For instance, with a capable group, the therapist might say, 'Move to the music in whatever way it suggests but emphasize wide stretching movements' or 'This music is forceful. Move to it with determination and confidence.' With a less capable group, say 'Show me how you can dance to this music. Make big movements.'

Problems with getting started, or perhaps trying too hard, are often solved by a gentle warm up or some relaxation exercises. Choose music people like.

Using an acceptable title, working in a circle and introducing dance gradually will all help people feel less self-conscious about moving in each other's company — the first requirement for expressive movement. People must be able to choose whether to be involved or not, but be aware that spectators can inhibit others. Coming to the session should indicate a commitment to participate. Sometimes people who are less active can clap a rhythm or sing to the music.

Practical Organization

The format of a dance/movement session is the same as for any physical exercise session; warm up, main activities and wind-down. This routine avoids physical problems caused by starting or ending exercise too rapidly. It also gives people a sense of security — they know what to expect.

The extent to which a dance session should be structured varies with the dependence of the group. With very dependent groups, such as people with moderate to severe intellectual disability or the confused elderly, there will need to be substantial amounts of repetition in both the form and content of each session. The emphasis should be on the stimulus of the music. Avoid too many different activities in a session. With people who are very capable, the session will still follow the same format, but themes and content can be varied considerably.

Warm up with slow, stretching and swinging movements that use every part of the body, then move through a variety of types of movement and imagery to orientate people to the content of the session. If relationships and imagery will play a significant part, include some work on these in the warm up too. This part of the session should be slow and thorough,

Warm up before the session

focusing on suppleness and preparing the cardiovascular system for action.

Use the initial part of a session to link it with any previous sessions by reviewing or using some of the concepts already covered. Such repetition gives continuity. A balanced session will have a variety of dances or movement routines, with vigorous dances mixed with quieter ones. Vary individual, pair and group work in each session, and plan more activities than you need so that you have alternatives to choose from if necessary. Are there any limitations in the venue or time available? What are the needs, abilities and interests of people in the group?

End sessions in a way that completes the action and sums it up. A series of full, gentle stretches will make stiffness less likely.

Leading a dance session includes planning the kind of atmosphere that will work best. Do you want a workshop, experimental style, a keep fit class, or a social dance setting? Can the venue be changed to suit the style of the session? How do people's expectations contribute to the nature of the session? If an event is described as a social dance, for example, print invitations, expect people to come dressed in their best, decorate the room and perhaps prepare a supper.

With expressive movement, sessions need not emphasize group interaction. People can move independently to the same stimulus as others, perhaps taking ideas from one another then returning to movements based on what the music suggests to them. Keep a balance between individual and group work to help the group remain cohesive.

Alison Lee (*A Handbook of Creative Dance and Drama*) makes excellent suggestions about how to develop children's abilities in expressive movement. She suggests that every dance start from a still, balanced position 'like a statue of someone asleep'. Next she gets them to 'create' rooms to dance in. To explore what it means to dance she gets her dancers to use each part of their bodies in isolation. As they focus on each body part, they become more aware of it and how it can be used. They can picture energy flowing out from different parts of their body: fingertips, knees, head and so on. Lee suggests they exaggerate and stylize every movement to make them as distinct as possible.

Lee describes a dance as a series of movements linked to form a sequence. She gets dancers to create pathways from one point to another, patterns of movements that can be repeated.

Encourage people to experiment with the quality and variety of movements they make. If possible, dance with them. Emphasize free expression, fun and creativity, but do not lose sight of therapeutic goals, for the group and for each individual.

Sessions of expressive movement can begin with everyone moving in their own way, then go on to interactions between people, then on to creating dances.

Work out a theme and concepts to explore, and use music which might trigger ideas for the group. Be prepared to change if an idea comes up which seem to interest the group. Invite suggestions, and expect mature groups to share the leadership.

Each aspect of expressive movement — action, expression of feelings and communication — can be developed. If people seem stuck, make suggestions after watching what they are doing — but do not intervene too quickly. It is important to develop the dance element of sessions as well as the therapeutic goals.

With client groups which are very dependent, offer some one-to-one input.

The Therapist's Role

- Keep a record of what worked well, met people's needs and was popular.

- Keep explanations brief and keep the group action-orientated.
- Practise giving the instructions before the session. Use simple words ('Float', 'Fast', 'Wide') and short sentences. Communicate energy with a lively voice rather than a hearty voice which might sound patronizing.
- Avoid demonstrating or showing off a star performer. This is likely to inhibit people from valuing their own ideas — the stimulus people get from seeing what others are doing when everyone is working is usually enough. In some contexts it is useful to 'show' someone how a movement feels by moving their limbs.
- If a dance is being polished for a performance the therapist's role changes and demonstration, following and copying are appropriate. To learn particular movements or routines people should copy the therapist at the time rather than after a demonstration. The therapist either demonstrates facing the group who mirror what is to be done or demonstrates from one end of a semicircle.
- The sense of achievement from creating something is limited if a piece of music or movement sequence is used only once. Working on something which can be refined, remembered and repeated is more satisfying. Encourage people to suggest types of music and theme ideas. Ideally, all aspects of movement will be worked on and incorporated to make a satisfying whole. Look for a cohesive balance of action, unity and variety.

Creating a Session

Stimuli for expressive movement   Use music of all kinds, songs, chants, stamped rhythms, spoken words, percussion, clapping, pictures, paintings, poetry, objects, concepts, images, space and relationship — both social and physical — and simply the pleasure of movement itself.

Props can suggest actions as can dances seen on television and performances. Scarves and ribbons can be twirled slowly or quickly. Short handheld sticks can be used to emphasize movements.

Themes   Themes can be built round introducing a particular type of movement, exploring a piece of music, a poem, an event, a feeling or a relationship. Choose imagery that will interest the group.

Types of movement   Movements can emphasize:
- Parts of the body leading or acting as the focus of the dance. Ask, 'Where do you want your energy to flow from? Show one part of your body as starting all your movements.' Or give instructions: 'Focus on your knees and do a knees dance'; 'Do a dance with limp arms and hands'; 'Follow your elbow'; 'Use only your face, head and shoulders' (Warn people to avoid excessive neck movements); 'Do a dance with

your shoulders and hips (fingers and face . . .) working together'; 'Do a group arm dance'; 'It all starts with your toes. It ends with your toes.'

- The kind of action. Instruction words can be: gallop, skip, spin, punch, lunge, hop, shake, dab, pat, plod, tiptoe, scurry, bunny hop, caterpillar walk, spider walk.
- The type of movement. 'Be mechanical, graceful, swinging, flexible, flowing, smooth, floundering, swaggering, swooping, shuddering, scurrying, stealthy.'
- Tension or relaxation. 'Be controlled, loose, firm, stretched, strained, floppy, oozing, rubbery, floating in warm water, relaxed, calm, tense, gentle.'
- Weight or force. 'Be heavy, plodding, floating, like gossamer. Resist imaginary force (mud, elastic bonds). Sink to the ground.'
- The strength of an action. 'Be punchy, gentle, intense, forceful, tentative, explosive, energetic, weak.'
- Time and pace. 'Be quick, steady, sudden, gradual, random, rhythmic, sustained. Be like a bionic man, an old lady, a toddler.'
- Duration. 'Be sustained, spasmodic, momentary.'
- Tempo. 'Be frenzied, staccato, pulsating, soothing, bouncing.'
- Space/size. 'Be huge, tiny, minute, shrinking, small.'
- Level. 'Be knee level, head height, the part of the body that's highest — bottom, shoulders, hand.
- Where to move. 'Move sideways, up, out, far, vertical, right, left.'
- Shape. 'Be curling, curving, angular, zigzagging, circling, direct, straight, weaving, symmetrical.'
- Making spaces. 'Fill space, make circles, make a taboo centre circle, make a box shape, divide space in half.'

Music   Music is a bond between movement and ideas. It can be a strong, leading beat or a background to movement.

People can choose music or a series of sounds, or they can clap a rhythm for everyone else to move to. Rhythm makes it easier for people to work together because words are not needed — sharing a rhythm is a kind of communication. The accent beat of a rhythm can come at the beginning, middle or end of a musical phrase or dance. When the accent comes at the beginning, the dance works through and dissipates the tension of the accent. A middle accent has the effect of connecting and stabilizing parts of the dance — as if working towards an event and through it. Or it may give the feeling of a pendulum swing of constant motion. An end accent creates the feeling of a climax, of achievement and change. Each type of accent can be explored in a dance and mirrored in the music.

Rhythms   Change tempo or create rhythms with music, body sounds (clapping, knee slapping, stamping), routines (brushing hair, a sports action such as swinging a golf club), or through repeating patterns of movement (shoulder shrugs, heel banging) or sounds (hiss, whimper, hum, sigh). Get people to say rhythms: 'ONE and two, ONE and two' 'one, two THREE, four, one, two, THREE, four . . .'

Tell people to 'Do what a rhythm suggests with your whole body' or 'Just with your fingertips'. Or to 'Take a sound, make a movement' or 'Take a movement, add a sound.'

Imagery   It is best to work on movements first and then imagery. As in drama, imagery provides a framework. If it is well chosen, it increases people's sense of security. What images will your group accept, find useful, enjoy? How can ideas be shown in action? Use only a selection of ideas in each session.

Get people to show the characteristics of whatever they are trying to be. For example, get people to 'be' a machine, bicycle, cat, balloon, flickering candle or butterfly caught in a net. Get them to rock a baby, knead bread show where they itch or hurt. People can watch one another and discuss the common features in what they are trying to show.

At the end of the session, debrief. Announce that the action/role play is over and describe what is going to happen next.

Ideas for imagery can come from:

- Natural sources: birds, animals, plants, pebbles in a stream, dragon, a porpoise. Show each subject over time and in different places.
- Sounds: motors, wind, the sea and so on. Show hiss, roar, glug, ping, swish in movement.
- Manmade things: a typewriter, revolving chair, telephone, bouncing ball, dentist's drill, marbles, a smell, a robot. Do a dance with a wall, on a tightrope or of a day in the life of . . .
- Feelings: hope, joy, serenity, rage, nervousness, relaxation, excitement, curiosity, chaos, confusion, serenity, mischievousness.
- Transitions: for example, dirty to clean, 'You're covered in porridge (foam, clay), scrape it off, splat it off, shower it off.'
- Changes: youth to age, a trickle to a great river, the tide in and out.
- Relationships: start/finish, meet/part, mother/daughter, nurse/child, boss/worker, pet/owner.
- Routines: domestic routines, sports routines, work routines. Or feed the cat, write a grocery list, eat with chopsticks for the first time, climb a mountain, wrestle, play golf, play a trumpet, draw in the air, chop wood.
- Mime a story: a poem, a children's story, a rescue, an anecdote, a newspaper item, a crash on the ski slopes, a hunt for a lost ring.
- National dance images: Indian dances, Spanish dances and so on.
- Using imaginary objects: a balloon, flag, hat, high heels, big boots, one-man yacht, rubberband.
- Time: caveman days, the 22nd century, yesterday, tomorrow, my 21st birthday.
- Texture: sticky, rough, slippery.
- Colours: aqua, magenta, violet.

- Place: the zoo, the beach, a mountain top, auction rooms, a courtroom.
- People. Try any of the roles people fill at work, at different ages, as part of a cultural group: nanny, karate expert, magician, racer, cowboy, fire walker.

Props   Props create imagery, give ideas and accentuate styles of movement — flowing, abrupt and so on. Possibilities include: scarves, crepe paper streamers, ribbons, ribbons on sticks, lengths of fabric, large towels, balloons, shawls, rope, frisbees, bean bags, drums, masks, hoops, scarves, parachutes, balls, dressing up equipment and gymnastics equipment such as mats, hoops and balance beams.

Example sessions

1. Theme: changing pace.

   Imagery: galloping horses, horses hiding . . .
   Rhythm: pounding hooves, muffled hooves.
   Type of action: gallop, rear, nuzzle.

2. Theme: the story of making a parachute jump.

   Imagery: planes, parachutes, instructor.
   Rhythm: rapid, staccato. Slow, forever. Stopped. Gentle, gentle, fast.
   Action: shake, quiver. Wait. Freeze. Leap, whirl, float, curve, turn, gaze. Stop, stumble, stretch, stagger. Leap.
   Props: parachute?

Targeting specific needs   From a therapeutic point of view expressive movement can be used to address specific medical and social problems, such as:

- Movement skills: for people with arthritis stress flexibility and mobility with smooth, gentle, swinging and stretching movements.
- Social skills: make opportunities for people to lead or work closely with others. Social skills sessions can be complemented with movement sequences involving turn-taking, miming greetings and requests and having conversations using body language only.
- Learning skills and information: the steps involved in doing the laundry, meal-making and similar activities can be reinforced in a dance role play. Concepts like size, position and pace can be taught.
- Relaxation: use movement rhythms that emphasize relaxation.
- Sight: for people who are blind, or have limited sight, use touch and physical contact to give instruction and involve people.
- Hearing: give deaf people a clear visual demonstration.
- Reminiscence sessions: choose music which was popular when the members of the group were teenagers. For adolescents and young adults use dances which are currently popular.

Traditional Dance

Many types of traditional dance can be adapted for therapeutic groups: folk, tap, national, ballroom, disco, old time, square, Latin American, Morris.

Start with simple versions of a dance, choosing ones you like and feel confident to teach. Initially, try out new dances as just a brief part of a session. As well as being a therapist, you will need to be able to demonstrate the dance steps.

Think about the movements or relationships you want to focus on. Start with a step which the group will manage easily; clap the tune through then walk through the actions.

If people have limited mobility (people in wheelchairs and some old people) use only those parts of dance routines which will be manageable (just upper body movements, for example).

Dances call for different levels of energy, fitness and memory, so there is scope for programmes which increase in physical and mental demand. Alternate strenuous and easy dances; pay plenty of complements and keep it fun.

One way to make a particular dance more simple is to use only the easiest movements in the dance and repeat them. Gradually introduce more complex steps.

Select dances with a clear rhythm. The best kind of music is live — fiddle, flute, guitar — as the pace of a tune can be altered to accommodate the learners' needs. Try playing records at slower speeds as a way of starting off. Approach schools and clubs to see what resources they have. Some records have accompanying booklets of instruction.

Folk and square dance In traditional dances, especially square dances, Scottish dances and other folk dances, people must remember dance sequences, relate to the right partner and keep in time with the music. There is opportunity too, for learning about the customs and values of other cultures. A good number for folk dancing is twenty-four — eight is the minimum.

Many traditional dances use similar steps and when people know even a small number of steps, they can make up simple dances to square or Scottish dance tunes. For example, 'Circle to the left, circle to the right, take four paces in, clap, take four paces back, turn to the person next to you, link arms and swing.'

An advantage of folk dance as a first dance experience is that it is group orientated. People can help each other remember what to do and give physical support by linking arms or hands. Manners and courtesy are an important feature of these dances.

It is easier to 'call' for a square dance if you have an assistant to lead the dance itself. Practise together and if possible teach a core of people the basic movements of the dances so they can teach others. Make the instructions brief and speak clearly and loudly in time with the music. Review the steps people have learnt regularly, and plan which ones will be added at each session.

Dance Games

Wheelchair dances and games   Use slow tunes and have plenty of space. If people are likely to become tired, get them to dance alternate dances. Warn people to be careful about collisions and hand and foot injuries.

Finger plays and action songs   Many already exist for children. Make some up to adult songs and music and tailor them to your group.

Songs which lend themselves to action   Make a group activity of putting actions to well-known songs, sing-a-long songs like sea shanties and old time songs.

Playback dance   One person in a group describes an event that was significant to them and a small group portray it in dance, each person taking a different aspect of what has been said, and including both the feelings and actions of the event.

Festivals and pageants   Build a play/dance round the music of a festival.

Marching routines   Make use of marching team routines and get the group to sing or clap as they march. Have an 'accompaniment' group to sing and clap a rhythm. Make up a chant to suit a march.

Mirror dances   People take turns to be the mirror-image of what their partner does. This can be started as a simple 'recognize-and-respond' exercise, and then developed into a complex dance dialogue. People can complement or contrast with one another, each taking it in turn to lead.

Pairs action   One person sits, stands or lies while their body is sculpted into different shapes by their partner. They can be sculpted as though they were a floppy rag doll or made of wire, clay or planks of wood.

Musical games   There are many musical games for children and a few for adults. As part of a reminiscence session, you could use traditional children's music and action games, such as Oranges and Lemons, Punchinello and The Farmer in the Dell. More adult musical games are the Hokey Tokey, Conga and Auld Lang Syne. Some traditional drinking songs may be useful.

Conga   The group lines up, one behind the other, hands on the hips or shoulders of the person in front. The leader sets off with the group copying them in what they do. The traditional routine is kick left, step one, step two, kick right, step one, step two and so on, with a bouncy rhythm. Caution the leader to go fairly slowly at first. Other movements which can be used are small jumps with both feet together, a pace to the right or left, tiptoeing, hopping and so on. Keep it simple.

Try getting people in a line to be ghosts, a roaring dragon or a sea serpent moving up and down with the waves.

The greatest person in the world   The leader asks the person on their left (say 'Janet') what they would like to mime (magician, hula dancer, acrobat, equestrian, tap dancer, conductor, traffic director . . .). Then everyone stands in a circle and the leader introduces Janet as the greatest person in the world, like this:

'Today I would like to introduce Janet, the greatest badminton player in the world.' The leader claps, urging everyone else to clap too: 'Give her a big hand. Janet will perform for us and we will follow her actions.'

After more clapping and cheering, Janet leads the group for a few minutes, smashing imaginary shuttle cocks with superb accuracy. Then it is her turn to introduce the person on her left in the same way.

If people are easily overstimulated, tone the activity down so that every member leads the group in action for a few minutes, but without the showmanship. If someone chooses an activity which is unsuitable, suggest modifications such as slowing the pace down or simplifying the movement.

Movement memory   A leader makes three movements (adapted to people's abilities) one after the other. After the demonstration the group repeats them.

CREATIVE WRITING

Writing: a pleasure, a chore or a responsibility? Writing is seen in different ways by different people. Potentially, it is a satisfying creative medium and a good social activity for a group. It can bring a real sense of achievement.

Creative writing can be a group or one-to-one activity. It can be the basis for a series of sessions or used to provide variety among other activities. There is some form of written activity to suit everyone, even those who cannot read and write, if a scribe writes for them. Poetry or prose in which vivid images are created quickly is particularly useful in therapeutic groups.

Therapeutic Application

In 'one-off' writing activities, people are often surprised by how easy it is to produce satisfying results. Lively, sensitive images seem to be just waiting to surface.

Creative writing sessions can be lightweight and fun or in-depth and skill-building.

As an extended therapeutic activity, creative writing best suits people who are used to expressing their ideas in writing. For them, the main pleasure, and much of the therapeutic value, comes from the self-expression and the discipline needed to put ideas on paper and refine them. With each redrafting the thinking process is sharpened. Writing is a way of ordering thoughts and being creative — words give structure to ideas. Through writing people see what they know. Some will find it easier to compare or express emotions on paper than in conversation or group discussion.

Keeping a diary of events and feelings is a good project for aiding insight. It can give people a sense of control over painful or bewildering events in their lives.

Planned sessions bring out many other potential benefits. Writing can:

- Reinforce workplace skills like decision making and perseverance.
- Enable people to get to know each other in a new way. It encourages careful, sympathetic listening.
- Be important in retraining a damaged dominant hand.
- Improve literacy.
- Help people become more fluent in a second language.
- Aid learning of any subject matter. The process of research followed by writing is an excellent way of learning.
- Be useful in social skills training. In shared writing each person must take the other's ideas, values and choice of words into account, to make the activity work. Listening, discussion and compromise are essential in this process. Groups working on the same piece of work should be small — two to four is the ideal. Alternatively, people can write separately on the same topic, then share what they have written, comparing similarities and differences.

  Exercises in writing dialogue can be useful to social skills groups. Starting points could be simple, familiar routines (greetings, partings, requests), followed by more complex social dialogues (conversations about a sport, hobby, controversial issue or emotionally charged situation).
- Be extended to sharing ideas on writers and writing, studying how particular effects are created, how newspapers and advertisements manipulate ideas and so on.
- Have potential reminiscence value. At times people need to go back to events in their past and recreate, review and resolve them.

Contraindications, Precautions and Limitations

A common problem is lack of confidence in writing skills. A less common but important problem is illiteracy. It is sometimes difficult to find out whether people can read and write because, through embarrassment, many such people have developed effective ways of hiding their illiteracy. Neither illiteracy nor lack of confidence are real barriers to participation if a scribe can listen to people or interview them and record what they say. The scribe may need to be able to read or follow a specific communication system, such as a Blissymbols board or Makaton (simple logical communication systems for people with communication difficulties). In group exercises one scribe to three or four people can work well.

A scribe/interpreter may be needed when people are not working in their own language.

People can be very shy about sharing what they have written. If a group works together as a unit from the beginning, this problem may be reduced. Try to generate a group atmosphere in which people are supportive of each other's efforts. (See WORKING IN GROUPS, *Cohesiveness: building group relationships* p. 204.)

If people cannot think clearly (through depression, anxiety, schizophrenia, brain damage and so on) writing activities should be kept fairly concrete — or avoided completely. If people experience hallucinations and delusions, projects should be structured so that they are unlikely to provoke unhealthy preoccupations. It is also important to take into account people's concentration spans.

The physical act of writing involves fine finger movements and hand control. Pens or pencils can be built up or weighted or a computer or typewriter used. Paper may need to be stabilized.

Written projects done to retrain hand function should be interesting to do, not just mechanical exercises. If the goal is purely creative, it is probably better for a scribe to do the writing.

People with limited sight may need a scribe. Some will find it easier to write with a bold felt-tip pen on a large page.

Writing to express feelings can lead people to avoid interacting with others and to deny their real-life problems. Encourage people to share what they have written so that they have the opportunity, either one-to-one or in a group, to see how others respond to what they have said. When the aim is to express feelings, a common finding among therapists is that: 'Ask for a feeling and you get a thought, ask for a thought and you get a feeling.'

The Therapist's Role

Expect to give support and encouragement, generate discussion and perhaps set the pace of work. Sometimes there will be a teaching role or a need to help people edit what they have written.

The early focus of any creative writing in therapy should be on expression rather than literary merit, spelling and grammar. Quantity and quality are unimportant. Explain this at the beginning so that people can leave behind memories of struggling with work reports or school essays. What matters is that the writer understands what they have written and enjoys writing — or at least gets some satisfaction from it! When writing is done regularly people can work to improve the quality of what they do.

Developing a Session

In an hour-long, one-off writing session there is time for five minutes explanation, twenty minutes writing, thirty minutes sharing and discussion and five minutes conclusion. If a group wants to develop their writing skills sessions must be longer so that some of the writing time can be spent on review and correction. At the sharing stage more time will be needed for comment on both the writing and the content. An hour and a half is a maximum stretch for actual writing but it may be better to do several quick activities than one that takes the whole time. If people talk for too long beforehand, they may lose the urge to write about a subject. If people go on talking in the writing time, steer them firmly into writing for that part of the session.

In the discussion stage, get people to first share only the opening part of what they have written, then the whole piece of writing. Endings too can be separated out and compared.

It is hard to make progress if people only write during group sessions so encourage them to do more between sessions. 'Half a page on . . .' may seem manageable, and if people get involved they may well edit and rewrite it several times.

Half a page is also a maximum if people are to share what they have done with the group. Writing letters or keeping a diary are other useful ways of doing more writing on a regular basis.

What kind of writing works best?   Carol Peck (*From Deep Within: Poetry Workshops in Nursing Homes*), working with the elderly and in short sessions which needed to be complete in themselves, stuck to poetry. She wanted to show people how to use language to bring ideas and feelings alive, how to make 'pictures with words'. As a starting phrase she gave 'Blue is . . .' People then used all their senses to build images with this phrase.

Alternatively, instruct people to start with a scene, anchor it with sensory images of size, space, time and sound, then bring on some characters. Something must happen. What happens can be gigantic or minute but it must lead to a change.

Hints   Coberly, McCormick and Updike (*Writers Have No Age*) make a number of suggestions for creative writing. First, that ideally the leader be a writer themselves (though this is not essential), second, that it is 'better to suggest things to write about rather than a form to use' and third, that editing should be tailored to the amount people can accept. Concerning editing they say 'let the spirit of the work override your ideas about how it should be done'. A fourth suggestion is that leaders of creative writing groups should encourage people to read as much as possible. Choose books and poetry to read aloud in sessions and they may stimulate people to read on.

Initially, people are likely to choose 'safe' topics like 'A day at the beach' rather than 'The day my sister died'. They are likely to over-idealize things and emphasize the good, positive and pretty, and avoid expressing their feelings. They are also likely to be too honest and tell things exactly as they are or were. Effective writing plays some things up and others down.

To help people write better provide them with good models, plenty of opportunity to practise and feedback that is supportive and constructive. Set clear attainable targets and praise what you like very specifically.

The first session in a series should consist of structured, straightforward projects which will help people get to know one another and give some scope for creativity. In groups where writing is the main activity, the first session should help people identify possible subject matter.

Mutual help   Some people are very sensitive about sharing what they have written. Before people listen to (or read) each other's writing, give them specific guidelines so that their comments will be useful and acceptable to each other. First, everyone should acknowledge that each person has a commitment to what they have written and that in sharing it they trust others to value their work and be constructive in the comments they make. Second, give people 'help' they can accept — avoid overloading them. As a therapist, monitor the total number of comments to each person — if everyone in the group contributes, the effect can be overwhelming. Be matter-of-fact about spelling and minor grammatical errors — it is often better to ignore them. 'Picky' corrections divert attention from the overall quality. Clarity and interest are much more important.

Questions for constructive comment
Use questions sparingly as they can imply criticism.
- What do you like best in this writing? Identify a sentence, phrase or idea.
- What is interesting?
- Can you pick a focusing statement or a key phrase? Does it work well? Is it in the best place?
- Can you identify where the introduction ends? Where the conclusion starts?
- Are there any effective similes or metaphors? Could they be extended and developed? (A simile is a comparison, a metaphor describes one thing as another).
- Is there anything the writer could make more of?
- Anything that is unclear?
- Do the ideas link one paragraph to the next?
- Could you draw a diagram-plan of the piece?
- If this person were to change just one thing what would you suggest? (Work in pairs — if several people make different suggestions the limiting effect of 'just one thing' is lost).

Practical Organization

Develop an atmosphere conducive to writing. Good physical conditions
are important (seating, lighting, tables — individual tables or a single large
one?). Choose a time of day for sessions when people are likely to be
wide-awake and able to concentrate. Morning or mid-afternoon sessions
are good 'working' times of day.

Essential equipment is paper, dark pencils and an eraser. Folders to keep
work in are a good idea and art materials like coloured inks, crayons
and felt-tip pens can be useful. Reference books such as a dictionary, a
thesaurus, dictionary of quotations, style book and perhaps some 'How to'
books are worthwhile. Poetry books, books which inspire and books which
give models of types of writing can also be helpful.

A closed group, or one in which the membership changes gradually
('slow open') is usually most appropriate. It is probably best if the people in
the group have fairly similar abilities although differences can be used to
encourage tolerance and to provide opportunities for people to help one
another and take leadership roles.

Activities

Warm-up and one-off activities

Poetry   Start with colourful images. Aim for the essence of concepts, vivid
images and meaning; ignore rhyme and metre. In group work simple
devices can be used to give unity to people's work, for example starting
phrases such as Robert Browning's 'These have I loved . . .' or Mother
Teresa's 'Life is . . .' At its simplest this can be a 'sentence completion
activity'. The same starting phrases can be used several times. For example,
the instruction might be, 'Write three sentences starting with 'Our hero . . .',
'Mary's old car . . .', 'A cat is . . .', 'Green is . . .', 'The flowers . . .', 'My
favourite . . .', 'An important (place, person, day, possession) in my life . . .'
(See *SELF-AWARENESS ACTIVITIES, Part sentences* p. 31.)

Captions   Cut out pictures, cartoons or advertisements from magazines
and get the group to write captions for them. Or use words cut out of
magazines for the captions. Have enough words to give people plenty of
choice. People piece the words together to make slogans and captions.

Words only collage   Topics for this activity can be insight-orientated, 'My
life', 'My dreams' or, more general, 'Motor bikes', 'The colour red'. (People
sometimes learn as much about themselves from a neutral topic as from an
emotionally loaded, insight-orientated one which may seem threatening.)

As a warm-up activity collages should be small, say 10 cm by 10 cm. If
used in the body of the session, the collages can be larger and done
individually, in pairs or in groups, with a more definite theme. Tiny mini-
collages glued onto shapes (circles, triangles) of card can be made into
badges.

Myself as People choose a picture and write about it as though they were part of the picture. 'Myself as a tree', 'Myself in Rome' and so on.

Word association chains Give the group a starting word and ask them to scribble down associated words as fast as they can for a set length of time. Twenty seconds to two minutes is long enough.

This exercise can be changed by stipulating the kind of word to use: nouns, verbs, adjectives or adverbs (for simplicity, define adverbs as words ending in 'ly'). Ask, 'Did any of the associations surprise or interest you?'

Alternatively, work in pairs and say words and phrases in turn as rapidly as possible. A third person acts as scribe.

Word shapes This is a cross between art and writing in that people write words in the shape of their meaning. For example, 'balloon' is a fat rounded shape and 'brick' an oblong. Coloured pens and pencils make this activity more interesting.

A calligram is a poem written in the shape of what it describes, for example a poem about a tree would be tree-shaped.

Stimuli for creative writing

Pictures Choose a picture which will interest your group or is related to a therapeutic goal (pictures of work and recreational activities, people interacting, schools, hospitals). Show the picture and get everyone to jot down ideas. Ask leading questions: 'Where is this place? What would you hear? Smell? Feel?' For a picture of a person: 'Who is this person? What is their name? Where are they? Where do they come from? What have they been doing? What are they going to do next?'

People write a paragraph or story based on the ideas they jotted down.

A piece of writing People write down their reactions to a phrase, a poem, a letter to an editor or a controversial article.

Music Play a piece of music and ask, 'What could it be called?', 'Where does it take you?', 'Is it telling a story?', 'What feeling does it suggest?', 'Does it remind you of a place? A person?'

Objects Anything can be used — toy animals, maps, photos, memorabilia of all kinds. First people jot down any words, phrase associations or impressions that come to mind. Next they decide on a style of writing (factual account, dialogue, poetry) and use the words and phrases to write a piece about the stimulus material.

Place, person, object People work in groups of three. One person has a picture of a place, one a picture of a person and the third an object. Each chooses what should be said about their item in a story. If a scribe is used he or she can prompt the group with questions about the place/person/object: 'John, tell us where this story is happening.'

Hat topics   Each person writes a topic on a slip of paper and puts it in a hat. The topics are mixed and everyone takes a slip of paper, making sure they do not get their own, and writes a piece about it. (You may want to specify the type of topic: place, time, subject and so on.)

Columns   People divide a page into three columns headed 'Nouns', 'Adjectives' and 'Verbs' (a fourth column for 'Adverbs' is optional). They then write as many words as they can under each column in response to a stimulus idea ('Winter', 'Hockey', 'Cats' . . .). After a set length of time (say three minutes), or when ideas are beginning to dry up, people use their words in a piece of writing.

Words for a story   In turn, each person in the group chooses one word. Everyone writes the words at the top of a piece of paper and then combines them in a story.
    If people have limited ability, choose only three or four people to give words.

Doggerel verse   Get people to write down all the words they can with the same ending (-ay, -ell, -ack, -ake, -ing, -ong) and then construct verse from them.

Threes   The group chooses a topic then everyone writes down three nouns, three adjectives and three verbs relating to it. Each person tries to use their nine words in a piece of writing.

Graffiti board   This group activity can be a quick warm up, a one-off session or an ongoing project. The group covers a board or large sheet of card with slogans, aphorisms, jokes and one-word statements, using a variety of pens, biros, pencils, crayons and chalk, and perhaps coloured paper shapes to write on. A theme can help: 'Favourite foods', 'Good books', 'Poetry', 'What's on', 'My hero'. Set limits beforehand if you think some material may be offensive.

Successes bulletin board   Get people to write about things they appreciate others in the group doing or saying. Use the board to recognize all levels of contribution, effort and cause for celebration. The items can be pinned up and changed at regular intervals.

News sheet   Exercises such as the preceding two can be expanded into a weekly typed and printed news sheet or magazine. A news sheet can include announcements, advertisements, poetry, welcomes, art, recipes, jokes, hobby tips, reviews. In miniature, it is a newspaper, so examine the contents and sections of newspapers for ideas.

Reminiscence   People can write about their family history, a particular period in their life, an important incident, a travel story. (See *VERBAL ACTIVITIES, Reminiscence* p. 140 for more topic ideas.) Working in pairs or threes can be a good idea with the very elderly. Use a scribe or interviewer if necessary.

Not what it seems   People think of an incident or thing 'that isn't what it seems' then develop a story round it, planning how they will build up one impression then alter it as the story unfolds.

   Alternatively, base a story on a misunderstanding involving a word with more than one meaning.

Guided-imagery fantasy trip   People shut their eyes and the therapist tells a story and asks questions to stimulate their imagination. When the story is finished everyone writes down their version of it. (See *RELAXATION, Fantasy trip* p. 186 for subject ideas.)

An interview   Each person thinks of something they could be interviewed about. Working in pairs, people take it in turns to be interviewer/interviewee. Both write up the interview for a magazine or a newspaper. Topics might be: 'Favourite foodstuffs', 'Races', 'The fire'. The interviewer can ask questions to bring out details about people, season, place and 'what happened'.

It happened to me   One person reads out a passage written in the third person to the group, and each person rewrites the story as though it happened to them.

   Or people can rewrite the incident as a poem.

Message   Working individually or as a group, people write a message or poem for a card (for example, a birthday, get well or thank you card). This is a good activity if one person in the group is ill or away for some reason.

No stops   People write without pause for a set length of time, say two minutes. Give a starting word or phrase such as, 'One day I will . . .', 'John . . .' (people use their own name) or 'I think . . .'

Consequence writing   Working in a group, each person writes the opening lines of a poem or story on a piece of paper, then passes the paper to the person on their left who adds one or two lines. The top part of the story or poem can either be left visible or turned down so that only the end shows for the next writer. If the writing is not hidden people try to continue the content of the story as a whole. Covering up the first contribution makes the activity more of a game.

   Variations: Everyone uses the same starting topic ('Snails', 'Adoption', 'Safety') and agrees to write poetry or prose. The elements of the story

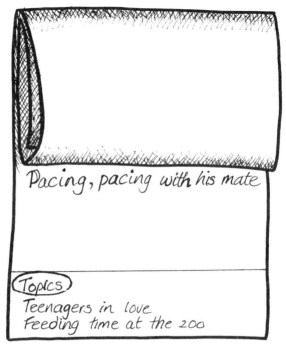

Pacing, pacing with his mate

Topics
Teenagers in love
Feeding time at the zoo

Consequence writing

can be listed at the bottom of the page: Topic/theme, Characters, Setting/props.

This activity can also be done with a self-awareness focus — see 'An interview' above — with people exploring personal stories and concerns.

Word associations   Each person has a long, narrow piece of paper and writes one word at the bottom. The type of word can be specified, for example, a word describing an emotion (anger, hope) or a work role (nurse, salesman). The papers are passed round and the next person writes a comment at the top of the paper in response to the word at the bottom. They then fold the top of the paper over and pass it on to the next person who repeats the process. If the group is large, decide how many statements you will get beforehand (six statements is generally enough). The papers are passed back to the original people, who read them out to the group in turn.

Variation: solutions to problems   Each person writes a problem on the bottom of their paper and each group member writes a possible solution. Papers can be folded over, or left open so that each person must think of something new for the list. It may be a good idea to mix the papers up so that who wrote what is less obvious to group members.

Extend this activity by having people write the first steps required to achieve the solution they have suggested. The steps should be stated in such a way that it is easy to tell when they have been achieved.

Clarify the activity with an example on a blackboard or large sheet of paper.

Types of writing

Particular forms of writing can be useful as a starting point but avoid sticking to them rigidly.

Descriptive piece   Write a word picture of an event, person, place or object.

Biographies   People choose someone to describe. It can be someone they know, have read about or seen on television. Ask for a detailed account of the way the person looks, dresses, acts and speaks, the events they are or were involved in and where they happened. Perhaps include an evaluation of what has happened, or what might happen in the future. The group as a whole could write a biography of one of its members or someone known to everyone.

Alternatively, people could write an autobiography or a curriculum vitae. Writing a curriculum vitae may sound more like a serious exercise than creative writing but if the writer explains their values and the significance of their life experiences, it becomes a creative exercise.

A diary   A day-by-day description of events can be a piece of creative writing. People can write about a day in their current life, a day in the past or a day in the future. They could also write a day as someone else might experience it. Or get people to talk to a partner about a day in their life. Each writes a diary day for the other.

Diary writing can be a way of collecting things to write about. It provides practice and is an aid to keeping track of progress.

Mock school report   People rule up a sheet of paper like a school report and write teacher's comments beside each subject heading.

Letters   Letters can be personal, quick memos, formal business communications or complaints to a politician. In a creative writing group, any of these types of letters can be composed.

Writing business letters, job applications or letters of request or complaint, clarifies the form these letters take and helps people to improve their letter writing skills.

Reports   Report writing provides people with a model of how to write a report and, as an exercise, is an opportunity to write something creative or serious for a bulletin board or newsletter.

The steps? Gather data then arrange it in a logical order. Write an opening which defines the concern or subject of the report and how it will be addressed. Elaborate each point in logical order, using headings if appropriate, and perhaps illustrating each main point with an example. Sum up and draw a conclusion and/or put a request. Check for completeness, directness, brevity and clarity.

Pen friends   A pen friend can be an old friend living far away or a local friend. People in the same hospital or institution can write to each other as pen friends.

Compose a letter for a partner   In pairs, each person takes it in turn to tell their partner what they want to say and the partner writes it down in letter form.

Alternatively, the group writes a letter on a blackboard for one person. The aim is to help the person whose letter is being written to clarify what they really want to say. Encourage the group to check repeatedly both the tone and content of the letter with the person they are writing for.

Job descriptions   Get people to write a job description for the ideal nurse, teacher, mother, son, boss.

Or tell them to 'Write a description of yourself in the words your best friend would use.'

Or ask them to write an item for the 'Work wanted' column of a newspaper, as though they were advertising their own 'position'. For example, 'Mother available, cooks a basic range of food . . .'

They could also write a 'Wanted' advertisement for an imaginary partner, child, friend, house, car or holiday.

Advertisement   Ask, 'If you were an advertising agent and had to sell yourself, what would you include in your product promotion?'

'What would you include in an advertisement for the film of your life?'

'What would you write on the dust jacket of your autobiography.' Remind people that the aim is to sell the book!

An appreciation   Write about a friend as though they were emigrating or leaving a job after a long period. This can be a good exercise when someone is leaving a group.

A reference   As an esteem-building activity, get people to write 'references' for each other. (As a precaution, make sure that the references will not be used in job applications. If there is any risk of this, collect them at the end of the session or get people to work on scrap paper of some kind).

Inventories   Write an inventory of 'The perfect desert island' or 'My ideal wardrobe'.

A 'wanted' ad

Or do a 'self-inventory'. Each person stocktakes their skills, interests and abilities.

Reviews   Find some reviews in magazines and newspapers and get people to examine their style, format, language and content. Then get people to write their own. Topics might be 'The television programme I dislike the most', or 'The best film I ever saw'.

Or, get them to review an imaginary autobiography of their lives. The review could tell what they have done, who the players were, when and where things happened, what they liked and disliked, what was successful and what was not.

Word puzzles and games   Common word games are crosswords, find-a-word, and acrostics (muddled word order puzzles). Small groups can make them up for each other.

Dialogue   Each person chooses two to four characters and a situation, and then writes an imaginary dialogue. This can also be done in pairs or small groups.

Plays   To write a play as a group activity, people first need to choose roles and a scene. They can then try out lines together, inventing them on the spot. After 'acting' the play out, the group can write down what happened and what was said, refining it as they go. Encourage people to stick with the roles they chose, rather than adding too many new ideas.

A log   People decide the elements of a journey — who, how, what, where and when — and then let a story about 'what happened' on the journey evolve out of them.

Poetry   Poetry uses the full vitality of language, including all its nuances.

Get each person to complete the same phrase several times, and then collect people's papers and put them together in an order which makes some kind of sense (for example, start with pragmatic comments and move on to sensory or abstract ones). Alternatively, get everyone to read out what they have written and write it on a blackboard or large sheet of newsprint and decide on the order as a group.

Topic ideas that have worked well with other groups are: Colour — 'Yellow is ...'; Time — 'Morning is ...'; Tastes — 'Bananas are ...'; 'Smells'; 'Things which are tiny (huge ...)'; 'How things feel'; 'Sounds like ...'; 'Opposites'. Other possibilities include:

- Events and places. 'I used to ...', 'An important day', 'Something I've learnt', 'Worst and Best', 'My favourite place', 'Do you remember ... ?', 'When I was ...'
- To ... 'A poem to the moon', 'To a cat', 'To spring', 'To love ...', 'A poem to welcome ...'
- A recipe for love, autumn, painting, grandparenting ...
- Likenesses. 'I am like ...', 'People are like ...', 'A tree is like ...', 'A stone is like ...'
- Special things. 'My time capsule', 'My favourite ...'

To develop poetry writing sessions, read a number of pieces in a particular style aloud to the group, then suggest they try writing in a similar style.

Or get people to try rewriting the rhythm and pattern of a well-known poem or song, perhaps keeping portions of the original words. Songs used in advertisements are often familiar and easy to adapt.

In discussion avoid too much intellectual concern about meaning. Instead, emphasize and enjoy the feelings and images of each poem.

An anthology   Collect together as many poetry books as possible and get people to browse and choose a poem they like for a group anthology.

Group poem
A Bath is...
For getting dirt off
Relaxing
Warm peace and quiet
A flood, a mess
Fun
A cocoon of warm silk
Luxury
Ease to aching bones
Cleans mental tiredness
Hot bubbles
A womb enveloping me

A poem by seven young mothers

Quiz What is a colloquialism, acrostic, connotation, pun, aphorism, metaphor, ambiguity . . . ?

Writing skills

Pointers for good writing:

- Keep it simple. Avoid complex phrases, obscure words or words which are overused. Aim for clarity.
- Use short words, short sentences and short paragraphs — they are easier to read than long ones. The length of sentences and paragraphs should vary, but make sure the longer ones are digestible.
- Write for human beings. Good writing has a lot in common with good speaking. In conversation, people take account of the person they are speaking to and in writing, too, it is important to have a picture of the people you are writing for. What are they interested in? An audience helps the writer get the amount of detail right and keeps the writing lively.
- Use dialogue — it adds variety to prose.
- Use contractions where appropriate (it's, they're). They make writing more direct and personal.
- Avoid the deadening effect of cliches and wornout phrases which have lost their meaning through overuse.

- Use active prose. The key to active prose is the active voice (John hit the ball). The passive voice (The ball was hit . . .) is indirect and can obscure who did what (sometimes that is just what is wanted of course!). It can also seem longwinded.
- Convey the story and feelings through nouns and verbs in preference to adjectives and adverbs ('He pondered . . .' rather than 'He thought carefully . . .'). Adjectives and adverbs are much less effective for creating strong, clear prose.
- Check words like 'each', 'they', 'it' and 'that'. Make sure it is clear which object or person they are referring to.
- Be specific. Concrete examples will hold the attention of the reader much better than abstract concepts. Referring, for example, to 'silks and satins, lace and electric blue' is more vivid than simply saying 'beautiful dresses', and 'a scone steaming bubbles of cheese' is more real than 'morning coffee'. Aim for coloured pictures!
- Write with confidence. 'Possibly', 'seems', 'rather', 'can be' and 'perhaps' make people doubt what is said. Sometimes it is preferable to be definite and wrong than vague and right.
- Avoid 'elegant variations'. Changing from 'the leader' to 'Sir Winston' or 'Churchill' can be confusing when they refer to the same person.
- Be enthusiastic. Instead of telling things just as they are, add impressions, feelings and what you think things mean. Select, exaggerate and omit in order to make a story out of flat facts.
- Construct strong beginnings and endings. The beginning of a story entices the reader to follow and when they finish it is the ending which stays with them. Endings draw ideas together and complete them. They can be punchy, a summary, memorable, sad, ambiguous, decisive.
- Keep yourself in the background.
- Choose a style and stick to it. Know how the kind of thing you are writing is normally done. What models are you following? Romance? Short story? Comedy? How are they written? What is the range of subject matter? How are particular effects created?
- Plan the layout. Good visual layout makes writing inviting. Vary the lengths of paragraphs and have plenty of white space and headings to break up solid blocks of writing.
- Make a plan, gather ideas, put them in a logical order, choose a suitable style, then start writing rapidly. Edit, chop, change and rearrange later.
- Expect to proofread. Check and recheck for repetition, clarity, correct spelling and grammar, and sensible links between paragraphs.

Word processing and creative writing

Liz Foster (*Writer's Workshop, the Word Processor and the Psychiatric Patient*) sums up the values of word processing in creative writing:

Together, the processor and printer provide three valuable functions:
- They enable the patient to produce an accurate and professionally presented piece of work.

- They facilitate the production of magazines and newsletters containing the patient's work.
- They allow the patient to be involved in the entire production process.

Where the physical process of writing is particularly slow, a word processor can give people the opportunity to edit their own work after someone else has typed it. Word processing guarantees a professional-looking end product. Learning to use a word processor is fun. It opens up a new world of communication and gives people a sense of being part of the twentieth century — a potential morale booster!

Publication

Basic criteria for offering material for publication are that the script is typed on A4 paper, one side of the page only and double spaced with wide margins. Many journals regularly publish their criteria and requirements for publication. Number the pages and keep a copy.

VERBAL ACTIVITIES

We talk to our friends for company, to ourselves to work out what we are thinking and we argue and debate because we enjoy it. Social interaction and intellectual stimulation are the most common reasons for using verbal activities as therapy.

Therapeutic Application

When people contribute to a discussion or a meeting, they listen and put their views. They form opinions, change their minds, disagree and learn to appreciate others' points of view. They learn how to be persuasive and how to share their ideas effectively. They get to know each other. They practise expressing their ideas. Discussion can orientate people in time and place, is a means of sharing information and helps a group develop a sense of unity. People may learn how to teach others or research information; they may improve their knowledge of the language.

Verbal activities and psychotherapeutic discussion are at either end of a continuum. In verbal activities, the focus is on the naturally therapeutic characteristics of discussion and includes any discussion engaged in for interest, information or enjoyment. The focus of psychotherapeutic discussion is on solving problems through discussion; the discussion is a means to an end. The activities described here range from a mid point on the continuum, with most at the verbal activities end.

Contraindications, Precautions and Limitations

To participate in verbal activities people must be able to think clearly, relate to others and have basic communication skills. Without these abilities verbal activities will be either impossible or emotionally threatening. Practical activities like a game or craft in which there is some scope for conversation may be a better choice.

Depression is common in treatment situations. When people are depressed they find it difficult to remember things and formulate their views. Again, a practical activity is a better choice.

People which delusional ideas will be unable to debate topics which overlap with the area of their delusions. If a topic unexpectedly triggers delusional ideas, bring the person firmly and quickly back to something relevant.

The Therapist's Role

The therapist chooses discussion topics or organizes the way they are chosen, plans a task that will make the discussion interesting and co-ordinates it. Clarifying and linking people's statements, identifying areas of agreement and disagreement and summing up at intervals are part of the responsibility. Also important are keeping people to the topic, monitoring time, controlling digressions and, sometimes, setting limits on behaviour. Direct the occasional question to a non-contributor. Be clear about the therapeutic objectives for the group but, within the constraints these impose, be prepared to be flexible.

Use warm-up activities which involve speaking. Once a person has spoken in the group, it is easier to speak up a second time — even getting each person to say their name in turn helps.

Expect people to join in but recognize that if you fill every silence, or give the group too many ideas, there will be no discussion.

Sometimes a 'discussion' is planned when another approach would have been more sensible. For example, if you want a particular point or attitude to emerge, it is probably better to explain or teach the material directly rather than plan a discussion and hope it will go the way you want. If a decision has already been made on something, this should be made clear so that the discussion addresses either how to get the decision changed or how to adjust to it, rather than what the decision should be.

The style of leadership, directive or democratic, and the level of structure that will work best, will vary with the maturity of the group and its purpose. With a group that is strongly task-orientated, or immature, the therapist usually has to work harder to keep the discussion going. Generate discussion by throwing questions to someone who is likely to respond, preferably someone who is physically situated across the group from you. Plan questions to draw ideas from the group and use activities to support the discussion.

In a mature group throw any general questions directed to you back to the group, 'I'd like to know what the group thinks about . . .' or 'How would you answer the question?'

Topics and presentation Topics can be presented in a variety of ways and each approach sets different expectations. The simplest format is to announce a topic and explain it clearly so that everyone starts from the same basic premise. The explanation can indicate likely sub-topics or issues, an order for covering them and a time allocation to guide the group. The therapist can also suggest sources of information people could use to orientate themselves (for example, 'You may have read . . .', 'You have all experienced . . .', 'You have all seen the effect of . . .').

Large groups can be subdivided and each small group given part of a topic to discuss. Explain the topic before arranging people in sub-groups because once the groups are formed people will first focus on each other rather than on what they are being asked to do.

With many topics pictures are useful — even a simple sketch helps people focus. Use a blackboard, white board, chart or sheet of paper or card.

Topics When you choose a topic or guide the group's choice, consider people's ages, abilities, interests and needs. When coverage of a topic depends on knowledge assess whether the group has enough information to get somewhere with the topic. Are all the group members able to contribute?

Avoid closed-ended topics unless the group has the resources to discover the 'correct' answers. Topics that call for creativity, opinion or imagination are safer because there is no 'right' answer.

Traditionally, controversial topics include sex, politics and religion. Examples of other topics which are potentially controversial are race, failure, crime and insanity. Such topics are more relevant to group therapy than to activity-oriented discussion groups.

Look for topics which are appropriate to the group — topics you might enjoy may be uninteresting to the group or, worse, make them feel out of their depth or envious.

Questions One way to keep any group moving is through asking questions. 'What', 'Where' and 'Who' questions explore what people know. They focus on facts. ('What have you heard about . . . ?')

Other questions explore agreement and difference: 'Why do you think this happened . . . ?', 'What caused . . . ?', 'How do you feel about that . . . ?' 'Why might . . . ?', 'What else could . . . ?'

Encourage elaboration and explore the reasoning behind people's statements: 'Tell us more about . . .', 'Do you mean . . . ?' Or perhaps the group could examine obstacles: 'What would make that difficult . . . ?', 'Would all the consequences be desirable . . . ?', 'Could you really . . . ?'. Or, provocatively: 'What if . . .', 'But perhaps . . . ?'

Some questions help draw ideas together: 'Does everyone agree that . . . ?', 'So you see the alternatives as . . .', 'So you want to . . . ?', 'Well, where does that get us?', 'So you want to try . . . ?'

Task-focused questions point the way to action: 'What are the steps we/you need to take?', 'How long is . . . likely to take?', 'What resources are needed?'

Discussion

A discussion can stand on its own as an activity or follow or precede activities like a play reading, talk, film or sports contest. The purposes of discussion before an activity may be practical, like planning or clarifying the activity. After an activity discussion helps sum up and review what happened. It consolidates and evaluates the experience.

Spontaneous or unstructured discussions start when people are together, have time to talk and have a topic which interests them. From a therapeutic point of view there will be times when it is important to make sure that these three elements — time, people and topic — come together. Think of questions to get people talking, then keep a low profile.

Making a planned discussion work

Planned discussions are more structured and for a structured discussion it is important to create an atmosphere that will suit the group and their skills and abilities. What levels of formality do they expect? What style of leadership will work? Is there enough physical and psychological privacy? How can relationships be developed? Consider each of these factors in relation to creating a discussion session which will suit the group.

Physically what is most practical? Sitting round a table, sitting in a casual circle or on formal lines of chairs? If you want to generate closeness, make sure that people are physically close together. An informal discussion calls for comfort without barriers between people. When the aim is to give and share information they can be more spread out. The place you meet needs to be a quiet area with few disturbances.

To make a discussion work people must share the time available, respect each other's views and keep to the topic. If there are several groups working in the same area they must also keep their voices down.

Small groups (four to eight) make it easier for everyone to contribute and as a result the discussion is likely to be more satisfying. It is often a good idea to divide larger groups into sub-groups.

Discussion can be brief and spontaneous or a planned event in which time has been allowed for preparation.

Keep planning and evaluative discussions constructive. Usually, people in a group will grow to enjoy each other's company, but people can also 'talk themselves' into unrealistic decisions or a negative frame of mind if one person or part of the group is forceful and persuasive. Encourage appreciation of differences and respect for others' views. Keep the focus on issues and ideas — on content rather than personality.

A traditional problem-solving approach can give a framework for discussion: gather information or brainstorm ideas, put the ideas in some kind of logical order and then discuss them until a level of consensus or decision is reached, or there is satisfaction with the exploration of the ideas.

Avoid a situation in which the most fluent and confident people dominate the discussion. Invite contributions from quieter members or design a task in which everyone's contribution is significant to the end result (for example, a survey of the group's views).

Ur (*Discussions that Work*) suggests that a key to successful discussion is having an immediate purpose or task, ideally one that cannot be done without communication. The task should be easily understood and everyone's contribution needed. It should be interesting to people and at a realistic level.

Examples of initial tasks for discussion groups:

- 'Make a list of the problems facing . . .', 'Make a list of what should be done about . . .' (Each person should contribute at least one idea and the order negotiated).
- 'On a mural show . . .' (In groups of two or three, each person must contribute and the connections between elements negotiated so that the group can explain them when the mural is complete.)
- 'Write a precis of the group's view on . . .'
- 'Compose a letter to . . . about . . .' (Agony column style.)
- 'Draw up a charter for . . .'
- 'Plan an item for a hospital or community news sheet on . . .'
- 'Tape record . . .'

Some games and puzzles also make excellent 'tasks' for discussion.

If sub-groups are expected to report to the whole group later they may need a scribe or reporter.

Resource books for teaching English as a second language usually include many useful activities. The following are examples:

Spot the differences Photocopy a clear black and white picture with plenty of detail and on each copy add a few additional details and white out others. The things added and deleted on each picture should be different. Photocopy the pictures again so that people cannot tell what the changes are. Make enough copies of the pictures so that there is one of each picture for each person. In pairs, each person looks only at the picture they have and, by talking to their partner, lists as many differences between their pictures as possible. (Option: tell people how many differences there are.)

Find the way Alter two maps in the same way as the pictures were changed in 'Spot the differences' (above). Use them for the 'Spot the differences' activity or for a route-finding activity in which one person's map is unlabelled and they need directions to buy a number of items.

Or people can plan efficient routes for buying a number of items on a shopping list.

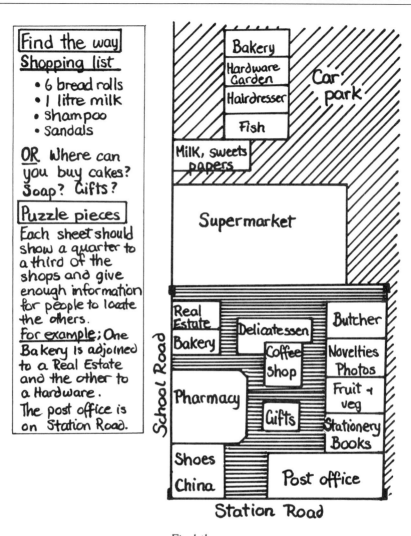

Find the way

Puzzle pieces Create a puzzle in which each person holds different pieces of information and all are essential to solving the puzzle.

Put the pictures in order Find or draw cartoon strips with three or four pictures. Photocopy the strips and then cut them into individual pictures. The task is to get the pictures back into the correct order.

Words for a story The group makes up a story using words chosen by the group members. Each person suggests how their word can be brought into the story.

Starting points for discussions

Television programme   The group plan to watch a particular television programme with the idea of discussing it later. Tasks might be to list the actors in order of effectiveness, write a review of the programme, re-enact part of it or plan a next episode.

Stories and vignettes   Read out typical (or atypical) life histories, problem stories, vignettes or role plays and plan questions to draw out discussion on the relevant issues in the story. ('How would you feel if this were you?', 'What would you have done?') Stories can be found in most newspapers and some texts for health professionals have case histories that could be used. A session could be made up of a number of these depending on the discussion potential of the scenario.

Ending a story   Tell a story and get the group to create a variety of endings. Newspaper stories are a good source of ideas.

Pictures and charts   Use information presented through pictures, on a graph, on a flow sheet, or in figures. Discuss what the information means.

Proverbs and common sayings   As a starting point for a dicussion, choose contrasting pairs of proverbs or sayings and get the group to discuss which they think is more valid. (For example, 'Out of sight, out of mind'/'Absence makes the heart grow fonder'.)

Alternatively, list sayings or proverbs on a handout sheet, a blackboard or overhead transparency, and get people to rank order them.

People could also give examples from their lives of times a proverb applied or did not apply.

Sentence starters   Get each person to end the same sentence. For example, 'When I go home it will be hard to . . .', 'Changes I've seen in my lifetime are . . .', 'How many ways can you think of to . . . ?', 'The effect (consequence) of . . . is/will be . . .', 'The best way to . . .', 'The best . . . is . . .', 'When the ladder gave way, the mother (boss, mechanic) said . . .', 'When the girl won the first round of the tennis competition . . . she (her mother) said . . .' (See *SELF-AWARENESS ACTIVITIES, Part sentences* p. 31.) Make people go further than finishing the sentence. Encourage elaboration and comparisons.

Pros and cons   Get people to 'Discuss the pros and cons of the law on . . .' or the pros and cons of different means of transport, types of accommodation, holidays . . .

'Have you ever . . .'   'Have you ever made a parachute jump (owned a restaurant, gone deep-sea diving . . .)?'

'I urge' telegram   The group discusses an issue they feel strongly about. They compose a telegram beginning with the words 'I urge . . .' to someone who has the authority to change the situation.

Question and answer   People take it in turns to ask someone in the group a question. For example, 'What is your favourite food?', 'Your favourite television programme', 'Your happiest moment', 'Your most valued possession'.

Brainstorming   Topics for brainstorming are usually problem-oriented — 'What should x do about y?' Brainstorming starts with getting as many ideas on a topic as possible, then the ideas are discussed and ranked. Rules for brainstorming are: all ideas are to be accepted without question, including ideas that build on or modify other ideas; there is to be no discussion until the group has run out of ideas; ideas can only be clumped together with the consent of both proposers.

'Problem' situations   The aim is to clarify people's values. Several example situations are given on p. 136 — they can be adapted to suit the group's situation or life experiences.
     Alternatively use agony column letters. Draft replies in small groups, then compare them among the whole group.

Quiz questions   These can be tailored to generate discussion. When a question is answered, ask people for more information or an opinion.

Questionnaires and rating scales   Get people to fill these out then discuss the results. A well-known rating scale is Holmes and Rahe's stress rating scale (see Bibliography). Some books on assertiveness contain rating scales and another source is popular magazine questionnaires.
     Or, get the group to design a rating scale or questionnaire themselves. For example, 'The qualities of a good teacher are . . .', 'Ten criteria for choosing friends are . . .'

Prepared discussions   A topic is chosen in advance so that people have time to prepare for it and think about what they want to contribute and what they want to find out. Prepared discussions are useful practice for contributing to meetings where the agenda is distributed beforehand.

Games   Some games lead easily to discussion, for example, Twenty questions. Commerical games which generate discussion are Pictionary, Trivial Pursuit, Scruples and Jumping to Conclusions.

Current affairs topics   Material on world or local affairs is readily available in newspapers, current affairs magazines and popular general magazines, as well as on television and radio. Check what bills are before parliament and what issues are being raised in editorials and letters to the editor.

A straightforward way to use newspaper articles is to cut them out over several days (or get people to select their own) and then read them out as a starting point for discussion.

Writing to a local Member of Parliament, a newspaper or public figure are ways in which people can act on a discussion and make their views known.

Social issues topics   Example topics: Child rearing practices, The distribution of resources in society, Conservation and ecological policies, Healthcare, The legal system, Social discrimination, Educational opportunities, Facilities in the community.

Make the topic specific: 'The effects of unemployment on local teenagers', 'Local healthcare spending'. A first step might be to produce a list of the positive and negative aspects of a policy or situation.

Relationship topics

These generally have a group therapy orientation. They examine things like friendship, childrearing, marriage, work relationships, social responsibility, mental health, leisure, ageing and the use of money and resources. Through discussion people become more aware of their beliefs and why they hold them. Assessing whether their values are constructive or destructive in their lives, and in what ways, are common therapeutic goals of these discussions.

Friendship   Start by brainstorming a list of proverbs or sayings about friendship (the sayings do not need to be well-known, simply things which people believe to be true) or make up a list. Examples are: 'Friends are like guitar strings, they should not be kept too tight', 'Absence makes the heart grow fonder', 'The more I see of human beings, the more I like my dog'.

When the list is complete get people to
- Rank the items in order of importance.
- Describe experiences they have had in relation to each.
- Respond to leading questions like, 'What does friendship mean to you?', 'What spoils friendships?', 'What can people do if they have difficulty making and keeping friends?'

Look for stories about friendships in newspapers and magazines.

Childrearing   Get people to complete a selection of sentence openers then share what they have written with the group.

> 'Children should be seen and not heard, but today . . .'
> 'Childhood is a time of . . .'
> 'Reading to children is . . .'
> '"A loved child has many names" but . . .' (Swedish proverb.)
> 'Children today . . .'
> 'Monitoring television, films and books for children is . . .'
> 'Talking to children is . . .'

'Religious training for children is . . .'
'The effect of praise/criticism on children is . . .'
'The best way to discipline children is . . .'
'Chores and responsibilities . . .'
'Having plenty of choices in life . . .'
'Self-esteem is . . .'

Many of the sentence openers can be the sole topic for discussion. For example, 'Reading to children . . .' could be a starting point for reminiscing about children's books or exchanging ideas on good books for children.

Maturity   The group brainstorms a list of attributes which indicate maturity. Ask, 'Do people have to be mature all the time?', 'How would you rank the statements on the list?'
One group's list of statements went like this:

- Being able to see several points of view.
- A knowledge of right and wrong.
- Humanitarian values and caring for other people.
- An interest in world affairs.
- The ability to exercise self-control.
- Being able to see the consequences of one's actions.
- The ability to make friends with all sorts of people.
- Serenity.
- Stability.
- Flexibility.
- A clear purpose in life.
- Self-acceptance — acknowledgement of strengths and weaknesses.

Problem situation topics

Setting up flat (Variations: Entertain toddlers, Survive in the jungle, Live on a desert island, Go on holiday, Buy food for a week, Plan a wardrobe.)
In small groups, the situation is presented as follows: 'You are about to set up flat. You have paid a deposit on a three-bedroom flat with no furniture or appliances. From the list below you must choose ten items to buy for the flat and rank them in order of importance.' (List: washing machine, beds and bedding, stove, hot plate, microwave, television, VCR, hot water jug, toaster, crockery, cutlery, dishwasher, bookshelf, table, dining chairs, couch and easy chairs, sewing machine, sideboard, wardrobe, dressing table, bureau, computer, lamps, rubbish tin, cushions, saucepans and kitchen implements, coffee table, side table, radio, carpet square, curtains, rugs, plant, mirror.)
The discussion can be theoretical or each person can be given a sum of homemade 'money' and a price put on each item. People must discuss how they will use the money so that the flat suits all of them. Using local prices as a guide, add up the cost of basic items and give each person an equal share of the total sum plus a little extra.

Variations

- People first choose twenty items from the list, then they halve it.
- Additional questions are added such as, 'If you were allowed one luxury item in the flat, what would you choose?' (The group can negotiate and make a collective answer or each person can respond for themselves.) 'If it was one book? One type of food? One record or tape?'
- 'You have to look after four toddlers for three hours on a rainy afternoon. They're not interested in television, but you have . . .' Give the group a list of resources available to them or get them to list what they would like.
- People choose a suitable wardrobe for a holiday. (Use cut-out or drawn pictures pasted on cards.)
- Have a 'Gripes auction'. Each person thinks of one thing that annoys them, then tries to sell it after explaining the effect it has on their life. They can sell it either by offering some of a good quality along with it, or by exchanging it for a gripe they would not mind so much.
- Auction several jobs, houses, dogs, cats, two children, a glasshouse, car, pick-up truck, boat and so on.
- 'Your plane has crashed in the jungle. On board are . . . The equipment that's intact is . . . You have time to grab ten things before the fire forces you back. What would you choose? Only five things?' (List: crate of dried fruit, crate of wheat, compass, map, pet cat, pet dog, matches, tent, sleeping bags, walkie-talkie, radio, rope gun, knife, flares, first-aid kit, barrel of water, box of books, pillows, knapsack, suitcase of clothes and footware.)

For this topic get people to choose individually first, then negotiate in small groups. The small groups come together to compare decisions after a predetermined time, say five minutes.

Who to hire? Choose a 'person to hire' whom your group is likely to be interested in: a medical superintendent, a mother, a teacher, two children, a boss, a nurse. The task for the group is to decide who to hire from a list of applicants. You can prepare the 'applicant' list or the group can be divided into two, with one half as the selection committee writing a job description for the person they want, and the other half preparing the applicant list.

Each applicant has strengths and limitations. Ideas for strengths are charm, physical strength, relevant experience, attractive appearance, commonsense, steadiness, patience, cheerfulness, education, enthusiasm, practical skills (good cook, woodwork skills). Limitations might be poor education, careless paperwork, aloofness, inefficiency, short temper, 'cold' personality, bossiness, extensive responsibilities outside work, talkativeness. (For example, Mr Jones, age thirty-two, is cheerful and practical. He has four pre-school children, four schoolage children and his wife works full-time. He is studying for a relevant qualification but so far has done poorly in his exams).

Who to hire?

A picture of each applicant, even a primitive sketch, will help people focus their ideas. Alternatively, the group which has prepared the list of applicants can role play them.

Other 'Who do you choose' topics are: 'Who should be president', 'Who should be sportsperson of the year?' and so on.

The life-boat game   A large yacht is sinking and the only life-boat is not big enough to hold all the people in the group. In this 'Who do you pick game' each person chooses someone they admire to go in the lifeboat (it can be someone they know, a well-known person or a historical figure) and speaks briefly about the person they have chosen, or pretends to be that person. When everyone has had a turn at putting their case the group votes on who is to be saved. It can be just one person or about half the group. Debriefing is important.

Alternatively, the voting can be omitted and the activity ended with a discussion on why people chose the people they did.

The best television programme   Each person chooses a 'best' or 'worst' television programme or advertisement to praise or criticize and then speaks briefly in defence of their choice. Encourage people to choose different programmes or assign programmes to people. The group votes first on the most persuasive speech, then according to their own views of the programmes.

Continuums   Topics for this activity must have two opposite points of view, with either end of the room being designated as these opposites. The group's task is to physically form themselves into a continuum of views across the room. Each person starts by choosing a place between the two endpoints which represents where they think they belong. After talking to the people standing next to them, they change places where appropriate. Discussion in pairs and threes continues until everyone feels they have found their correct place on the continuum. (In practice, people often end up in clusters).

The topics can be lightweight: 'City lovers versus country lovers', 'Television is good/television is bad'. Or more serious: 'There should be no film censorship versus there should be rigorous censorship', 'Religion is dead versus religion is a vital force in our community', 'Alcohol should be banned versus alcohol should be freely available'. If there are several likely clusters of opinion rather than two opposite poles, use the same format but get people to choose one of three or more groups.

Discussion in teaching and learning

Discussion can be a systematic and efficient method of learning. People examine what they know or feel about a topic and, in the course of discussion, change or integrate their ideas. This kind of discussion is only effective when the group has a knowledge base to draw on — they must have enough information, either in their collective knowledge or in the resources available to them. Sometimes the process seems slow but the consequent learning is likely to be well integrated and in depth.

People need to be tolerant of each other's views, accept that the task is worthwhile and be prepared to share the leadership. Ideally, everyone should participate and feel positive about discussion as a means of learning.

They need to come regularly and to prepare themselves so that material can be covered efficiently. Evaluate the group regularly to make sure it is meeting people's needs.

An example of a therapeutic setting in which the learning-through-discussion approach can be effective, is in groups with a firsthand knowledge of a medical condition or community resource. Collectively, the group is likely to have more information to share in a well-led discussion than the therapist can offer through direct teaching or one-to-one counselling. With perceptive observation, the therapist usually has only to steer the discussion so that a range of key issues is covered.

Learning through discussion is useful when social attitudes impinge on the subject area. People learn from each other how other members of society view the subject being discussed.

There are potential problems to watch out for. First, as stated, if people lack knowledge, or time to prepare, issues will be poorly covered. Second, too many people in a group can be a problem because the time available for each person to speak will be limited. Third, people may have very different levels of verbal ability and status differences, real or imagined, can inhibit people from speaking freely. For this reason, or through personality, group members may either dominate or fail to participate.

Study groups   A study group must first decide what it will study and how the discussion will be organized. One common approach is to get everyone to read a book in sections and then discuss it. People can all read the same material or each person can read something different and lead the discussion on their own section. This gives each person something unique to contribute.

Other starting points are regularly reading a newspaper or magazine column, following a television programme, seeing a film, inviting a guest speaker or following a correspondence course.

Reminiscence

Reminiscence means discussing and reliving the past. It helps people resolve their feelings about what they have done and about what has happened to them. It has a social value and it links past to present.

With the elderly, try to find out about their lives in advance in order to generate material for reminiscence sessions. Relatives and friends may be able to give supplementary information for people with memory loss. Find out the names of family members, occupations and hobbies they have had, likes and dislikes.

Reminiscence sessions can be fun and worthwhile with all age groups — reliving past pleasures will usually improve cohesiveness in any group. Possible topics include outings, holidays or a sports series.

Begin with a specific topic and plan a number of leading questions round it. If people are easily confused, questions to stimulate ideas should be simple and direct.

Props to complement the topics are helpful. Some old school books, a school cap or hat and photographs could be used for a discussion about school days. Trigger ideas and anecdotes with music, photographs, books, objects, old newspapers, bric-a-brac, recordings, clothing and coins. Or use smells: linseed oil, pinewood, spices, new carpet, leaf mould. Anniversary and festival days will bring back memories. The items need not be museum pieces. Some reels of cotton and a plastic peg were everyday items one group used as the basis for a lively then-and-now discussion. A quiz can be a good way to get a discussion going.

Activities such as a cooking session, a singsong or re-enacting a scene from the past work well. A life review would follow the stages of life: early childhood, family and cultural roots, parents and grandparents (their jobs, interests, what they wore), nicknames, school days, friendships, brothers and sisters (early days, recent days), childhood holidays, sports, hobbies, work, courtship, mail (the most important letter/gift/phone call ever received), marriage, role of spouse, children's lives, children's twenty-first birthdays, places lived, holidays in adulthood, festivals, clothing, prices, household equipment, war, achievements, picnics, customs, music, dance, pets, illnesses, community service and retirement.

Alternatively, use topics: 'Sad times', 'Proud times', 'Happy times', 'What I've valued', 'What I'd miss if I was young now.'

Debating

Debating allows several aspects of a topic to be aired in a format which structures the way people take turns and the way they speak.

The requirements for a debate are a carefully worded motion, two reasonably equal teams, a chairperson who the teams address, an audience willing to participate and an adjudicator who can give balanced comment on people's arguments.

Debates can be formal encounters between people who are serious about debating or impromptu affairs arranged on the spot to stimulate thought and discussion.

In a full debate, each team investigates the topic by reading round it and discussing it, then they decide which speaker will say what. Speakers usually prepare notes to remind themselves of the main points they want to make.

The topic for a debate should interest the group and have enough substance to get people involved without being so controversial that people are unable to be objective. They are worded as brief, clear affirmative motions. For example, 'I move that women are equal to men'. Decide on the topic then work out an exact working, taking care to avoid ambiguities. If the wording can be taken to mean different things the teams may do just that, with the result that they will not be debating the same issue.

How a debate is run   Debating teams are usually made up of three people. One team, the 'affirmative' team, supports the motion and the other, the 'negative' team, opposes it. The teams take it in turns to speak, starting with the affirmative team. Team leaders have twelve minutes to speak and the other team members ten minutes each. When all six people have spoken, members of the audience may speak, if they want to, once only, for two minutes each. Finally, each leader has five minutes to sum up and reply, first the leader of the negative team, then the leader of the affirmative team.

When all the speaking is over the chairperson 'Puts the motion to the floor', that is, they repeat the motion to the audience, who are asked to vote on it with a show of hands according to how convincing the teams have been. The adjudicator counts the votes and declares the result.

The chairperson has several other responsibilities. Before the debate he or she checks the time available and the practical arrangements. He or she opens the debate by stating the motion, telling the teams how they will know when they have used their time and explaining any ground rules for the debate. As well, the chairperson welcomes the audience, introduces each speaker, restores order if necessary, restrains speakers who go over their time and rules on points of order.

Each person in the team has a different part to play. The leader of the affirmative team defines the words in the motion, the boundaries of the affirmative team's argument and delivers a prepared speech supporting the motion. The leader of the negative team gives a prepared argument and makes some reply to the affirmative leader. The other team members prepare arguments which will fill out and substantiate their leader's case and they also rebut the previous speaker. They speak through the chairperson rather than directly to the other team. Each team tries to finish on a strong, positive note, reinforcing their main points and appealing to the audience.

For a good debate teams should prepare well, have divided the material carefully between them and be positive about their case regardless of what they really think. They should aim to use arguments which are simple, direct and easily illustrated. The thrust of the arguments should be directed towards convincing the audience, rather than towards the other team. In their rebuttals, team members should concentrate on the other team's arguments and logic rather than on aspects of their personalities or presentation.

Impromptu debates   In activity-oriented healthcare settings the rules for a debate are usually modified. Commonly the size of the teams is reduced (two members) and the time for each speaker is shortened (say one to three minutes for each speaker). The whole group can select the topic (it should not be debated as it is chosen!). Teams draw for the affirmative or negative role and then have five minutes to divide the topic and prepare their arguments. The challenges are to work as a team, stay with the idea and develop it.

Speeches

Memory   Get people to select a newspaper item and plan a brief speech about it. They can have three to five minutes reading time, then they must put the paper down and start speaking without referring to the article they have chosen. Encourage people to plan interesting beginnings and persuasive endings. As each person speaks, the audience can make notes on the points which would be responded to if the speech was part of a debate.

Debating topics   Get people to give an impromptu speech on a debating topic.

Beginnings and endings   One person starts a speech and someone else, picked at random, ends it.

Chain speaking   Speakers take it in turns to carry on a story or speech, each trying to relate their contribution to the ideas already expressed.

'Chicago forum'   Each person has the same length of time to speak (one to two minutes) and starts with the same opening phrase. For example, 'The only hope for civilization is . . .' 'The only way to improve the health services is . . .', 'Unemployment is . . .', 'Children today . . .'

Panel discussions   Select a topic which people in the group will find relevant and interesting, and let everyone know what it is ahead of time so that they can plan questions to ask the panel.

Traditionally, people on the panel have expertise in the subject area being discussed, but as an informal activity you can bestow imaginary expertise on panel members. Simply select any three or four people to be the panel and tell them what they know. For example, 'Jim, you're the Mayor, and an authority on funding local health services.' Introduce each person with a good build up. If the panel get really stuck answering a question, they can call for comment from the audience or even swap places. For example, a panel member might say, 'I'd like to put that question to the audience. Can anyone help me out?'

Topics: 'Problems which face the recovering alcoholic', 'Coping with dependence', 'The best . . .', 'The penal system . . .', 'Hospitals', 'Zoos', 'Junk food', 'Nuclear power', 'Being rich', 'Our environment', 'Equality', 'The consequences of . . .', 'Alternatives to . . .'

Look in newspapers for topical issues.

4 | *Communication Skills*

Communication skills, divided here into social skills and assertiveness skills, can be taught in order to complement other treatments or as skills in their own right. Here, the term 'social skills' refers to basic communication skills: knowing what to talk about, how to take turns in conversation and how to speak at a socially acceptable pace and volume. Assertiveness training is at a more advanced level. Its aim is to help people communicate clearly and honestly while respecting others' feelings.

Although being able to communicate is essential in work, leisure and educational settings, courses in social or assertiveness skills can be threatening because they are about very personal skills. Previous social failures make people reluctant to try again. The first step is to build an expectation of success. Courses must be pitched within, or close to, people's comfort levels. As well as learning *how* to communicate, people need to develop the confidence to communicate.

Progress is often rapid at first which generates confidence, but establishing new skills as part of someone's normal way of responding takes persistent effort. Feedback must be frequent and clear, with plenty of positive reinforcement so that the new skills become habits.

SOCIAL SKILLS

Social skills training is about communication: Social graces, how to use a knife and fork and how often to change one's clothes can be included in the course but they are secondary to learning what to say and how to say it.

Therapeutic Application

Training in social skills is needed when people have lost skills through trauma or illness, when they have never had an adequate opportunity to develop skills or when they need a different range of skills from the ones they currently have. They must be able to tolerate some closeness with others.

Groups who may benefit from training are:

- People in the adolescent to middle adult age group who have significant problems with communication. The elderly are often reluctant to change lifetime patterns of interaction.
- People with physical disability who find others interact with them inappropriately, or feel socially discriminated against because others interpret their disability as being more global than it is.
- People with mild psychiatric disorders or in recovery from serious psychiatric disorder (chronic schizophrenia, severe depression).
- People with mild to moderate mental retardation. When retardation is severe, people need extended teaching or ongoing support to master social skills.
- People who move from one cultural group to another and need to learn the connotations of body language, turntaking and so on in the new culture. For the main cultural group in a society, learning how other cultural groups express emotion can save a great deal of confusion and misunderstanding.
- People whose circumstances have changed significantly for other reasons (such as through trauma or disease). The change can relate to social class, work role, increased or decreased dependency and so on.

Every life stage and social setting requires a slightly different range of social skills. These are usually acquired or altered without difficulty if the change is slight and the person's existing social skills are sound.

Assessment   Start by listening to people's voices — a person's tone of voice and style of speaking will usually indicate how they feel about themselves and their level of social skill. Use specific assessments to pinpoint problems. Assessments explore either particular situations in which people have difficulties (job interviews, shopping, talking to someone they feel is important, participating in a group), or check a range of skills including: voice quality (volume, pitch), quality of speech (interest, silences, pace), eye contact, body language (stance, facial expression, dress), speech content (relevance, appropriateness), conversation style, approach to people (taking turns, appropriate self-disclosure, initiative), use of questions and skills in opening and closing conversations or giving explanations. Vocabulary and grammar may be a problem (correct tenses, correct use of common words).

Skills, and the settings they are used in, are interrelated. In assessment establish clearly and specifically which skills need to be developed and in which settings.

Contraindications, Precautions and Limitations

Courses are of little use if people are reluctant to attend, confused, severely depressed, anxious, psychotic, drowsy through medication, or have other more pressing treatment needs. (See *SELF-AWARENESS ACTIVITIES*,

Therapeutic application p. 9 and *Contraindications, precautions and limitations* p. 10.)

The Therapist's Role

In a social skills course the therapist is more clearly a teacher and leader than in an assertiveness course.

Choosing the level and pace to work at   Courses can be designed for people who have very few skills or for people who are functioning well but want to be more confident in particular situations.

Work in small steps, demonstrating each skill first. Be matter-of-fact about people's difficulties and very specific about what to change. Move on only when people are comfortable. People must be successful — and know they have succeeded. Praise good or acceptable responses, do not just take them for granted.

Practical Organization

Teach social skills in small, closed groups where an atmosphere of trust and support can be built up. In some circumstances one-to-one teaching/ coaching is the best approach. A small group is essential for social skills training. (Basic information on assertiveness can be covered in large groups — ten to thirty — but obviously opportunities for activities, discussion and role play will be more limited.)

The less capable people are the more behaviourally based the training should be — that is, concepts should be presented through activities rather than as straight theory.

Use role play, games, creative writing and discussion to reinforce information. You can focus on conversation skills in any activity; before a cooking session, for example, discuss the social skills that will be needed, work on them while the activity is in progress and review them afterwards. Incorporate these skills into as many activities as possible.

Contracts   Some therapists find attendance contracts useful. People commit themselves, in writing, to coming to a set number of sessions and to participating actively in ways which are negotiated and specified in the contract (See *WORKING IN GROUPS, Setting clear ground rules* p. 215.)

Timing and length of sessions   A series of between four and ten sessions, with each session between half an hour and one and a half hours in length, usually works well. In each session focus on just one or two main concepts. Short sessions should target one concept only.

The first session should give an overview of the goals and methods of the course. First sessions especially should be gently paced with plenty of reassurance. Aim for a work atmosphere in which learning is taken seriously. Each subsequent session should be linked to the previous session with a brief review of what was covered and an opportunity for questions or comment on relevant experiences people have had since then. Occasionally, reviewing information is more effective after the new topic has been introduced in that the links between the topics will be more obvious.

Before you begin discuss the importance of mutual support and confidentiality. Set ground rules concerning these issues and remind people of them regularly. Explain the format of the session.

Between sessions set people a task to reinforce what has been covered or to prepare them for the next session.

Environment   The course location helps set people's expectations. Privacy is important because it gives people the freedom to role play. There should be enough space for a variety of activities. Ideally, have tables and chairs available for drawn and written activities and more comfortable seating — with no physical barrier between people — for discussion. If only one seating area is available, clipboards can be a satisfactory option for drawn or written activities.

Examples   Relevant examples bring concepts to life. However, examples from resource books may not reach people because their experiences have been different; prepare examples with the group in mind. The language in resource books can also be a problem if it is different from the way the group speaks. Terms like 'psychological space' and 'negative consequences' are outside many people's everyday vocabulary and need to be reworded!

Handouts   A sheet of information listing key points will help reinforce learning. Illustrations help.

Role plays and discussion   Like any activity, role plays break up the pattern of sitting and listening and make the content of a session more personal.

Select typical or actual problems which people encounter, so that they can try out alternative ways of dealing with them and find one which suits them. Note that although the activities/games described in this chapter are useful, working through 'real' material is far more valuable. (See *DRAMA, Role play* p. 48, *Therapeutic application* p. 36 and *Contraindications, precautions and limitations* p. 38 and *WORKING IN GROUPS, Emotional issues* p. 212.)

Activities   Activities make an occupational therapy session different from those organized by other health professionals. Activities are especially useful when people need long-term teaching. Through feedback from practical, concrete experiences, people see themselves more clearly and identify what they want to change in their attitudes and behaviour.

Activities illustrate concepts in a way that is interesting and hopefully enjoyable. After each activity reinforce the links between activity and concepts.

In a session choose activities which contrast with each other: pencil and paper activities, physical games, drawing and drama activities. The content of activities should emphasize positive personal characteristics rather than problems, and focus on strengths rather than limitations; people are generally overaware of their weaknesses anyway.

Tapes and videos Tapes and videos give people information about how they look and sound and over time can provide a useful record of progress. Make sure you know how the equipment works before the session.

Social Skills Activities

Topics are described here in an order which reflects a gradual increase in skills. You can combine several sessions if people have the basic skills or expand one topic to fill several sessions if people have few skills. The demands of a session will also depend on the length of the session, the number in the group and the teaching style used.

1. Observation, body language, eye contact and social distance

A high proportion of social communication takes place through the body language of posture, eye contact, movement and expression.

A key part of teaching social skills is getting people to be aware of body language, their own and other people's. Body language (nods, amount of eye contact, tenseness, gestures, posture) gives a speaker information about the acceptability of what they are saying and whether to go on. Speakers need to be able to recognize messages of interest, boredom, confusion, irritation and so on. And when they are speaking, their body language should match what they say and convey relaxed confidence.

Cultural differences add another dimension to body language and should be explored if they are relevant. Even when the group has the same cultural background, it is worth spending a little time discussing the differences between cultural groups.

Eye contact should be discussed. Both too little and too much interfere with comfortable communication and, in this area particularly, different cultural groups have different expectations.

Physical distance between people is important; people need to be aware of how far apart people expect to be in different social, educational and work contexts.

The conventions surrounding touch also need to be understood.

Relaxation techniques usefully complement information about body language. When people are relaxed, their verbal and non-verbal messages are more likely to match.

Observation activities

Kim's game Show a selection of objects to the group for half to one and a half minutes, then take the objects away and ask the players to list all the things they can remember.

Variations on 'Kim's game' are:

- Lay out the items in a definite pattern on a tray. After people have studied it, take the display away and move some of the items round. Players try to remember where things were and what has been moved.
- Show a draught board with a pattern of draughts on it, then take it away and ask people to reproduce the pattern.
- Divide the group into two teams, Let each team observe the other for a minute. Each team then moves out of sight of the other and alters a set number of things about the appearance of people in their team. They might undo a top shirt button, remove glasses or add earrings. The teams return and each tries to identify the changes in the other team.
- One person leaves the room and alters certain aspects of their appearance. The rest of the group tries to identity what has changed. Have props such as belts, ties, combs and lipsticks available.
- With the whole group together, one person (the 'guesser') leaves the room and then a second person either hides or leaves the room by another door. The first person is called back in and must work out who is missing.
- Divide the group into two sub-groups and get them to form a line. Each sub-group then tries to memorize the order of the line of people in the other group. After a minute or so everyone moves about, and each group has a turn at reassembling the other group in its original order.
- In pairs, people talk to and observe each other for one minute and then stand back to back. The group asks questions such as, 'Was your partner wearing a belt?', 'Who has a partner with a watch?', 'What colour are your partner's eyes?'
- Spot the difference: photocopy a line drawing (clear cartoons or advertisements can be suitable) and add or white out some items on each copy. Photocopy both drawings so that the changes are less obvious. Make copies for each group member or get people to work in pairs and spot the differences. (See *VERBAL ACTIVITIES*, *Spot the differences* and Find the way p. 131.)

Ask, 'What do you notice about people's facial expressions, eye contact and body position?'

Drawn whispers Each person has a pencil and paper. Someone is chosen to go first and has thirty seconds to draw a picture with as much detail in it as possible. They show their drawing to the player on their left and count to three slowly. The second player draws what he or she has seen, shows it to the third player for the count of three and so on. When each player has had a turn the pictures are compared to see how much they changed and what people observed or failed to observe.

A second picture can be started by every third (or fourth) player so that in a group of nine, three pictures might be circulating at the same time. This means fewer people are waiting for a turn. Alternatively, continue a discussion about observation at the same time as the activity, with people dropping out briefly when it is their turn to draw.

Another option is for everyone to be shown one drawing, which they all try to memorize and then copy down.

Eyewitness   Plan a 'surprise' incident to happen in front of the group. Afterwards, a 'detective' interviews the group to get details of what happened. Possible incidents are a snatch burglary, a kidnapping or a visit from a VIP. You can get someone who is not in the group to burst in or prime a group member to act the part. They could dress up to add more challenge to people's powers of observation.

Traditional games involving observation

I Spy	Up Jenkins
Hide and Seek	Blindfold games
Hunt the Thimble	

Discussion points   What details are people most likely to miss in social communication? What makes it easier or harder to notice social cues? Are observations always accurate? What reasons might there be for inaccuracies?

Body language activities

These activities are based mostly on mime.

Show and guess   People work in pairs or small groups and take turns to show an emotion or guess what their partner is showing. (See DRAMA p. 54 for more activity ideas.) They can use just their face or their whole body.

The activity is simpler if a selection of emotions are listed on a chart, blackboard or overhead transparency in front of the group.

Variations on 'Show and guess' are:
- Give each person a topic card with a feeling to portray. The others guess the feeling.
- Each person writes a feeling on a card and puts it in a hat. (With this approach people may get a topic which is harder than one they would have chosen.) Increase the level of difficulty gradually.
- Using either of the topic card systems above, people try to show how an emotion looks when someone feels the emotion but wants to hide it. Discuss times in life when this happens.
- Each person draws feeling-expressions for the group to guess.
- Paste magazine pictures of people on cards and discuss what feelings they are showing. Discuss the effects of dress, facial expression and stance on the feeling or mood a person conveys.

Social message quadrant

- Working in pairs, one person moulds the other's body and face to show a chosen emotion. Try this sitting or standing. This can also be used as the basis of a guessing game.
- One person (or half the group) leaves the room and the rest decide on an emotion and an action to show, for example, walking sadly, sitting hopefully. The person/group returns to guess what the rest of the group is showing.

Discussion When facial expression and body language convey conflicting emotions, which is more important? When is this likely to occur?

Social messages Get people to examine two continuums, such as friendly/unfriendly, and submissive/dominant.

This activity can also be done as a magazine picture exercise or a drawn activity. People find or draw pictures which are appropriate to each quadrant. It may be relevant to look at cultural differences in the ways feelings are expressed.

The chart below gives cues for the continuum friendly/unfriendly. Get the group to construct a similar chart for dominant/submissive. People then act out an emotion using one or two cues. Initially, both cues should be from the same column.

Possible emotions to act out are: hostility, anger, surprise, joy, sadness, curiosity, amazement, grief, boredom, frustration, worry, impatience, concern, preoccupation, stress, enthusiasm and excitement.

CHART:

	Friendly	*Unfriendly*
Tone of voice	soft, warm	hard, cold
Facial expression	smiling, interested	blank, sneering, frowning, bored uninterested
Posture	leans toward speaker; relaxed	leans away from speaker; tense
Eye contact	makes eye contact	avoids eye contact
Touching	touches other softly — upper arm, shoulder (check with people if touch is acceptable)	no touch
Gestures	open, welcoming	closed, arms folded
Spatial distance	stands close	stands at a distance

Discussion   Which emotions are easiest/hardest to portray or guess. What happens when body language and words do not match?

Passports

Passports Find pictures in magazines in which people show particular emotions. Paste these onto the inside of a piece of card folded in half, and make window holes to reveal parts of the faces. The group discusses the expressions and tries to guess the emotions. When the card is opened the people and their setting can be seen and/or there is a caption telling what has just happened.

Discussion 'Making assumptions about people's feelings can be a mistake'.

Card spotters Use an ordinary deck of cards (two packs for a large group) and make a chart or information cards showing the emotion each playing card represents:

Ace	— Love	Seven	— Loneliness/worry
Two	— Contentment/	Eight	— Sorrow/sadness
	happiness	Nine	— Anger
Three	— Shyness	Ten	— Hope
Four	— Indifference	Jack	— Joy
Five	— Fear	Queen	— Surprise/shock
Six	— Frustration	King	— Warmth/friendliness

Deal out all the cards keeping back a minimum of ten for a draw deck which is left face down in the centre of the table.

The first person to get rid of all their cards wins. Alternatively, play for a set length of time and the person with the fewest cards wins.

Players can part with cards by accurately expressing emotions or by identifying the emotions shown by other players.

To play: The player on the dealer's left (first Expresser) selects a card from their hand, puts it face down on the table in front of them and shows the emotion that was on the card.

All the other players silently guess what emotion is being expressed and if they have a card or cards matching their guess they put them face down on the table in front of them. When everyone has done this all the face down cards on the table are turned over.

If any match the Expresser's, the Expresser puts their card, and any others they hold of that number, at the bottom of the kitty pile.

If no player has matched the Expresser's card, ask if any player had cards of that number in their hands. If anyone did, then the Expresser has failed to show the emotion so keeps the card in their hand and takes one from the kitty. If no one had a card of that number the group votes on whether they could guess the feeling or not.

Anyone who puts out a card which is different from the Expresser's takes their card(s) back and, in addition, receives the same number of cards from the top of the kitty.

While the kitty is small, Expressers should not use cards they have picked up recently in case all the others are still in the kitty. For a shorter, simpler game, use only the twos, fours, sixes, eights and tens.

Mimes   People move round the room in a circle. At intervals, call out emotions or situations. On each call, players stop and mime the emotion or situation, and then move on. Ideas for calls are, 'Greet a friend', 'Say goodbye', 'Angry encounter', 'Sad greeting', 'Joyful reunion', 'Greet a business partner'.

Body whispers   The group forms a line with everyone facing the same way. The person at the end of the line picks a feeling to show (or is given one on a prepared cue card). They tap the second player on the shoulder, the second player turns round and is 'shown' the feeling by the first. Player two gets player three to turn round and see the feeling and so on. Everyone shows what they expressed at the end. Were there any misinterpretations along the way?

Throw a feeling   Throw a ball (real or imaginary) in a way that shows a feeling. It can be the way the person is feeling at that moment, the predominant feeling they have had recently or just a feeling they choose for the group to guess.

Contradictions   Work in pairs. Each person picks an emotion to show and something to say which contradicts it. For example, they smile and say 'I'm really angry'; they look sad and say 'I'm in love'; they look anxious and say 'I don't mind at all'.

Eye contact and social distance activities

Activities involving eye contact and exploration of social distance can be extremely threatening to some people. If this is the case, either avoid these activities or modify them to a level at which the participants can cope. Observe people's reactions carefully.

Eye contact conversations   People try holding a conversation for between thirty seconds and two minutes in each of the following three positions, back to back, face to face, face to back, with one person avoiding the eye contact of the other. You may want to suggest topics of conversation. Some party games call for eye contact, for example, Winks.

The space I need   The group stands in a wide circle. Each person takes it in turn to stand in the middle and one by one, the others walk slowly towards them. The person in the middle tells the person walking towards them to 'Stop' when they are at a distance which feels comfortable for conversation. Try the activity with two or three people walking towards the person at once.

How does it feel having a person or group close to you? Does it make a difference if the person in the middle is standing, sitting, lying or kneeling?

Variation: Do the exercise again with more complex instructions. For example, 'An old schoolfriend you haven't seen for several years rushes up to you' or 'An angry boss walks up to an employee who has just crashed the firm's car.'

Discuss when people feel comfortable with others close to them and when they need more space. Which people can come close? What sized crowds do people comfortable in?

Seating arrangements   In pairs, people communicate from different sitting or standing positions, then discuss the effects of position on their interaction. First they talk for two minutes face to face to get acquainted. Then, for at least half a minute:

- They talk sitting or standing back to back.
- They face each other without talking (first close together, then at a distance).
- They sit close together, facing each other, and communicate using only hand gestures.
- They face each other, hands behind their backs, and keep completely still.
- They sit opposite and close together; opposite and far apart; at various angles; side by side; side by side with one person a foot ahead of the other.
- They try a variety of positions round a desk.
- In groups, they try close circles, spread-out circles, two rows sitting opposite, a teacher/classroom arrangement, a V-shape, an X-shape and a line.

Ask, 'Which was easiest? Hardest? How did the positions affect what you said?'

2. Listening skills

People who communicate poorly are often poor listeners — they jump to conclusions and miss what others are saying.

Listening skills activities

What made that sound?   People identify sounds made behind a screen or under a table, or pieces of music, instruments or recorded voices.

Introductions   In pairs, people interview each other and later introduce each other to the group. The type of information they are to find out can be specified, for example, likes and dislikes in food, favourite music, hobbies.

Finishing sentences   People talk in pairs about a set subject. At any point, you 'cut' the conversation and the listener must go on. They should continue both the content and feeling of what was being said. (See *SELF-AWARENESS ACTIVITIES*, *Part sentences* p. 31 for topics.)

Send a message   Divide the group into two or more teams (each team must have at least two members). Each team works out a ten-word message to send to a partner team. The message is divided into an equal number of words for each team member. The teams stand on opposite sides of the room and, on a signal from the therapist, everyone starts to say their part of the message and continues to repeat it. The first team to work out the message they are being sent wins.

Remember and repeat   In pairs, one person relates an incident to the other person. It can be true or just a story. The other person has to retell the incident using the same tone and emphasis.

Or, in a small group, one person relates an incident then picks someone else to repeat it. Encourage people to dramatize their incidents.

Listening   Pairs sit facing each other. First one person talks for a minute while the other listens, then they exchange roles. The talker attempts to get their partner to respond either physically or verbally. The listener is as unresponsive as possible.

Discuss how people felt about talking to someone who was unresponsive. Ask, 'What are the differences between a question and a statement?', 'What hidden messages are there in conversations?'

3. The content of conversation

The three main content aspects of conversation are general statements (G), specific statements (S), factual ideas expanding the general statements, and related opinions or feelings (F) (see Trower, Bryant and Argyle *Social Skills and Mental Health*). Most conversations begin with a general statement. Next, either the speaker or the listener elaborates with a specific statement or question. To join a conversation a listener identifies these two aspects of what is being said and adds a statement that alters or adds to only one or two of the ideas — they keep the rest the same so that there is continuity in the conversation. If a contribution has too little overlap with what has been said, either in content or feeling, the topic of conversation may lapse and the first speaker is likely to feel they have been cut across. If there is too much overlap in the content the conversation will be dull.

Many conversations are structured around established rituals; for example, greetings, starting conversations, partings, apologizing, making introductions, explaining things and making requests.

Content of conversation activities

Soap box oratory   Speak for thirty seconds on:
- The sports news this week.
- A national incident this week.

- One piece of news in this group was . . .

Go round the group asking each person what could be added to the topic. (See *VERBAL ACTIVITIES*, *Starting points for discussions* p. 133 for more topic ideas.)

'Score GSF'   Work in pairs using pencil and paper. Each pair selects a topic (or give people topics) and each person makes some jottings about what they want to say under the headings 'General' (G), 'Specific' (S) and 'Feeling' (F). One person talks first, with their partner joining in only minimally (nods and so on). After one minute the speaker stops and the listener must identify the G, S and F content in what was said. Each time the listener is right they score a 'Yes'. The partners then swap over.

Radio and television, GSF   Identify the G,S,F elements in taped excerpts from television and radio or in recorded songs and dialogue. Or read aloud passages of dialogue from books or magazines and identify the G,S,F elements.

Cue cards   Work in a group or pairs. Give each person a card with a General topic and a Feeling. People make up a sentence using the topics and add details as well. Example topics: 'Vegetables (G) I hate' (F), 'People (S) I admire (F)', 'A pet (G) I'd love (F) to have'.

Self-disclosure   Work in a group or pairs. Each person picks some aspect of their life as a topic (high school, last job, hobbies). In turn, each person tells the group their topic. Go round the group a second time, getting each person to add a specific detail. On the third round each person adds a feeling or an opinion.

For example, 'My hobby is jogging (G), I run about three times a week (S), I enjoy being fit (F).'

Ask, 'What is the role of self-disclosure in making friends?'

Conversation starters   Using a blackboard or chart to record them, brainstorm topics which make good or poor conversation starters. Jot specific and feeling elements round each topic.

Belinda's journey   This activity is played in three rounds. First make a set of cue cards, one for each person, with questions on them like: 'Where would you like to go?', 'Who with?', 'What will you take?', 'Eat?', 'See?', 'What do you hope to do there?' (this one can be used several times), 'Where will you stay?'. Go round the group in turn. In the first round each person makes an initial general statement (G) about a journey, working from their cue card. In the second round people use the same card to add a specific (S) comment to their first statement, and on the third round a feeling or opinion comment. Encourage the group to make their comments fit together so that everyone shares the same fantasy trip.

Free information   Get people to respond to a cue card question (What sport/television programme/food/type of job do you like best?) with two pieces of information (G, F or S) joined by 'and'. For example, 'I like cricket and I watch it on TV.' (See *DRAMA*, *Progressive introductions* p. 56.)

4. Topics of conversation

People can build up their range of conversation topics through selective television viewing, reading or trying new activities. Suggest they make daily notes about their experiences, focusing on the kinds of things they might talk about.

It is important for people to know which subjects are appropriate in particular settings. Train them to notice the topics others use and the responses they get. Part of this skill is being aware of one's status in a situation and the role-related expectations of other people. What are the differences between addressing a workmate and a boss, for example?

Vocabulary can be built up through crossword puzzles and other word games, reading and discussion. Choose games based on everyday words rather than obscure ones. Discuss words which are likely to be new to people.

Actively listen for repeated grammatical errors in what people say and build exercises round them.

Precautions   People may have difficulty with:
- Appropriate self-disclosure.
- Delusional ideas. They may find it hard to move from delusional topics.
- Suspiciousness. These people will share little of themselves.
- Keeping relationships appropriate. They may ask for sympathy un-realistically or take too great a share of a conversation.

So what do you do? Discuss self-disclosure and social expectations, giving concerete examples of what is and is not appropriate. Sometimes one-to-one work should precede group work. At other times you will need to move on firmly and set limits on how time will be shared. At some point inappropriate behaviour must be dealt with — people need to be coached in acceptable alternatives or any skills they learn will be undermined by their problem.

Topics of conversation activities

Leading questions

'List three things which make you different from other people.'

'My favourite . . . is . . .'

'Two unusual things which happened this week are . . .' (See *SELF-AWARENESS ACTIVITIES*, *Part sentences* p. 31.)

Throw the ball, ask a question   Using a real or imaginary ball, people throw the ball to each other and ask questions which cannot be answered with 'yes' or 'no'. Give example topics or cue cards.

Ask, 'Why is it important to give leads to others in conversation?'

'And' ball talk   Play in a group. Form a circle and throw a ball or bean bag from one person to another in any order. People speak only when they have the ball. They can start a new subject or go on from what the previous person said starting with 'And'. The speaker throws the ball to someone else when they have no more to say or, after fifteen seconds, whichever somes first (the therapist calls time).

Similarity   Paste a large number of pictures onto cards or use a selection of objects. Participants have to pick up any two and explain a similarity or connection between them.

Ask, 'How do people move from one topic of conversation to another?'

Thesaurus   Explain how a Thesaurus works (choose one at a suitable level). Each person has a turn at being 'Keeper of the Book'. They pick a word and ask the group, 'How many different ways do you know of saying . . .' (See *VERBAL ACTIVITIES, Discussion* p. 130 and *Reminiscence* p. 140 and *DRAMA, Activities* p. 54.)

Who am I talking to?   Make a set of cards with occupations on them (bank manager, checkout operator, mother). People pick one and discuss the kinds of conversation topics they would use initially with that person. How would they move on from that topic?

Or, use the cards in pairs, with each person taking the role of the occupation on their card. They begin a conversation . . .

Nonsense talk   This exercise, commonly used to develop drama skills, can also be used to highlight conversation skills. Get people to talk to each other in pairs, using meaningless sounds instead of words. People must try to imitate the pattern of a conversation. Encourage them to let their partner know clearly when they want to end their turn or take a turn.

Variations: one person uses gibberish for their part of the conversation while the other talks freely. Or, one person talks freely while their partner responds with the same nonsense phrase at appropriate intervals.

Give each person a role (mother, teenager) and a topic so that they know what they are trying to talk about (a tree blown down, fashions, a sports topic).

Use this exercise to look at voice qualities — volume, variety and pace.

Everyone's story   Work in a group seated in a circle. One person begins a story and after developing their opening ideas, hands over to the next person. This activity works best when people try to make a cohesive story by developing the initial ideas rather than introducing too many new ideas.

Weave a conversation   Prepare a ball of wool with knots tied in it at intervals. People unwind the wool round their hand until they reach the next knot, talking until they get to it. Then, holding onto the wool round their hand, they toss the ball to someone else. People must be ready to think of appropriate ways to end what they are saying when they reach a knot.

Collecting signatures   Make a task sheet for each person with two vertical columns. The first column contains sentences to be completed and the second is for people's names.
- My favourite food is . . .   Name
- The type of garden I like best is . . . Name
- The sport I like best is . . .   Name
   Each person circulates and collects information and signatures.

5. Taking turns in conversations

Knowing when to contribute to a conversation and when to let others have a turn is an important skill. People feel uncomfortable when they are left out, spend too long talking or when they are expected to go on talking because the person they are talking to contributes very little. Recognizing patterns of conversation and understanding the turntaking process is the first step towards joining in appropriately. People signal when they want others to take a turn, or when they want to go on, by changes in body language and changes in the pace and tone of what they say. Get people to observe how this is done by watching people talk to each other (friends, people in a cafeteria, on television).

Activities to practise taking turns in conversation

Well-known games which involve taking turns are card games, dominoes, dice, board games and some verbal games. Most of the activities under 'Topics of conversation' can also be used to focus on this aspect of conversation.

6. Voice and speech qualities

Volume, pitch, pace, clarity, variety of tone and other aspects of voice all affect how readily people are listened to. Voice qualities project images which can be either positive or negative. They depend considerably on self-confidence so build up people's confidence in their ability to contribute. Confidence grows with practice, clear feedback and enthusiastic but realistic reinforcement of success. Relaxation exercises or singing and rhythm activities before a session can make it easier for people to get started.

Voice activities

Voice games Get people to say words or phrases in different ways (sadly, angrily, joyfully). Tape them so that people can hear how they sound. Ideas for words to begin with or to use on their own are: 'I . . .', 'We . . .', 'If . . .', 'How . . .', 'Yes'. Ask, 'How did people change the meanings of words?'

Get people to read passages of prose or poetry and record them so that they can hear how they sound.

Distance Get people to walk backwards away from a partner or group, talking as they go. Compare the distances at which people can be heard easily. (See *MUSIC, Voice exercises and singing* p. 95. Many of the activities in *DRAMA* p. 54 and *VERBAL ACTIVITIES* p. 130 can be used.)

7. Specific situations and individual problems

Choose social situations which are relevant to people's needs. Possible topics are: speaking to strangers, speaking in a group, party small talk, disagreeing with others in specific relationships, responding to criticism, giving and accepting praise. Individual problems can also be covered.

Courses for communicating in specific situations such as job interviews, selling, public speaking or teaching may be relevant. They could be added at the end of a general course in social skills or form the basis of a stand-alone course. The general components of conversation skills (observation, body language, listening skills and so on) can all be applied in such courses.

Practise coping with mundane but infrequent situations, such as visits by door-to-door salespeople or using a neighbour's phone. Use a problem-solving format to identify options for dealing with the situation and role play the approach that seems the most appropriate.

Activities for specific situations

Role play Exercises in gibberish or 'games' in which people make a lot of noise may help 'free people up'. (See *DRAMA, Role play* p. 48 and *MUSIC, Activities* p. 95.)

Role play situations which people have found difficult and encourage the group to give each other feedback. If possible, video role plays and give the person an opportunity to play the same role again several times in quick succession.

Making requests The card game, 'Happy Families', provides a good opportunity to practise making requests. Get people to be creative in the way they ask rather than sticking to the traditional format of the game. It may be worth making sets of cards which are designed specially for the group, such as members of a sports team, the cast of a television show or a music group.

Cue cards   Make cue cards which specify a situation, two roles and a task. For example, *Situation*: at work/at home in front of television; *Role*: co-worker/mother/visitor; *Task*: give praise/make an apology.

Ask, 'How does conversation change in different situations?'

Conflict consequences   Each person needs:
- A small piece of paper (say 10 cm by 10 cm) with 'Conflict' written at the top.
- Two larger pieces of paper, say A4. One piece is folded in half length-ways and labelled 'Said' on the top left and 'Felt' on the top right. The other piece is labelled 'Consequences'.

First, each person writes a conflict situation on their small piece of paper and passes it to the person on their right. (You may want to specify the kind of situation: at work, between husband and wife.)

Everyone reads the paper they have been given and writes a response under the 'Said' side of their large paper. They hand both papers to the person on their right.

Each person reads the small and large papers they have and writes an entry under 'Felt', folds the paper over so that both the entries on the larger paper cannot be seen, and passes the papers to the person on their right. People alternate entries' in the 'Said' and 'Felt' columns until four to six have contributed.

The next person reads all the entries so far then fills in the 'Consequence' paper. Read the results out and discuss them.

In summary, the entries are: write conflict situation, write alternate 'Said' and 'Felt' remarks, write a consequence.

ASSERTIVENESS SKILLS

Assertiveness training is about refining and fine tuning social skills and developing a personal style.

The aims of assertive communication are to be clear and honest while respecting others' views and feelings. It is a 'goal directed' way of communicating, a kind of verbal problem solving which fosters confidence and decision making.

People sometimes assume that assertiveness is about 'getting your own way' but in fact it is more accurate to see it as about being heard — whether what is being said is a compliment or a concern.

Therapeutic Application

A course in assertiveness skills is useful when people are unhappy with the way they are functioning in particular relationships (marriage, at work, living with a domineering teenager). They want to develop alternatives to losing their temper or feeling like a doormat. It is useful when people have difficulty taking the initiative, refusing requests or expressing their feelings.

Other common goals of assertiveness training are anger management and pain management. In anger management people examine the causes of their feelings. They seek to avoid making accusations and learn to tackle problems not people. In pain management, being assertive may reduce chronic pain. Research suggests that some chronic pain can be related to poorly expressed feelings.

Assertive people are able to express their feelings spontaneously and considerately. There is no 'beating about the bush' or trying to communicate through hints. Once people have mastered the skills involved, acting assertively becomes a matter of personal choice.

Physically, people with good assertivness skills hold eye contact, move smoothly rather than jerkily, hold their head still as they speak, use complete sentences and vary the pace of their speech. Their smile will show warmth rather than nervousness.

The first requirement for assertiveness training is that people believe that they can change themselves.

Assertiveness skills must be built up carefully. They are likely to be seen as doing more harm than good if people who are changing their style of communication 'overdo it' in their initial enthusiasm. For example, a normally passive person may swing beyond being assertive into an aggressive mode. Warn people to practise on a small scale initially!

Excessive politeness interferes with assertive communication.

(See *SOCIAL SKILLS*, *Contraindications, precautions and limitations* p. 145 and *Practical organization* p. 146.)

Basic Concepts in Assertiveness Training and Activities

1. Styles of communication

In the following, several styles of communication (aggressive, passive, indirect and assertive) and the short- and long-term effects of each are described, in order to help people identify which they use and when.

Aggressive communication In aggressive communication people are over-dominant. Aggressive people may gain short-term satisfaction from venting their feelings but in the long term their relationships are likely to be damaged. The people to whom aggressive people relate will be unduly passive or aggressive in response to them. Relationships involving warmth, trust and respect will be limited.

Passive communication In passive communication, people maintain a situation as it is, comfortably familiar, but they rarely express their feelings and opt out of managing their own lives. They are over-concerned to please others and avoid conflict. Generally, their self-esteem is low and people find them uninteresting company. A sense of helplessness, guilt, inadequacy and obligation are common.

Passive people are likely to use excessive thanks and apologies. They are also likely to be aggressive on occasions when their pent-up feelings break out.

There are times when a passive response is appropriate (being tactful, allowing someone else to lead) but as a regular way of communicating it is poor.

Indirect communication   Hints and body language are the primary method of communicating in indirect communication. Others are expected to guess what is meant. Ambiguity is common and wrong assumptions are easily made and the communicator will become frustrated when their cues are missed, or misread. In the short term such people are likely to bottle up their frustration. In the long term their frustration will emerge as sporadic verbal aggression, ill health or long-lasting low-grade depression.

Assertive communication   Assertive communication is open and direct. People know where they stand. Speech will be clear and audible, stance upright and eye contact and body language will reinforce what is being said. Assertive people speak for themselves and expect others do the same. Gestures are expressive and used for emphasis. In the short term communication is clear and in the long term it generates respect in relationships.

Polite communication   Politeness cuts across the other types of response. It relies strongly on social convention and may be aggressive, indirect, passive or assertive. Where social conventions are well understood polite communication will be clear. By definition, assertive communication is sensitive to other people's feelings and acknowledges them, so it is only impolite when social convention calls for a passive or indirect response. The assertive speaker will acknowledge the convention and state that they wish to be more clear and direct than is normally expected. At other times they may choose to defer to convention and give the expected passive or indirect response.

Most people use more than one style of communication, changing styles from setting to setting, though one style will usually predominate day to day. Being able to recognize and use a number of styles gives people the flexibility to change if they want to.

Activities for identifying styles of communication
Choose situations which are as realistic as possible for your group.

Role play   Get people to try out the same words or phrases in the four styles of communication: aggressive, passive, indirect and assertive. Encourage each person to use body language and facial expressions which match the style of communication they are using. Phrases to try: 'Hello', 'I don't agree', 'Could you help me?'

Next get them to use the same tones of voice but with body language which does not match. Discuss the effect this has on communication.

Try longer role plays in each style. Suggest topics or write full scripts. For example: Ask workmates or family for a loan (book, car, umbrella). Ask for a date. Ask workmates how to do a job.

Persuasion   Work in groups of three or four. One person in the group is chosen to sit in a particular place. They stay there until someone persuades them to move. Taking turns, members of the group use all the methods of persuasion they can think of: passive hints, indirect gentle persuasion, aggressive and assertive vigorous persuasion. If the sitter stays put they can say which method came nearest to persuading them to move after everyone has had a turn.

Or, one group can persuade another group to do something.

Do the same exercise with one person trying to persuade the other to buy something.

A romance   Cast people as 'the Indirect father', 'the Passive mother', 'the Aggressive daughter', 'the Assertive older son' (or whatever selection of people will suit the group). The situation: 'One day the aggressive daughter decides to leave the job she has and look for another one.' Together, the group plan out a story with each character acting in their designated style.

Sentence completion   These part sentences can be used as prompts for discussion or as a written activity. 'I am likely to be passive (assertive, aggressive, indirect) when ... because ...'; with ... because ...'; at ... because ...'

The journey   This is a pencil and paper activity. Each person draws a roadway and along the way puts stick figures to represent the people they meet. They can either put people in their lives or choose kinds of people (bank manager, physiotherapist, pharmacist, farmer, timber merchant, energetic three-year-old and so on). They label the people in each encounter and state the kind of relationship they usually have with that person or type of person. Follow this with each person explaining their roadway to a partner or the group.

Responses   Make a set of picture cards (using newspaper and magazine pictures) which show passive, aggressive and indirect people. Discuss how the people on the cards would respond in a variety of situations, such as being asked to give a donation to a charity they have no interest in, being shortchanged in a shop where several others are waiting to be served, asking — or being asked — for a dance and so on.

What advice would group members give to the people in the pictures?

High chair   Examine the effects on a relationship when one person sits in a higher chair than another (say a high stool and kitchen chair) or where one person sits while the other stands.

2. Rights, responsibilities and barriers to assertiveness

Rights   A basic concept of assertiveness training is that everyone has certain rights as a human being. Examples of such rights are the right to communicate openly and honestly and the right to choose one's friends.

Responsibilities   As well as rights, everyone has responsibilities which complement their rights in social relationships. For example, the right to speak is complemented by a responsibility to listen and the right to be assertive includes the responsibility of allowing/expecting others to be assertive too. It is worth exploring this last example in some detail.

Personal barriers to assertiveness   At a personal level people may see themselves as having little or no right to express themselves. They may be anxious about other people's reactions, the 'What if' syndrome. This fear of social rejection is based on 'should' and 'ought' feelings learnt from parents, peers and authority figures ('If I say that people will think . . .'). The underlying problem is low self-esteem.

People tend to talk themselves out of taking the risks of a direct approach. They say to themselves:
- 'People might laugh at me', 'I'll only speak up if someone else does' (lack of confidence).
- 'I'll sound grouchy', 'It might hurt people's feelings' (guilt).
- 'People might not like me' (irrational belief).

These ways of thinking have vivid but easily remembered names in the literature on assertiveness: 'catastrophizing' (expecting a catastrophic outcome), 'absolutizing' (seeing things in absolute terms with no 'possiblys' or 'perhapses'). People may be unaware that it is possible to learn to express themselves differently. They may not know how to start.

Social status barriers to assertiveness   Social and cultural values often assume that some people have more 'rights' than others. The rights of the fit and the disabled, the wealthy and the poor, men and women, the young and the old are often viewed differently. Work and social roles can influence the status people have in their social groups and how readily their views are listened to and under what circumstances (bank manager/cleaner, father/child). People's real ability to speak for themselves is not always assessed. In healthcare settings, examples of social status barriers to communication may come from the hierarchy of medical personnel and their patients.

The way people interact with others is a guide to how they see themselves and the kind of status they think they have; when people see themselves as inferior or incapable they often relate to others in unsatis-

Rights and responsibilities

factory ways. Of course people must operate within some social rules and constraints in order to be accepted by their peers, keep their jobs and so on. However, everyone has basic rights as a human being regardless of their socio-cultural situation and their life roles. Assertive communication recognizes the needs and rights common to all people.

Activities on rights, responsibilities and barriers to assertiveness

Listing rights and responsibilities Make a short list of examples of people's rights and responsibilities on a blackboard or chart. Put two or three to start with, then get the group to add more. It may be easier for people to think of examples if they look at a range of situations and roles. For example, 'A boss has the right to . . . and the responsibility to . . .', 'A working mother has the right to . . . and the responsibility to . . .'

Personal barriers — the brick wall Make a set of card 'building bricks'. They should all be the same size, like bricks. People write their personal barriers to being assertive on the brick cards, using as many as they need. (Examples are: 'People might laugh at me', 'I don't have a good vocabulary'.) Build a wall with the cards using Blu-tack or pins to attach the blocks to a background sheet or wall. Look for the common components in people's contributions and discuss how each could be dealt with or accepted if it cannot be changed. As each is dealt with, take it down from the wall.

Alternatively, use round cards and build a mountain of 'boulders'. (See *RELAXATION, Mental relaxation techniques* p. 182.)

Pushed down First, get people to write down two to four negative things they say to themselves in certain situations. For example: when speaking to someone they think of as important, someone they do not know, someone who is in a position to influence what happens to them; when they are asked to do something they do not want to do; when someone criticizes them.

Then, in pairs, one person sits down and the other person stands behind them with their hands on the seated person's shoulders. The seated person reads out one of their statements and the standing partner gives them a push downwards on their shoulders. The seated person reads the next statement and gets another push down. When the seated person's list is finished, the pair reverse roles.

The idea is to give people a graphic demonstration of the effect of giving oneself negative messages. Put a time limit on this part of the activity to make sure that there is time for the second part of the activity.

For the second part of the activity, get people to write a list of their strengths and statements which they could make to themselves to build and maintain their confidence. When people run out of ideas get them to work as a group and add to each other's lists. (See *SELF-AWARENESS ACTIVITIES*, Building esteem p. 27.)

When 'When I feel like saying I can't do something . . . I can stop myself by saying . . .' Each person fills in this sentence one or more times. Get people to compare lists. (See *SELF-AWARENESS ACTIVITIES*, 'Who am I?' topics p. 16.)

Ask, 'Why do people talk themselves out of using their abilities? What are the sources of self-perception? What 'should' messages do people live by? What is their effect? Follow the discussion with an esteem-building activity (see *SELF-AWARENESS ACTIVITIES*, Building esteem p. 27.)

Self-talk snakes and ladders Make a large model of a snakes and ladders board on a piece of card, blackboard or white board. Get the group to offer suggestions for labels on each snake and ladder.

To play, each person or team has a counter (place marker) and they take it in turns to throw a dice. The counter is moved the number of spaces shown on the dice. If the counter lands at the bottom of a ladder it moves up it, if it lands at the top of a snake, it slides down.

3. How to be assertive

Assertive communication is brief, clear and uncluttered by excessive detail. A commonly used formula for creating assertive messages is the DESC script where DESC stands for DESCRIBE, EXPRESS, SPECIFY and CONSEQUENCES (see Bower and Bower, *Asserting Yourself*).

Assertive communication begins with a factual statement in which the subject is DESCRIBED (D). The feelings and thoughts are EXPRESSED (E), goals or requests are SPECIFIED (S), and finally the CONSEQUENCE (C)

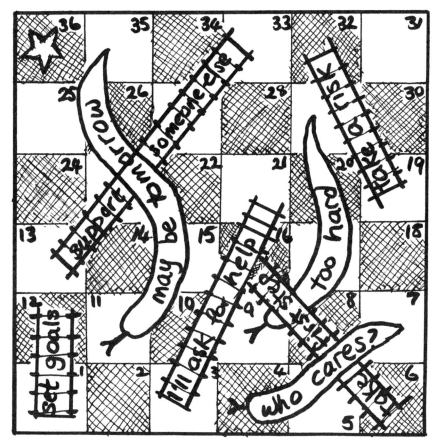

Self-talk snakes and ladders

which the person expects to follow is stated. (S) and (C) are sometimes omitted.

Examples First, the subject the person is speaking about is stated simply and clearly (D), closely followed by an expression of their main feeling about it (F).

(D) 'The rent is late' (no negative adjectives are used).

(E) 'and I am worrying about it.'

Feelings are expressed with a statement which begins with 'I' rather than 'you' — statements starting with 'you' can have a judgmental tone. 'I' statements put the responsibility for the feeling on the speaker rather than the listener.

This is usually followed by more factual information about why the speaker has developed the feeling: 'because the landlord could evict us if it is regularly overdue' or 'because I hate owing money'. Said assertively, the tone will be matter-of-fact and nonjudgmental.

(S) The goal is what the speaker hopes will happen next. It is solution-oriented and phrased as a request: 'I'd like you to put in your share before tomorrow.'

(C) The communication is concluded with a consequence: 'then I will stop worrying' and/or' . . . if you can't do this we need to discuss our options.'

The speaker's stance, movement and voice are matter-of-fact. The speaker looks at the listener and is ready to negotiate a compromise.

Assertive statements can be used to give praise and compliments as well as to express concerns. Assertive compliments, like assertive requests, are clear and simple.

Longer conversations: negotiation   In longer conversations, where people want to maintain an assertive style, the same four elements, (D), (E), (S) and (C) are present, but the feelings expressed are more complex, the other person's feelings can be acknowledged and topics connected to the main one can be raised. There is a broader analysis of options and outcomes and possible compromises can be discussed. In-depth conversations often both start and end with a brief assertive statement as an introduction and a summing up. The brief formula is used when people want to express a concern which will be heard, or give praise that cannot be missed.

Techniques   In assertiveness training, role play, personal rehearsal, writing out messages to clarify feelings and planning communication, can all help people put theory into practice. Explore people's personal concerns through discussion and role play to help them see how the theory applies to their own lives.

More topics   Other concepts frequently included in assertiveness courses are how to persist with an assertive statement, how to handle aggressive, passive or indirect responses and how to avoid weakening an assertive message. The key is to keep messages simple and clear, repeat them if necessary ('broken record') and answer only relevant questions.

Specific situations can be covered, such as expressing anger, negotiating, giving compliments, admitting a mistake, apologizing, participating in meetings, giving talks and presentations.

For other topics which contribute to effective assertiveness skills see *SELF-AWARENESS, Building esteem* p. 27 and *WORKING IN GROUPS, Feedback and praise* p. 218 and *Self-disclosure* p. 220.

Activities for practice in being assertive

DESC scripts   Get the group to compose a number of statements and write them up on a blackboard or white board so that everyone can see them (get four people to stand in a line holding up the four parts of the statement written on large cards). If the group does not have enough ideas for the statements, make cue cards describing the situation and the people involved. Remove sections of each statement and discuss the effect on the overall message if part of the statement is left out. Alternatively, write the statement on four separate bits on cards. Try them in different orders, three at a time or any other variation you can think of.

Role play   Someone in the group describes a situation in which they were unassertive. Get them to role play the situation up to the point where they responded unassertively, then de-role people and, working in pairs or individually, write four-part assertive statements which could be used in the situation. Compare the results and discuss how each might work.

Rerun the role play trying a selection of the endings.

Situations   Prepare a set of pictures of social situations with captions giving a brief description of the scene. Ask, 'What will each person say next if they are appropriately assertive?' The pictures can also be used to practise differentiating between styles of communication.

Observation   Get people to listen for the components of assertive statements in conversations or in television programmes. Are any elements regularly omitted?

5 | *Relaxation and Massage*

RELAXATION

Stress, mental or physical, makes people tense and unrelaxed. Posture is stiff and muscles are taut from using energy unproductively.

These characteristics of stress are reversible. Learning to relax can break the negative cycle and is often the first step towards a better quality of life because, when people are relaxed, they have move energy to learn the skills which make life satisfying and productive.

Therapeutic Application

As part of stress management, relaxation techniques are useful for problems which are primarily psychological. They help people cope with acute and chronic anxiety, temporary stress and more prolonged periods of chronic stress. Physically, they can reduce muscle spasm, headaches, blood pressure and pain. They are important in a balanced life.

Being able to relax reduces people's apprehension before experiences they expect to be painful or unpleasant and can actually lessen an experience of acute pain. Often, it is not the stressful event itself which causes problems, but people's physical and mental reactions to it.

Understanding relaxation techniques and the way they work gives people useful knowledge about how the body reacts to stress and about how to cope with it. Relaxation can usefully precede activities which need a clear, relaxed frame of mind. In drama or self-awareness activities, for example, people are likely to be more receptive to ideas if they are relaxed.

Like any skill, relaxation takes time to learn and improvement comes with practice. It is similar to exercise — with training there is steady and considerable improvement in the quality and effectiveness of performance. Eventually, techniques become a matter of habit and can be used quickly and confidently.

People must be motivated to learn relaxation. They need to view relaxation as a relevant, worthwhile, learnable skill rather than something a therapist does to or for them.

As it is hard to predict which technique will work best for a particular person, it is sensible to try a number of different techniques several times, before choosing one to develop more fully. Whatever relaxation technique is chosen, it should be combined with other stress management strategies to form a comprehensive programme.

An initial one-to-one session is often useful to assess people's individual needs and check that they understand and accept what relaxation involves. Explain that there is no 'success' or 'failure' and orientate them as to how to get the most out of a course. An attitude of self-acceptance is important. Programmes that run from ten to thirty minutes a day, several days a week, work well for learning most techniques.

Contraindications, Precautions and Limitations

When people are learning relaxation techniques, common initial problems are:

- Self-consciousness (giggling, laughter), cramp and discomfort (wriggling, scratching). It is best to ignore these things and to convey an expectation that people will quickly settle.
- Some people fear losing control when they relax, and it is true that occasionally strong, unexpected feelings will well up in relaxation sessions. Explain that if this does happen, it is normal and is the release of buried feelings. Usually people feel better afterwards.
- Disorders which involve muscular tension make relaxation techniques difficult to learn. For example, people with schizophrenia are invariably tense, although they may not appear so to the casual observer. Instruction in relaxation is best left until the acute phase of the illness has past. Neurological damage resulting in muscle spasm or poor muscular control (as in cerebral palsy) seriously limits people's ability to learn relaxation. However, N. Barnett from the Cerebral Palsy Unit in Rotorua, New Zealand, reports that the techniques, progressive relaxation (p. 192) and breathing for relaxation (p. 193), have been used to good effect with such people on the muscles that are under voluntary control.
- Severe depression brings cognitive limitations so mental relaxation techniques are contraindicated until people are well on the way to recovery.
- Chronic pain syndromes usually involve considerable tension and muscle spasm and although this makes relaxation difficult to learn, it is usually worth the time and effort.
- Medications which affect muscular tension will interfere with the ability to relax.
- People who are agitated and restless will disrupt a group and have great difficulty relaxing.
- Some relaxation techniques are contraindicated for people who suffer from hallucinations. 'Fantasy trip' methods are particularly risky because they encourage retreat into an imaginary world. Meditation and thought stopping can involve similar risks. Autogenic training (p. 186) may be

contraindicated for people with hypertension because it is said to affect basic metabolism and possibly increase hypertension.

The Therapist's Role

It is important to know the theory behind the techniques you use, and to have tried each method. This enables you to explain theories in simple terms which will make the techniques easier to remember.

Encourage people to set realistic goals in relation to practice. It's difficult to practise at times of low stress (if people feel relaxed the techniques seem irrelevant) and at times of high stress the techniques are harder to learn. Although real mastery requires determined, steady effort, 'dabbling' and experimenting can give people a knowledge base to build on.

People may feel uncomfortable if they are aware of being watched so keep this in mind when choosing where to sit or stand in relation to the person or group. Being touched can make some people feel uncomfortable.

Plan what you will say and rehearse it; practise on friends if you can. The pitch of your voice should be quiet and the pace even. There should be plenty of time to carry out the instructions.

Check if anyone is hard of hearing and if they are put them in the best position to hear. Observe people's responses to see how easily they are following your instructions. It is usually impractical to do the relaxation exercise at the same time as giving the instructions.

When people are trying to select an approach, discussion and feedback are important. At the end of a session discuss the advantages and drawbacks of the methods tried, the time and space required to do them and how to keep the experience satisfying.

Debriefing — the way a session ends is important. Get people to sit or lie for a minute or two, perhaps with their eyes closed, then with them open, as they begin to think about what they are going to do next. The transition to other activities should not be too abrupt.

Practical Organization

The time available is important. How much time is needed for teaching mastery of a particular technique? How frequent should sessions be and what is the ideal length of a session? How long will each stage of a session take? What is the best time of day to do them? Most techniques can be learnt quite quickly but practice needs to be daily or at least several times a week to consolidate learning and get real benefit. Note the danger of showing people a number of techniques in one session. It is beneficial for people to try a variety of techniques but they need time to get a real feeling for each one.

Should teaching be done in a group or individually? Group teaching has several advantages. People see others with the same problems as themselves and they can share ideas about what works for them. Generally, groups of four to eight work well but for some techniques larger groups are acceptable (autogenic training, progressive relaxation and exercise).

Should practice or self-monitoring between sessions be planned? Is a contract to attend and practise a good idea? Would keeping a stress diary be useful? What materials will be needed — tapes, mats, handouts? Books about relaxation and hand-out sheets are useful as back-up to practical sessions.

Issues related to the male/female and age composition of the group are sometimes significant, as are the size and cohesiveness of the group. People need to feel comfortable relaxing with others around them. A sense of security can be built up by discussion before and after the relaxation itself, and through social contact within the group (see *WORKING IN GROUPS*, *Cohesiveness: building group relationships* p. 204).

Avoid scheduling sessions for times when people are tired or have just eaten. Alcohol immediately before a session is not a good idea either. Suggest people attend to physical needs like going to the toilet, washing hands and face, blowing their noses and so on before the session. Recommend loose-fitting clothing and removal of shoes.

A place to relax   Find a quiet room which is free of distractions and warm without being too bright and sunny. Lights should be dim, or indirect if they are on, and a warm coloured light is preferable to a cooler, bluer one. If the temperature is too warm people may fall asleep, if it is too cool they will find it difficult to relax. Sometimes a sign on the door is useful to prevent interruptions. There should be as little movement as possible in the room and no haste in the session.

Provide small pillows and work on a carpet or mats of some type. The surface should be reasonably firm or, again, people may go to sleep. On the other hand, too hard a surface will mean people think about their physical discomfort rather than relaxing.

Some relaxation techniques are best done lying down, others can be done sitting. Techniques designed to be done anywhere and at any time (autogenic training, physiological relaxation) should be practised sitting on a couch, at a desk and so on, to encourage people to do them in these places in everyday life.

When people plan their own relaxation suggest they use the same place each time. It should be somewhere where they will not be disturbed and the requirements regarding dim lighting, quietness and comfort are the same as for groups. Taking the phone off the hook may be advisable.

Instruction tapes   Instruction tapes can be used to teach relaxation or for regular personal relaxation sessions. The drawbacks are that some people may depend on them too heavily, they cannot be used at any time or place and aspects of the speaker's voice or part of the content may be unsuitable for a particular person. Check that there is enough time for people to carry out the instructions and that the tempo and volume are suitable. If possible, have people try several tapes to see which suits them best. Helping people to record their own tape is another possibility.

Music If music is perceived as soothing then it is likely to have a soothing effect — but of course the reverse is true too. When you are planning a session ask people how they feel about different types of music and which kinds they find the most relaxing.

Music is more appropriate with some types of relaxation than others — it is very useful with breathing exercises (if the pace is right) and where imagery is a focus. Lyrics or strongly emotional music are likely to interfere with relaxation. In relaxation music should be used in a definite way — to dictate the pace of breathing, relaxation or exercise, or to set a mood and focus for contemplation. If people develop a strong association of relaxation with a particular piece of music, then simply hearing the music may relax them. Music works less well as a background although there is sometimes benefit in this. (See *MUSIC, Music and relaxation* p. 97.)

Stress and Its Consequences

Relaxation techniques are easier to learn if people have a clear sense of the difference in their bodies depending on whether they are tense or relaxed. Start by getting people to identify their tensions and the causes of those tensions. They need to identify situations in which they experience stress during a day, specific events which cause them stress and stressful interactions with specific people. Stress can came from the environment (people, things, events), the person's body (discomfort, pain), or their thought processes and attitudes (negative perceptions of self and ability to cope).

Next, look at the effects of the stressors, both positive and negative. A moderate amount of stress or tension is useful. It is stimulating, a spur to action. Or, still in a positive way, a brief sense of overload is a warning to be heeded.

The physiological changes that occur as a result of stress are caused by adrenaline being released into the bloodstream to prepare the body for action, the 'fight or flight' mechanism. However, in many stressful experiences, vigorous action is inappropriate so the body is left in a state of tension that is difficult to relieve. (An adrenaline surge is sometimes useful — for an athlete in a race, for example.) Short-term stress can be exhilarating, but in the medium term a sense of unease develops, a sense of being trapped, and in the long term it causes unpleasant mental and physical symptoms.

Adrenaline produces changes in the body: breathing becomes rapid and shallow; oxygen use increases; heartbeat rate increases; blood pressure rises; blood flow to the brain and major muscles increases but is reduced to the digestive system and hands and feet; muscles become tense, usually in the shoulders, neck and scalp first; all sensory perceptions are heightened.

Stress in a work situation can cause mistakes, absences and accidents. It is usually the result of poor work methods, fatigue, boredom and poor time management.

Common signs of stress From the bodily changes listed above unpleasant symptoms may develop. The commonest are headache, dizziness, sleep disturbance, swallowing difficulties and aching muscles, particularly in the neck and shoulders. Spasms in back muscles are common, leading to back-ache problems. Stress generally plays a significant part in chronic pain syndromes, either as a precursor to the pain, a product of it, or both.

Every bodily system is affected; there may be circulatory effects like palpitations and breathlessness, skin rashes, cold, clammy hands and feet, and, in the digestive system, problems like nausea, indigestion and diarrhoea. In the reproductive system there may be menstrual and sexual difficulties.

More serious is the role stress plays in disease and illness, appearing to contribute to the onset of many disorders when the symptoms listed above go on for a long time.

Stress has psychological effects as well: accident proneness, persistent tiredness, loss of appetite, worrisome thoughts, angry or resentful feelings, irritation and loss of concentration. Other effects which have both psychological and physical features are allergic reactions, low-grade infections, low back pain, wind and burping. People under stress may compound their problems by getting little rest, taking on too much and being poorly organized — their activities consume all their time and energy with little useful result.

Severity The severity of stress depends on the magnitude of the stressor. Numerous small stressors have a cumulative effect and can be as severe as one large stress. The effects are worse if people dwell on the stressor but are unable to take action to lessen it. As well, the more recent the stress, the more significant it is likely to be. The effects are also more severe if the stress is outside the person's control, relentless and ill-defined, or coming from many sources at the same time.

People's attitudes determine how severe a stress will be. If their perception of a stressor is very negative ('This is a disaster' rather than 'This is a nuisance') the effects are much worse. Thresholds for stress can be low because of previous stresses — the 'final straw' situation. People with few, or poor, support systems are less able to tolerate stress than those who have good support systems.

Types of stress Discussing types of stress (conflict, pressure, frustration) can help people pinpoint the sources of stress in their lives. *Conflict* results from one person's values and desires being in opposition to another's, or from two or more wishes of the same person being in opposition. *Pressure* results from the constraints of time and task demands. *Frustration* results from there being barriers or obstacles which prevent a person from reaching their goals; it also results from unmet needs.

Coping with stress   Practical solutions to stress are:
- Limiting the amount of change in life and avoiding or moving away from stressful events. If people recognize their stress tolerance levels they can conserve their energy to deal with those things which are most important to them. Accepting that some stress — and distress — is inevitable in life is important too. It is possible to get used to a particular stressor by gradually increasing tolerance to it. (See *Systematic desensitization* p. 191.)
- Finding and developing support systems. This gives people friends and contacts to turn to when they need help.
- Widening the range of leisure pursuits. Satisfying, involving activities build up self-esteem and act as a distraction from stress.
- Learning to relax. To some, relaxation means doing less, to others, doing something different or dealing directly with physical tension by using relaxation techniques. Specific techniques in exercise and relaxation are part of the armoury which help people to cope with stress.

Stress Management Techniques and Activities

A stress management session can be a one-off event or a series of sessions. No technique is unique to this area. A stress management programme should educate people about stress, increase awareness of personal stressors, and provide work, diet, exercise, leisure planning and relaxation skills.

Rest, work, social life and selfcare activities need to be balanced for each individual. As well, people need a sense of commitment — self-investment — in realistic activities and goals. Commitment to goals establishes and maintains a feeling of control, whereas simply responding to outside pressures leads to a sense of powerlessness.

People who find that they rush, vacillate, miss deadlines, have too little time for rest or are easily overwhelmed can usually regain control by planning. Realistic goals, based on personal values, are planned for each life area after first getting an overview of the existing balance of activities.

Planning includes dealing with problems. Problems are identified in detail, divided into small units and put into a personal order of priority so that they are easier to tackle.

Activities

Activity configurations   People list what they do over a set length of time (a day, or a week) and make notes about specified regular intervals (for example, each half hour, or morning, afternoon and evening). It may be important to record who was present. At the end of each day they make notes about what seemed to be out of balance. Which part of the day did they feel happiest about, least happy with? Was there anything unusual about this day?

Graphic activity configurations

- *Bar graph*   Colour in squares on a ruled grid or piece of graph paper, each square representing half an hour. Main colour categories might be work/education, selfcare, leisure, rest/sleep. Social, creative, sports/ physical activities are other possible categories. The result is a bar graph of how time is spent.

  Or, using the same basic data, colour in squares in categories such as 'Enjoy', 'Have to do', 'Want to do', 'Do because there's nothing better to do'.

- *Pie graph*   People make a pie graph of how they spend their time and another, for comparison, of how they would like to spend their time. This can be an off-the-cuff activity or based on records kept over a period of time. (Note that accuracy may be less important than the person's perception of what they do.) (See *SELF-AWARENESS ACTIVITIES, Things I've done* p. 19.)

- *Key area quadrants*   People divide a large sheet of paper into four areas: work/education, leisure (sports/creative activities), selfcare (ironing, cleaning car) and social/friends/family. In each quadrant, they list all the concrete things they do in that sphere of their life.

Brainstorm on Paper   People brainstorm using the heading 'Everything I do'. When they run out of new points to add to the list, they put grade ratings beside each item.

Focused activity configurations   These concentrate on just one type of information. Possibilities are situations that were upsetting, cigarettes smoked, headaches, backache or other health problems, diet, exercise

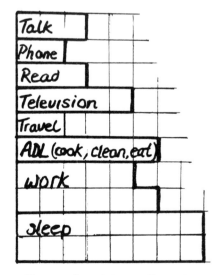

Bar-graph activity configuration

Pie-graph activity configuration

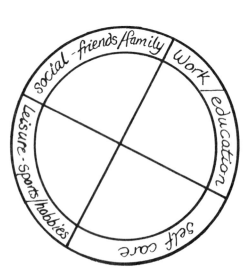

Key-area quadrants activity configuration

taken (amount, nature), contacts with people (social, household management, work), recreational activities (alone/with others, passive/active), resting time or time spent on work. Notes should be made on any significant circumstances which affected the pattern and/or made it atypical.

Stress overview

- People write down all the stressors in their lives on a piece of paper.
- They pick one and write it in the centre of another piece of paper.
- Round the edge they jot all the causes and contributory factors. If it is a problem they specify who contributes and their own role.
- At the bottom of the page they write, 'What am I going to do about it?' and then answer as specifically as possible.
- Identify any strategies that have worked in the past.

Other problems on the initial sheet can be examined in the same way. (See *SELF-AWARENESS, Choices and decisions* p. 26 and *Building esteem* p. 27.)

Time planning (or self-pacing) activity configurations heighten people's awareness of the things they want to do more or less of. Make 'More' and 'Less' lists and plan how to make changes.

Plus and minus In this activity people identify which activities are of low/ high priority in their lives and which could be rescheduled or eliminated. They first make a list of what they do, and then grade each item by putting between zero and three pluses or minuses beside it. Next, they divide a piece of paper into three columns, headed 'Important', 'Should do', 'Unimportant'. Each activity is written in the appropriate column. From this visual picture long- and short-term goals can be set. The overall plan should include time for interruption and relaxation. It should also anticipate some progress towards the important goals each day or at least weekly, so that there is a regular feeling of accomplishment. The short-term goals should be small enough for people to tell easily when they have been accomplished.

Role play putting plans into action and saying 'No' to low priority activities. Discuss each proposed change. Identify obstacles to change and clarify what needs to be done. Who can give support? How often should goals be reviewed?

Stress management and work problems People who experience chronic pain may need education about body mechanics, lifting, posture and so on. Plan a realistic pace of work with plenty of breaks to conserve energy.

Building a support network People may need counselling about community resources and leisure activities available to them. They may need to learn how to establish social contacts and make friends.

Diet   Diet has an effect on people's state of tension/relaxation. Most people should eat more fruit, vegetables and cereals and less oil/fat, sugar, alcohol and salt. Some foods, such as caffeine, make stress worse because they are stimulants. Tobacco and tranquillizers can be short-term relaxants but are counter-productive in long-term use.

It takes many months for people to alter their eating patterns; ongoing support is needed.

Hot baths   A short hot bath has good sedative effects but long hot baths are likely to leave people feeling mentally and physically restless.

Leisure   Leisure skills help reduce stress. Enjoyable, absorbing activities are a source of relief and distraction from stress.

Mental Relaxation Techniques and Activities

People's thoughts shape their experiences. Thinking, 'I can't do it' or 'This is awful' will only make stressful experiences worse.

1. Straight thinking

This is also called Relabelling, Dealing with irrational beliefs, Cognitive restructuring, Rational emotive therapy or Reframing.

People tend to judge things that happen to them by measuring them against their own values. This step between event and emotion can play a positive or negative role. It usually includes 'must, should, ought, always, never...' which can prevent people taking a flexible, relaxed view of events in their lives. If thought processes play a major part in stress, get people to examine how their thinking contributes to their stress. They must first recognize any irrational ideas or beliefs they hold. These are usually learned early in life and are reinforced by friends, family and workmates. They can create a negative emotional climate. For example, when a person who makes a mistake at work says to themselves, 'Everyone knows, I'll never live this down, everyone is talking about me...', this will hinder their ability to work. Other examples of unhelpful messages which people give to themselves are, 'I must be liked by everyone', 'I must be perfect', 'It's wrong to...' Harmful messages are likely to start with absolutes: 'It's never...', 'I can't...', 'I must...', 'I am...'

Pinpointing the message   Make an activity of identifying problem messages. Get people to rethink situations and ask themselves, 'What did I say to myself? How rational was that? Was there another way to look at the situation?'

Art, drama, creative writing or discussion activities can also be used to increase people's awareness of their self-talk.

At the root of negative, irrational thinking is the feeling that one is a pawn in the game of life, with no control over events. 'Straight thinking' counteracts this and encourages people to see things differently.

While the idea of 'positive thinking' may seem simplistic, with effort, it can be very effective. It takes steady, persistent, hard work to change habits of self-talk.

Self-talk columns At the top of a sheet of paper people write a major stressor in their lives. Immediately below they draw three columns. In the first they write their self-talk about the stressor; in the second their emotional response; and in the third alternative ways of looking at the stressor.

As a second phase to the activity each person chooses one item from the self-talk column to share with the group. The group suggests alternatives for column three.

Role play In a group, one person describes a problem they have experienced in which their attitude has contributed to the stress. The others play out a variety of self-talk responses as Mr Must, Miss Should, Mrs Everyone-will-think, Mr Blame, Miss Punish, Mr Tolerant, Miss Commonsense, Mr Reasonable, Mrs Creative and so on. Suggestions may be needed to get the group started, 'Describe something that makes you angry', 'Something that makes you feel inferior . . .'

Concentric consequences Each person draws three concentric circles on a sheet of paper. In the centre circle they put their name. In the second they write things they 'should', 'ought', 'must' do. In the outer circle they draw or write the consequences, both positive and negative.

Relabelling Each member of the group divides a piece of paper into three columns. They head the first column 'Values and aims' or 'Things

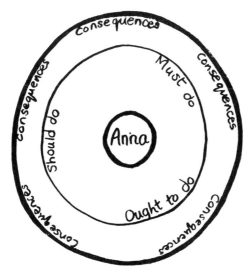

Concentric consequences

Aims	Barriers	Relabelled
① Improve work output	I'm not getting anywhere	Every bit helps
	This isn't good enough	It's OK to redo things
② Speak at the ward meeting	I'll blush	I can concentrate on what I want to say

Relabelling

which are important to me', the second 'Barrier thoughts', that is, thoughts which prevent them doing something about the things which are important to them, and the third 'Barriers relabelled'.

Group discussion 'Common irrational beliefs' is usually a productive discussion topic.

2. Social and assertive skills

Relationships are often the major source of stress for people, so teaching communication skills in combination with other relaxation techniques can be an effective way to help people relax in social situations.

Poor communication can also play a role in chronic pain if people internalize feelings and problems rather than express them; the pain can become the expression of feelings and be used to avoid honest communication.

Assertiveness skills help people retake control of their lives and can break the chronic pain cycle by decreasing a major source of regular emotional stress. (See *COMMUNICATION SKILLS* p. 144.)

3. Thought stopping

Teach concepts in small groups or one-to-one, preferably in frequent, short sessions. This technique is particularly useful for obsessive thoughts. It is based on the idea that negative thoughts precede negative feelings and it works best when combined with exercise or some other absorbing physical activity. Thought stopping must be done with real energy — an aggressive determination to make it work.

Suggest people start with a mild problem or one that regularly recurs. Or, for the purposes of learning the technique, people can practise with any thought, so that they will understand how to use the procedure when they are next troubled by an intrusive, repetitive worry or emotion. The technique can also be used for other types of negative feelings like jealousy, anger and anxiety.

Method People concentrate on the unwanted thought briefly, then aloud (or in their minds) shout 'Stop'. The 'Stop' can be accompanied by a physical action such as jumping up, snapping fingers or slapping one hand on the leg. Vigorous action helps stop the thought. With enough repetition the action alone may be enough to stop the thoughts. Next, reassuring, self-accepting statements are substituted and repeated firmly and continuously. It is a good idea to have a variety of statements ready so that no one statement loses its impact through being too familiar. The substitute statements can either be positive but related to the thought or entirely unrelated and distracting. Examples of statements are: 'Not now, not when you're tired', 'Get on with the job you are doing . . .' or 'What would my therapist say to me now?' Or they might choose a song to sing in their heads. Tell people they can shout, say or whisper whatever they choose, aloud or to themselves. It is vital to start as soon as the unwanted thoughts begin — they are harder to shift when they have been repeated for some time.

Ideally, people should also turn firmly to an interesting, absorbing activity, preferably with others, and they should engage in it as actively as possible. However, these kinds of activities will only work in a positive sense if the person uses them positively, that is, with determination to reach a point of catharsis, relaxation or release.

4. Positive imagination

This technique works well as a one-off activity. People visualize themselves as they want to be. It is an approach that follows naturally from thought stopping but it can be used as a separate technique. (Beware of the potential risk of inhibiting realistic assessment of a situation.)

The theory behind positive imagination is that as people can only have one thought at a time, they should work at making that thought as positive as possible for as much of the time as possible. Positive thoughts can be reinforced by deliberately 'feeling' the positive mood and physical state that goes with them. Examples of thoughts people might use are: 'I can relax', 'I can cope with this', 'I can enjoy . . . in this situation', 'Many people have coped with this problem and I can too', 'This setback doesn't mean I'll fail the whole thing', 'I'll get on with this and do my best'. Outgoing acts of cheerfulness and smiling can have an effect on mental processes. A confident posture and walk will add to the positive messages.

As a role play exercise, ask, 'How would a person stand, sit, move, breathe if they believed the positive things they were thinking?' Get people to act out situations, showing positive thoughts reflected in positive body language.

5. Autogenic training

This technique works best in a series of sessions fairly close together and can be done with groups of up to twenty people. People give instructions to their bodies with the aim of normalizing their body processes. The instructions or suggestions are about, first heaviness, then warmth, then heaviness and warmth together. The technique is useful for dealing with specific problems or symptoms such as circulatory disorders or hyperventilation and is also a good way of achieving general relaxation. It is often used with biofeedback and is similar to meditation in nature. To be effective it should be done briefly several times a day.

Suggest people start with just their arms, then add work on their legs and gradually increase the body parts they include. In a group session it may be more practical to teach the method in a comprehensive way from the beginning.

Contraindications and precautions   The authors of autogenic training suggest that the 'warmth' command be avoided with women who are pregnant. They also warn that there may be some risks for people with blood pressure problems.

Method   Keep external stimuli to a minimum and get people to lie down with their eyes closed (this is the ideal but it should be optional).

First people mentally scan their bodies for tension and consciously relax each part. Next comes instruction from either a leader, a tape or the person themselves. First about heaviness: 'My right arm is heavy' (pause long enough to feel the sensation), 'My left arm is heavy.' The same order is then given to both arms together, each leg, then both legs together.

Next come instructions to feel warmth: 'My right arm is warm . . .' and so on through each limb. Then the heartbeat is pictured as calm and regular, and breathing as calm and even.

The whole body is pictured: forehead cool and body warm, heavy and relaxed in a peaceful setting. The images of warmth and heaviness can be reinforced with mental pictures such as being bathed in warm water, lying on warm sand, head in the shade or being gently covered by warm sand.

As a technique autogenic training goes well with progressive relaxation.

After the session the person should rest briefly, then get up and stretch to fully wake themselves.

6. Fantasy trip

Fantasy trips or creative visualization work best in a small group. They can be done either as a one-off activity or at regular intervals for variety in a relaxation programme. The experience is like a planned, creative day-dream. An imaginary haven is created where people are able to relax. The fantasy can be described in detail or be just a guide.

Occasionally, people who are normally very controlled may be upset by this technique because buried feelings well up unexpectedly. As well, fantasy trips can reinforce retreat into hallucinations so they *must* be avoided with people who are actively psychotic or at high risk for psychoses. Monitor the effects with drug addicts too. In spite of its potential limitations, this relaxation technique works well for many people because it is easier to imagine being relaxed than to will it.

Method Talk about a scene, giving plenty of detail and describing it slowly enough for people to savour the experience. For example, 'Imagine you are lying on a comfortable couch by a fire listening to music' (describe the couch, the fire, the music, the room and the situation beyond). Or, describe a well-known walk, watching a seagull gliding over a millpond sea, lying on a warm beach, walking by a gently ripplng lake under autumnal trees . . . In a more abstract sphere, get people to imagine pastel colours or smooth, flowing shapes.

People could also imagine themselves as a river, a soaring bird or any similar image which appeals to them.

Another option is to have a group fantasy to music: people lie on the floor like the spokes of a wheel, heads towords the centre. One person starts describing what the music is saying to them, others speak at intervals. Choose music which all members of the group find soothing and restful.

At the end of the session bring everyone gently back to the present by saying something like, 'Lie (sit) for a few minutes and enjoy the feeling of relaxation as our session ends'. Reorient people to what they are going to do next.

Personal fantasy trip Each person in the group imagines a favourite place. Makes suggestions about the type of place (see above) and encourage people to bodily snuggle into their scene by asking questions to help them think of details. For example, 'Can you feel the sun, a breeze?', 'What colours are you enjoying?' Pause between questions.

To complete the experience get people to talk in pairs or threes about the place they imagined, what they saw, how it looked and how they felt. Tell everyone to let each person take their time, and to accept the day-dream at face value without trying to interpret it or find meaning in it.

7. Drama

Theatre games can give people practice at speaking and moving in a relaxed way. For example, tell people to act 'A relaxed group on the beach', 'A group who get on well together cooking a meal'. The role a person chooses can be near to a real life role they have (relaxed mother bathing her toddler) so that what they learn is more easily generalized to their everyday life.

Or, the role can be very different from the person's life roles but one in which relaxed confidence is easily conjured up as part of the character (cheerful oldfashioned cobbler, pianist playing a lullaby).

Relaxation techniques are, in turn, also useful in drama. They can help people get started when they are nervous about performing in front of others. Simplest to use in this context are breathing techniques, Jacobsen's progressive relaxation (speed technique), and positive imagination (picturing oneself as relaxed and successful).

8. Meditation

The concepts of meditation are more familiar nowadays but still have mystical overtones for many people. Explain to people that meditation is a way of clearing the mind and soothing inner turmoil through quiet, relaxed concentration. It is calming and establishes a deep sense of relaxation. It is a state of mind rather than an active process. Meditation is easy to learn and the benefits improve with practice. It encourages people to be positive, optimistic, interested and serene, all good goals for life. Ideally, meditation should be done for fifteen minutes each day.

When meditation is a familiar routine it can be used as a way of withdrawing from stressful situations, a period of 'time out', so that the person can deal with the stressor later in a calmer frame of mind. Or, when the person feels more relaxed, the situation may no longer seem as stressful anyway.

A limitation to meditation methods is that they are time consuming and people must be able to withdraw from circulation to do them.

The key factor in meditation is attention. In each type there is something to focus on: a thought, a sensation, a sound, a sight.

Two types of meditation are described here, transcendental meditation and contemplation. In both cases a quiet environment, a comfortable, relaxed position, a passive attitude and an object to dwell on are essential. Meditation should be done an hour or more after food, in loose, comfortable clothing and sitting in a position which can be held for fifteen to twenty minutes. It is best if people sit because if they lie down they are likely to go to sleep.

First, people relax physically, scanning their bodies for tension and relaxing each part as fully as possible. Some will find it helps to work down the body, tensing then relaxing each part. Other movements which can help produce quick relaxation are shrugging the shoulders, rocking the head gently forward and back then side to side, shaking or wriggling limbs, taking a few deep breaths and swallowing just once to relax neck and jaw. Suggest people close their eyes, breathe through their noses and listen to their breath moving slowly and evenly in and out.

Attitude is a key to successful meditation. People must have a passive attitude of 'let it happen', a relaxed frame of mind. They must be unconcerned about how well they are doing at meditation. If their attention wanders suggest they notice the distraction in an unworried way then return to meditating.

At the end of the session people sit with their eyes closed for a minute or two, then sit on with their eyes open for a few moments longer before moving on to their next activity.

The main difference between transcendental meditation and contemplation is the focus of attention.

Transcendental meditation

Also called mantra meditation, transcendental meditation is said to be good for blood pressure problems and obsessional thoughts.

People concentrate on one word, thought, sound or musical phrase and repeat it to themselves slowly and quietly as they breathe out. Whatever the person focuses on is called a mantra (the word comes from rajah yoga, the yoga of meditation). Breathing should be normal and even to avoid hyperventilation (over-breathing).

Focusing attention consistently on only one thing, the mantra, has the effect of slowing body metabolism and relaxing the body, and this state is deepened with mental relaxation. Traditionally, the words people use are a secret and specially chosen for them by a yogi. However, many simple words work well and some that are often used are the sound 'om', or the words 'one' or 'relax'. People may choose to say the mantra aloud or aloud in their minds but should avoid whispering the mantra because this makes hyperventilating more likely. The word should either be said to last the length of each exhalation or to last over both an inhalation and exhalation.

A variation of traditional transcendental meditation is for an instructor, working with one person or a small group, to aid the process of meditation by making statements encouraging concentration every twenty to forty seconds. At first strong tension is encouraged followed by letting go. Gradually, through the session, people are just reminded of the way releasing tension feels. For example, early in the session you might say, 'Grip your fist hard — let the tension go' and later, 'Feel just a tiny amount of tension in your fist, let go, relax.' And later still, 'Remember how the tension felt when you were letting go.'

Go through each area of the body, with regular pauses: 'Check your hands . . . say "relax" to them', 'Check your torso, say "relax"'. Each part of the body is searched in turn for tension spots then relaxed. You may want to prepare a list of things to say beforehand.

Contemplation

In contemplation people focus their attention on an object. The object helps them to refocus their thoughts when they are distracted. Possible objects are a picture, a round stone, a marble, a twig. The object is held or placed at arm's length.

Alternatively people can choose a mental image of something moving like drips of water falling steadily, bubbles rising in a pool or a candle flame. Their eyes should be open but unfocused as they picture the object.

9. Self-hypnosis techniques

There are two techniques of self-hypnosis. They are both quick, easy ways to relax and share some features in common with meditation. They work well for minor physical problems and, with practice, for major ones as well. They are good for relieving tension and anxiety. For many people, they are probably the best technique to use for visits to the dentist, childbirth or other situations in which physical endurance is called for. They are also useful for helping people persist in a sports activity when they are tired. Self-hypnosis is best taught in two or three sessions close together.

Self-hypnosis occurs naturally when people are intensely involved in what they are doing. An example of this is the sports competitor who ignores an injury, or the absorbed bookworm who does not hear the dinner bell. Hypnosis is a state in which people's consciousness is limited to a very narrow awareness, a controlled absentmindedness. It should be easy for people to become fully alert again.

The technique of self-hypnosis should be avoided with people who are actively psychotic.

Self-hypnosis

In self-hypnosis two processes are involved. First, achieving and maintaining an altered state of consciousness which blocks out other thoughts, and second, making positive suggestions to oneself. Either aspect can be emphasized.

Method   The hypnotic state is reached by a similar method to that used in contemplation. People sit or lie in a comfortable position and close their eyes or look slightly above their normal line of vision without focusing. They try to feel drowsy, inert, passive, unmoving, with their limbs heavy and immobile, and their attention narrowed. They check that their breathing is deep, slow and even. Some people can switch to this state simply by narrowing their attention, relaxing and breathing deeply.

Another way to achieve a hypnotic state is to suggest people focus on one hand held at arm's length and bring it slowly towards them. When it touches their forehead they close their eyes. Repeat three times.

In this state of heightened receptiveness people make hypnotic suggestions to themselves. Effective suggestions are direct and positive and made for the immediate future rather than the present. For example, 'Straight after this session I'll be able to . . .', 'I can relax . . .' There should be no element of doubt in the suggestions. Get people to say 'can', 'will be able to' rather than 'will try', or 'must'. The sentences can be long, with the person talking their body and mind into a calm, steady state of hypnotic relaxation. The voice should be even, unhurried and each suggestion repeated several times.

End the session in a definite way by getting up and stretching.

Narrowed consciousness

Narrowed consciousness can be used:

- When people experience guilt, grief or worry and can take no action to change the situation.
- In pain management and in sport as a means of enduring discomfort.

The aim of the technique is to block out other thoughts. People focus hard on a distracter which will keep their mind fully occupied. They attempt to experience every detail of it. For example, they recite times tables steadily and loudly inside their head, picturing each number and sign without a break, or they recite a poem or sing a song, picturing the words or the scene described in detail. Some people find simply counting enough. Engrossing, detailed practical activity or rhythmic physical activity can also be used. Whatever is chosen, it must be carried out with determination and fast enough to block out other thoughts and maintain the hypnotic state.

An example of a situation in which it is used is when someone performs 'on automatic' to overcome pain or their nervousness. For example, a person giving a speech may focus on just one aspect of a situation, preferably the speech itself. Extraneous, painful or irrelevant information is blocked out of consciousness. Of course, this is undesirable if people need to think actively about the situation; taken too far it diminishes people's ability to problem-solve.

10. Systematic desensitization

This behavioural technique helps people face a problem step by step. With careful planning they work from the least stressful aspects of the problem to the most stressful using progressive relaxation and deep breathing.

Systematic desensitization is usually done by trained psychologists and for seriously disruptive problems people should consult a professional with experience in monitoring the pace of the desensitization and in breaking the problem into a workable progression of small steps.

However, if the problems are minor, people can do it for themselves or each other. First, help the person break the problem into steps (imagine the problem as a series of pictures or imagine describing it to a stranger in detail). Try to get about twenty steps listed in order of difficulty.

Write each step on a separate sheet of paper or card and describe it quite specifically. People, events and places should be given in enough detail to conjure up a mental picture of a situation so that the person can easily visualize it later on.

Method   The person takes the first card, visualizes the situation it describes and relaxes at the same time. When they find they can do this comfortably they go on to the next most difficult card, gradually working through to the hardest at a pace which is comfortable for them. Go too slowly rather than too fast.

People can use the cards on their own or have a friend or partner read out the situations. They should hold the mental picture of each scene for at least twenty seconds before going on to the next one. When working with a partner the person should give a signal to indicate if they feel unable to relax.

Reinforce people's success and make sure they move slowly and steadily through the steps. It is essential to avoid rushing or people will make no progress. They may even become panicky.

Next, people go through each card visualizing themselves actively coping with the situation described.

The final step is to seek out the stressful situation and cope with it in reality, again taking a gradual approach with plenty of support.

Physical Relaxation Techniques

1. Progressive relaxation, or Jacobsen's relaxation

This type of relaxation and control can be done in groups of up to thirty. It emphasizes relaxation of the voluntary skeletal muscles. As well as being a technique to use in its own right, there is a speed technique, described at the end of this section, which can be useful before other techniques such as meditation or systematic desensitization. For most people, progressive relaxation can be learnt in one or two weeks of daily sessions. A passive attitude of self-acceptance is needed.

People lie on their backs on a soft but firm surface. A light squab on the floor works well. People's arms should be curved loosely by their sides or resting on the top of their thighs. Some people need a low pillow under their head to be comfortable and others one under the thighs as well. Get people to close their eyes and breathe gently through their noses, emphasizing breaths out more than breaths in.

Method   In turn, each muscle group is contracted for five to seven seconds then relaxed for twenty to thirty seconds. The contraction and relaxation are repeated then the next body part is contracted and relaxed in the same way. Talk people through the steps. For example, 'Clench or tighten your calf muscles, (pause) feel the sensation, (pause) let the tension go, feel the relaxed weight of your legs'. This process is repeated for each part of the body. With some body parts muscles can be tensed in more than one way (lips, jaw, shoulder girdle). Do each in turn.

As people become experienced the instructions can be simplified. 'Tell your muscles to contract (clench, tighten)', 'Tell your muscles to relax'.

Start with hands and arms, go on to the head (forehead, face, back of the head, chin and neck), chest, stomach, lower back, buttocks, thighs, then calves and feet. Or start at the feet and work up to the scalp. With the forehead suggest people feel the smoothness of their relaxed forehead rather than its weight, and with the head suggest they press it back into the pillow instead of contracting or tightening any muscles. In progressive relaxation people identify the difference between a state of tension and a state of deep relaxation in each muscle group. When they want to relax quickly they recall the sensation of relaxation and perform it at will.

Tapes work well; people can make their own with a timing and sequence to suit themselves.

Speed relaxation When the process of progressive relaxation is familiar it can be simplified and done more rapidly. People can either contract then relax whole groups of muscles: head and shoulders, arms, torso, trunk, legs. Or they can let tension creep up gradually from their feet and through their whole body to a count of ten, then let the tension flow gradually out again.

2. Breathing for relaxation

This approach is good for generalized anxiety and specific times of tension such as sitting exams or giving a speech. It is also useful before other relaxation techniques. Breathing is one of the first things to change when people are under stress. Breath-holding, hyperventilation and shallow breathing are all likely to occur when people experience stress — they contribute to a sense of tension and can become habitual. Breathing exercises are designed to break habit cycles like these but they must be done carefully or they can actually worsen an abnormal breathing pattern. The aim is to achieve slow, deep, rhythmic breathing. Exhalations should be at least as long as inhalations — breathing problems often relate more to incomplete breathing out than shallow breathing in. Relaxation breathing is best done in a small group where it is easy to see each person.

Get people to lie on their backs with their knees up, stand 'straight and tall', or sit crosslegged or in some position which requires little physical effort. Some people find it helps to close their eyes and breathe through their nose. Stress the importance of following the instructions and not holding a breath for too long, or breathing too quickly.

Instructions for the exercises

- Place one hand on the abdomen and one on the chest and give a relaxing sigh. Try to send out all your tension with the breath. Feel the out and up movement of the diaphragm.
- Take a deep breath through the nose and fill the lungs from the bottom. Feel the shape of your lungs then breathe out slowly and quietly.
- Take deep breaths using each nostril in turn. There should be no pause between breathing in and breathing out.
- Count in and out breaths, or only the out breaths. Saying a one syllable word on each out breath links this exercise with meditation.
- Shrug your shoulders up as you breathe in, then lower and relax them as you breathe out.

- Tap your chest all over with your fingertips.

Repeat the instructions for each exercise three times at a slow even pace and without a pause. Practise the pace of instructions beforehand — judge the pace from your own breathing.

When people are more familiar with breathing exercises they can count through each routine or say a mantra to maintain concentration.

Other useful activities are feeling the diaphragm movements without expelling any air, giving a huge yawn, adding sounds to both inhalations and exhalations — mmm, uhh.

Mental images can increase the effectiveness of breathing exercises. People can imagine:

- Their breath coming from inside their whole body and their tensions flowing out with each breathing out.
- Their emotions being released with each breathing out.
- Light, white air flowing in and wastes flowing out.
- 'Being' their breath.

Breathing and circulation   Exercises to encourage deep breathing should be done at a steady, even pace. If standing, the feet should be flat on the floor and slightly apart for stability.

3. Physiological relaxation — Laura Mitchell's method

This popular relaxation method (Mitchell, *Simple Relaxation*) works well anywhere, in a car, at meetings and so on. It involves getting the body into a position of relaxation and is effective as a starting point for other relaxation techniques. It combines well with breathing techniques. For states of acute tension or anxiety it would need to be combined with techniques like self-hypnosis and thought stopping.

The principle underlying physiological relaxation is that it is difficult to remain tense when body postures of relaxation are adopted. The technique trains people to recognize positions of tension and correct them.

Method   To change posture people need to give their body definite orders in the general sequence: 'Move the position. Feel it. Stop. Feel the position.' Examples of orders are: 'Pull your shoulders down. Stop.' (Rather than 'Drop your shoulders'.) Then, 'Feel it.' (Consciously register the feeling of the position in the joints and skin rather than the muscles.)

Relax body parts starting with the arms, then the legs, chest (breathing), body, head, face. Once the method is learnt people often find that one key action (changing shoulder or leg positions, for example) can be used to relax the entire posture. This method should be practised in a number of positions: lying, sitting at a desk or sitting in an easy chair.

The key instructions

- To the body: 'Push your body into the support (mattress, chair). Feel the contact your body makes with the support. Stop pushing. Feel the position.'

- To shoulders and arms: 'Pull your shoulders towards your feet. Feel your neck as longer. Move your elbows out and open. Feel the weight of both your arms resting on the chair arms or pillows. Stretch your fingers out. Feel them long and stretched. Stop. Feel them rested and supported.'
- To legs: 'Turn your hips outwards. Stop. Move your knees until they are comfortable. Push your feet away gently, but keep them bent.'
- To breathing: 'Breathe low in your chest, through your nose if possible, with an easy rhythm. Expand the area above and in front of your waist.'
- To the head: 'Push your head into the support. Feel the support holding the weight of your head.' Face: 'Draw your chin downwards with mouth closed but teeth separated. Stop with a feeling of your jaw heavy, lips loose, teeth separate, tongue loose. Close your eyes by lowering your upper lids without tightening the muscles round your eyes. Enjoy the darkness.'
- To the forehead: 'Begin above your eyebrows and think of your skin being smoothed gently up to your hair, over the top of your head and down the back of your neck.'
- To face and body language: 'Get your face and body to say what you want to feel.'

People should return to full activity gradually. Get them to wait a minute before getting up, and then to stretch in all directions.

4. Exercise

Exercise has an important role in relaxation. It should be increased gradually and systematically.

Any kind of regular exercise which makes people breathe heavily and increases their heart rate will, over time, improve their ability to relax. To produce relaxation, exercise should be done for at least ten to twenty minutes. However, even three to five minutes at a warm-up level of deep breathing with most body parts fully stretched will help. When the main purpose of exercise is relaxation, stretching, flowing actions are good but vigorous exercise which really extends people within their level of fitness is even better, and will produce a positive mood and relaxed tiredness.

In yoga exercises, relaxation is a specific goal, with the exercises designed to calm and relax both mind and body. Dance and movement can also be used to produce a healthy state of relaxation. Choose music and imagery which suggest the type of movement you want.

For full relaxation, people's minds should be occupied as well as their muscles, or, the exercise should predominate so that there is very little thought other than about the exercise.

Complete relaxation can be produced at either end of the mental involvement continuum. Sports/exercise routines at the high end of the mental involvement continuum are yoga combined with meditation, tai chi and orienteering. Swimming and jogging are at the other end. When people swim or jog their minds can go into neutral — they either think very little or they go into a gentle reverie and thus are rested from anxieties. If worrying thoughts intrude, combine with 'Fantasy trip' p. 186 or meditation.

Action images for relaxation Be a rag doll; dance in the sun; float weightless; move to soothing music; waft in a cool breeze; shake each part of your body (except the head), gradually increasing the number of parts involved; rise onto your toes and stretch your arms up, then lower your arms and curl downwards, breathing out; act a huge yawn.

Posture Posture is important in relaxation. A basic aim is to ease upwards — tell people to imagine that they are suspended by their hair. The body should be straight and balanced, with the parts not in use relaxed.

5. Biofeedback

Using a biofeedback machine, people get information not normally available to them about their body and the effect they are having on it.

Biofeedback is time-consuming but gives people effective feedback on how successful they are at relaxing. It is done on an individual basis and is often used to combat hypertension. The idea is to bring some functions of the autonomic nervous system (heart rate, brain-wave activity, muscular tension, blood pressure) under voluntary control.

People using biofeedback need to understand how it works. The machine only gives information, it plays no active role in the treatment. The changes are brought about by the person him or herself, using relaxation techniques. The advantage of a biofeedback machine is that it helps people see the results of their efforts. It is often used when other approaches have been ineffective.

Regular opportunities to practise relaxing with the machine, and coaching and encouragement from the therapist will help people make the most of the technique. The therapist should demonstrate how the machine works and be involved in the person's progress, rather than leaving the person simply to the machine.

MASSAGE

Massage should be a pleasure to receive and a pleasure to give. From a therapeutic point of view, vigorous massage (Swedish massage) has a positive, enlivening effect on circulation, skin and muscle tone. It gets muscles stretched, toned and ready for action. It is also relaxing because muscular tension is reduced. With gentle massage, the primary effect is relaxation and a soothing sense of wellbeing. It also aids circulation. Both vigorous and gentle massage are valuable for people who have problems with body image and both are easy to learn.

In a sense, massage is a form of communication through touch. The person giving the massage (masseur or masseuse) tries to understand and respond to the needs and feelings of the person they are massaging. For the person receiving the massage, it is reassuring because it brings a feeling of being cared for — it is companionable.

In most situations it is essential to get approval for massage sessions from the person's physician or case supervisor. You may be advised to get patients/clients to sign a consent form. In occupational therapy, massage can be appropriate for groups being taught relaxation skills.

Contraindications, Precautions and Limitations

Physically, massage is contraindicated with most skin disorders (unless they are very mild) and when people have damaged or healing skin or bruises from whatever cause. Arthritic conditions call for only gentle kneading or stroking of unaffected parts of the body. When there is no active inflammation it can ease the stiffness of arthritic joints. With neurological disorders it is important to check what types of massage can be done without provoking undesirable reactions. Avoid the area of a tumour, thrombosis or phlebitis. If you have doubts about massage in relation to a physical condition check with a medical authority first.

People who have sexual problems or are obsessed with hygiene may dislike massage. It may be disturbing to people who have problems with identity (insecure adolescents, for example) or who are actively psychotic. As with other relaxation techniques, people may experience a welling up of buried feelings. Give them reassurance and support if this happens.

People who have experienced little touch may find massage hard to accept. If you are unsure, start very gradually. The shoulder girdle seems to be the area where massage is most readily accepted and it is also an area in which tensions are particularly obvious. With the very ill, foot massage may be a good place to start.

Practical Organization

The role of leader or masseur/se   The leader's role is to teach and demonstrate techniques.

Get people to work with a partner. When they are being massaged they can feel what works. When they are giving the massage, they can say what they find pleasant.

As a group activity   Massage should be learnt and done in small groups in which people have chosen to be. The members of the group need to feel comfortable with each other. Clarify how the session will be organized and set any ground rules you or group members feel to be necessary. Aim for a practical, matter-of-fact atmosphere. The way massage is introduced and explained dictates how it will be received.

Although talk is a distraction to massage and should be kept to a minimum, it is important for a learner masseur/se to ask for feedback on how much pressure to use, how long to continue in each area and so on. The person receiving the massage should be prepared to give feedback at intervals — it is very easy to enjoy the massage and say very little.

Clothing, oils Massage can be done effectively through loose, light clothing. On bare skin oil or fine talcum powder is often used, but as long as the masseur/se's hands are cool and dry, skin on skin massage is fine. Oil is most likely to be needed on feet and legs where skin is often dry. Take special care if skin is chapped or sensitive.

Any skin oils or lotions or vegetable oil with a pleasant odour will be satisfactory. Herbs or perfumes can be added to odourless oils — a 'fresh' perfume rather than a sweet one will be less cloying. The oil can be warmed by standing the container in hot water for a few minutes before beginning. It is a good idea to have two bottles of oil, one at the person's head and one at their feet. It is also sensible to put the bottle of oil in a bowl so that it is less likely to be knocked over. The masseur/se should use just enough oil to make hand movements flow smoothly.

Music Assess the music people enjoy — does it lend itself to massage? Music for massage should be chosen for its pace and the kind of images it conjures up. It should be used for variety in massage sessions, rather than as an automatic accompaniment. It should be a definite choice rather than 'background' music. The masseur/se should work actively with the rhythm and mood of the music.

Environment The room should be quiet and warm, with soft lighting. Make sure there are no distractions.

Advise the person receiving the massage to relax and close their eyes if they feel like it. They should not 'help' the person giving the massage.

How to Massage

The masseur/se should have everything ready before starting; all equipment assembled, fingernails trimmed, jewellery removed and hands washed. They should wear clothing that is easy to move round in.

The best stance for the masseur/se is feet apart, which gives a wide base of support. The masseur/se should always take the time to get into a physically comfortable position before they start.

They should then relax their hands — stretch them, shake them, get them warm.

Both speed and pressure can be varied considerably in massage. Pressure should be even and steady for each phase of the massage. The pressure and movement of massage should come more from the masseur/se's bodyweight and whole, rhythmic body movement than from their hand muscles.

The masseur/se should think about the underlying structure of the human body, where there is more and less soft tissue. The soft tissues are a kind of 'play dough' or clay to be kneaded and moulded with the fingertips, ball of the thumb, whole hand or heel of the hand; all parts of the hands can be used. The masseur/se should be intuitive and relaxed, but also alert.

Vigorous massage stimulates circulation. It is useful before taking part in a sport. If the aim is to promote a sense of wellbeing and relaxation, the masseur/se should use gentle, slow stroking and kneading. Both vigorous and gentle massage can be combined with deep breathing and imagery.

Movements to use Lidell (*The Book of Massage*) divides massage into four types or levels of action: gliding, percussion, medium depth and deep tissue. All parts of the hands can be used.

Gliding: rub (palms or fingertips in circular movements — small or broad circles), stroke (fingertips, generally in one direction only), feather lightly backwards and forwards, rub firmly (knuckles) and make long, firm or light 'connecting' strokes (palm of the hand down) the full length of arms or legs.

Percussion: slap/pat (palms down with hands flat or cupped), chop (using the edge of the hand), tap (fingertips), walk (using the fingertips as though they are legs).

Medium depth or deep tissue: knead, pummel, pluck, rub with more vigour or pressure. Movements can be wide or localized.

Work in a continuous sequence. It is important to cover whatever area is being massaged fully and not leave bits out. Work right to the ends of arms and legs.

Limbs can also be gently pulled and stretched or moved in different directions, however avoid forcing joint movement.

A shoulder massage The masseur/se places their hands over the person's shoulders and firmly kneads the centre, top and sides of the back with the balls of their thumbs.

Foot massage Oil is usually needed in foot massage because the skin on the feet tends to be dry.

An Asian theory holds that each area of the foot represents a different part of the body, meaning that work on the foot will benefit the whole body. The masseur/se starts by washing the person's feet in warm water, then applying oil or lotion. Next, they make a fist and use their knuckles to apply firm, even pressure to the bottom of the foot with small circular movements. They use their fingertips for the upper surface of the foot and the ankle, covering every part of the foot and circling round the ankle applying pressure several times. The lower end of the heel is massaged with fingers and thumb. Then they run their fingertips down the valleys between the tendons and squeeze the webs between the toes. Next, they hold each foot in the middle with hands on either side, and let the hands slip to the edge several times. Finally, the masseur/se holds each foot in turn, one hand on each side, and slides their hands off the person's toes.

Hand massage The masseur/se applies oil or handcream. They rub the back of each hand, and knead and rub each finger and the thumb. The fingers are pressed gently apart and then squeezed tightly together. Finally, the masseur/se kneads and strokes the wrists.

Self-head massage First people flex their hands together, then they move them over the whole surface of their face. All kinds of actions can be used: circular movements with the fingertips, gently pulling at the skin in different directions, kneading and tapping. People can run their fingertips through their hair and gently massage their ears and neck.

Self-massage In a group session, teach people how to work on the easily accessible parts of their body: feet, head, hands and forearms.

Massage for the elderly The masseur/se should use stroking, gentle kneading and quick, light tapping movements.

Pairs massage Concentrate on an easily accessible area — back, hands, feet, arms, shoulders/neck, lower leg, head. It is probably easiest to practise on arms and lower legs.

Group massage The person to be massaged lies on their stomach with their eyes closed. Show the group (two to four people) what to do next, co-ordinating the massage from the receiver's head by gesture (talking spoils the mood of the massage for the receiver). Work on each part of the body. Begin very gently so that the initial contact is not too sudden. The massage is best broken into twenty-second episodes with pauses between them. Each episode should be a little more vigorous than the one before, and then become more gentle towards the end. Everyone tries to massage in the same way with the same strength.

Other forms of massage Roll a tennis ball over any muscular part of the body, roll a golf ball under the feet. Brush the body with soft dry fabric.

PART II
The Group Setting

1 | *Working in Groups*

In groups people experience life. They adapt, succeed or fail, are productive or unproductive. Needs for companionship, love and belonging and esteem are met, or not met. A therapist who knows how groups work can organize or change them to meet therapeutic goals. Many of the ideas presented here are as relevant to one-to-one work as they are to group work.

To participate in a group people need to be able to focus on a task with others present for ten or more minutes, to have some idea of the purpose of the group and to have basic communication skills.

The Therapeutic Values and Limitations of Group Work

There are many social advantages to doing activities in groups. Compared to one-to-one work there is a range of relationships and a bigger pool of skills and ideas to share. There are opportunities to develop social skills, self-awareness and to try new roles. People learn how to take the lead or act as a team member.

People who find one-to-one work threatening may be more comfortable working in a group, especially one that is low key and activity-based. Conversely, others may find the close relationship of an insight-oriented group threatening, or have difficulty relating to a large number of people at once.

Each group will offer a variety of role models. People may come to see themselves more clearly, through other people's reactions to them. In this sense, people 'show' each other the choices, limitations and resources in their lives. They see that others have similar concerns and difficulties to themselves and they can give one another support.

A drawback to group work is that the members get less individual attention and privacy and confidentiality cannot be guaranteed. People who have few, or poor, group skills will have difficulty contributing to the group or getting much out of it for themselves.

Another drawback is that problems can get overshadowed or magnified by the group, relationships may go to extremes and a group may be at the wrong level for some members. Sometimes groups give too much 'free

advice', rather than providing a forum for sharing and exploring feelings.

People come to a group in different moods, some enthusiastic, others tired and dispirited. Of course, when people choose to join a group, they come with an expectation that it will meet some of their needs. At some level they have already identified goals they have in common with the group. Problems are likely to occur if everyone in the group has different goals. People who have been directed to join a group may be reluctant to attend and their personal goals may be very different from the group's goals.

If people in a group are very dissimilar it is difficult to lead the group. On the other hand, a group of people who are very similar in outlook and abilities may not be able to provide each other with a range of points of view. If the people in a group are vulnerable for any reason (suspicious, physically unwell, withdrawn, depressed), it is more sensible to work on a one-to-one basis, at least initially.

For the therapist, positive aspects of group work are that people are less dependent on them and groups are usually economical in terms of time. On the other hand, group sessions are often more complex to organize and run than one-to-one activities and the demands on resources, such as space and so on, are greater.

There are limitations to group work but the support provided by other people can be very helpful. The stimulus of competition can be important and people usually come to enjoy each other's company.

Cohesiveness: Building Group Relationships

Cohesiveness refers to the bonds and relationships which enable a collection of people to function as a group. It is that sense of belonging which stems from shared concerns and it is a key factor in how well a group works.

In a cohesive group, people are comfortable sharing ideas and feelings and trying out new approaches. They can listen to each other, disagree, work together, encourage each other and be themselves. A cohesive group will accomplish a great deal more than a group that is fragmented.

Cohesive groups always share certain goals and needs. As well as this, cohesiveness in a group depends on:

- The similarity of the people in the group.
- How well the people know each other and how much time they spend together.
- The way the group is planned and started.
- The way goals are set.
- Personalities and alliances.
- The ground rules of the group.
- Turnover of membership.
- The size of the group.
- Leadership style and group maturity.
  These will be discussed in turn.

Similarity Groups of people are similar or dissimilar in age, sex, cultural background, medical condition and so on. Similarity makes it easier for people to understand each other.

It is important to be selective about the composition of groups and ready to bridge differences when dissimilarities cause problems in understanding.

Ideally, groups learning new skills should be fairly similar in their need or desire to learn what is being taught. When people are very dissimilar in their capacity to learn the therapist's task is much more difficult.

However, similarity can be unimportant and even be a disadvantage. Dissimilar people offer each other a wider range of views and opinions, and represent the cross-section of society more accurately.

Getting to know each other/time spent together Make sure people know each other's names and a bit about each other. Time spent together generally increases liking unless there is a reason for antagonism to develop. Meet frequently!

Starting a group The initial session of a new group sets the tone of the group so work out the kind of atmosphere you want and steer the group towards it.
- Discuss the choice of goals.
- Discuss the choice of activities and the style of the group.
- Point out things people have in common and emphasize similarities.
- Encourage camaraderie, mutual respect and good working relationships.
- Stress the importance of confidentiality.
- Role model by relating to each person in a positive way. Give people an equal share of your attention and take them seriously.
- Outline ground rules for sessions in a positive, matter-of-fact way.

Although you provide conditions in which a high level of trust and cohesiveness is likely to develop, a particular group climate cannot be forced or guaranteed.

Goal setting   As far as possible group members should choose their own goals. These goals need to be relevant, challenging, realistic and understood by the group.

To help a group set realistic goals review common needs in the group. What therapeutic activities will be useful to them and accepted by them? The answers lie in the reasons each person is in a treatment relationship, and in their shared values, sociocultural background, roles and abilities. Age range and gender are also significant.

Goal setting with the group gives people the opportunity to consider what they hope to get out of the group and where their goals and the group's overlap and differ. Encourage people to negotiate to bring their goals as close together as possible. Shared goals will aid cohesiveness. However, if goals are held too rigidly they may limit people's ability to solve problems as situations change.

With groups which function at a more immature level, the therapist may have to select goals, explain their relevance, then encourage people to get on with the tasks and activities designed to achieve them. People need to be given as much choice as they can handle. For example, the therapist might say, 'Tomorrow it's cooking and we're going to make lunch together. What do you want to eat for lunch, Donna?', 'Mary?' or 'Today we're going to have some fun. We're going to . . .' In this way the therapist makes the most of choices, and goal setting is simplified to what is realistic. A relaxed, playful atmosphere will encourage participation and allow people to gain skills and confidence.

Broad, long-term goals are reached through short-term sub-goals set for each activity session. There is scope for flexibility; the therapist monitors progress and will modify goals where appropriate.

Personalities and alliances   Any friendships and alliances that form will affect the way the group works. Be alert to these social processes. Support trends that are positive but intervene if they are destructive to the group.

People participate in groups in different ways. Examples of positive participation are offering new ideas, asking questions, taking the lead, encouraging others, holding back when appropriate, letting others shine, offering to do chores, taking the activity seriously. Examples of poor participation are attention seeking, under- or over-contributing or sabotaging the group in some way. In general, the more mature the level of the group, the more varied will be the ways people participate — they will take more roles. When you want to improve the overall quality of a group's performance, help people extend the ways in which they participate. Explain the roles people can try and teach them the skills involved.

Setting ground rules   There are always ground rules and expectations in a group. If they are clear, people feel secure; they know what is going on and where they stand. In cohesive groups the rules will be consistent and well accepted, while in a group where there is little cohesion the opposite will be the case.

Some group rules are obvious, others are not. The therapist and group establish the ground rules but there will be other more subtle expectations which people have of each other, and these can also act as 'rules' for the group. Discuss these expectations and if possible bring them into the open but be cautious about challenging people's hidden agendas too directly; their sense of autonomy may depend on them.

Written or verbal contracts are one way in which the therapist can set or clarify expectations. Each person agrees to act in certain ways (for example, to attend, be punctual, share chores, respect confidentiality, not smoke and so on). A written contract signed by each person is a way of negotiating a stronger commitment to the group and its goals. Contracts can be designed to protect and help the group as a unit, or to help individuals make the most of their opportunities in the group.

Turnover of membership   When should groups have a fixed membership? When can the membership change freely? The answers depend on the kind of group and its level of maturity and cohesiveness.

In a 'closed' group, the membership is established when the group is set up and no one else joins after that point. In 'open' groups new people can join at any stage, and in a 'slow open' group membership changes gradually. Each arrangement has advantages and disadvantages.

Closed groups usually run for a defined length of time. For example, a group may be made up of six people, run for six weeks and be established to teach basic assertiveness skills, relaxation techniques or budgeting. The arrangement allows the therapist to plan a course which forms a logical whole and has realistic sub-goals for the time available. If people joined the group half way through they would find it hard to follow what was happening and could hold the group up.

A time-limited closed group also allows the therapist to reconvene the groups in a new form at a later date with a new set of expectations and goals. Closed groups can be very cohesive over the period they operate.

In groups where each session is complete in itself, membership changes will be unimportant to the main goals of the group. However, some peripheral benefits will be lost. Generally, relationships will be more superficial and the therapist will need to be more directive, regardless of the abilities of the group members. It is important to aim for cohesiveness within the length of the session at least.

'Slow open' groups have an important advantage — existing members socialize new members. Such groups work well when there is a set amount of material to be covered in a limited time because, like closed groups, there is little waiting time for new members to catch up. And again, like closed groups, they work well when the emotional depth of the relation-ships in the group is important. A sense of group confidentiality can be maintained by the way the therapist introduces new members to the group. If possible, get group members to share in explaining the group's rules, goals and activities to new members.

Group size   It is usually easier for small groups to be cohesive than large; people get to know one another quickly and the therapist can build a relationship with each person. It is also easier to express feelings, try out ideas and take risks.

For insight-oriented groups, where cohesiveness is particularly import-ant, seven is said to be the ideal number. It may be practical to begin with one or two more than that so that the group will still be viable even if some people drop out at an early stage.

In large groups it is harder to generate supportive relationships and to make sure that everyone's views are heard. It is likely that some people's participation will be limited or that sub-groups will form.

With large groups it is often practical to start with the whole group together then divide it into sub-groups. Plan topics/activities which enable people to share skills and knowledge easily.

Sub-groups can all work on the same task or on different but related tasks. Indicate how long the groups have for their task and how their results and experiences will be shared. To avoid excessive repetition, when a large number of sub-groups have been set the same task, ask only a proportion of the groups to give feedback when the task is completed. Ask the other groups if they have additional comments to those already covered.

Dividing into sub-groups   If people are asked to form groups they are likely to choose others whose functioning is at a similar level to their own, and/or people who they already know and like.

If a more random mixing seems a good idea, number people off around the group. Count the group beforehand and work out how many sub-groups you need. For example, say three groups are needed, the therapist counts 'one', 'two', 'three', 'one', 'two' . . . and when the counting is com-plete all the ones go to one area, all the twos to another and so on. If you want to be sure that a sub-group within the larger group (for example, a group of staff or children) is mixed evenly through the sub-groups, number these people off first.

Factors that work against cohesiveness   External pressures on the group, such as unfavourable comments from care givers, staff or friends, expense, and commitments and interests that compete for time, are likely to reduce group cohesiveness. Cohesiveness will also suffer when goals and expec-tations within a group differ.

Cohesiveness can also depend on the social status of the group, 'high' status groups being more cohesive than 'low' status groups. Success will maintain or improve a group's status. (In 'high' status groups members have chosen to belong and the group engages in activities regarded as prestigious in the social setting.)

Leadership Style

Expertise in leading groups comes from understanding the principles of group management and from coupling this knowledge with experience. Theoretical information cues therapists in to what to observe in groups and enables them to respond to events while the group is in progress. It alerts them to their management choices.

Confidence as a therapist starts with careful planning. Planning cannot guarantee success but it gives a sense of assurance and increases the likelihood of handling difficulties well.

What are the therapist's responsibilities as leader? Does the group need a leader who is directive? One who facilitates democratic decision making? One who supports a natural evolution or separation of the group according to the members' needs? A co-member? A resource? A teacher? Demonstrator? Co-ordinator? Advocate? Role model? The roles and responsibilities of the leader must match the level of function of the group, the kind of task it is engaged in, the time available and the demands of continuity.

Generally, the leader plays a key part in setting rules and goals, choosing activities and establishing a suitable working relationship within the group. The leader will also have responsibilities outside the group situation, such as recording results for ongoing planning, report writing and liaison with other staff and agencies.

A liaison responsibility involves explaining the group to others; its goals, and the methods and activities being used to reach them. Outsiders may also want information about how success is measured and the group evaluated, and about entry and discharge criteria.

When a therapist and co-therapist are involved, they can share responsibility for the group, stimulate ideas in each other and cross-check perceptions of people, material covered and activities. Plan who will do what with care to make the best use possible of having two people. In small groups co-therapists should sit apart to avoid an 'us/them' feeling. It is often practical to have one person focusing on the activity the group is engaged in and the other on the relationships in the group.

Two key orientations Key overlapping orientations for leaders in any group are:
- A task orientation; keeping the group focused on their goals and the tasks, methods and activities they can use to reach them.
- A relationship orientation; maintaining the group as a cohesive unit.

A task orientation requires the therapist to arrange activities, teach skills, get people started, demonstrate tasks/activities, cajole people to greater effort and help anyone who gets stuck.

Therapists in a task-oriented group often need to be definite and decisive in order to get information across in the time available and enable the group to accomplish their task.

A task orientation is important when groups are immature, newly formed or have only a limited time to accomplish a definite task. In these kinds of groups, the therapist should choose activities that are easily structured and expect to do most of the decision making. Choice and ambiguity need to be reduced to a minimum.

A task orientation is more obvious with concrete activities like pottery or gardening but it is also important in insight-oriented groups and should not be underestimated or ignored.

When working from a relationship orientation, the therapist helps people to understand one other and balances contributions so that everyone is involved and no one person dominates. The therapist links one contribution to another and to the group's goals. He or she supports people when they take risks and try new things, offers reassurance if needed and reinforces people's strengths. The therapist also helps others to learn leadership skills.

In a relationship orientation therapists need to treat members as equals; that is, they need to be obviously fair and consistent, in order to make people feel accepted. They need to take a nurturing role and promote interpersonal skills.

The task and relationship orientations are a useful dichotomy for structuring observation; what roles do people take that contribute to each orientation? Examples of task orientation roles are contributing practical ideas, asking factual questions, organizing things, co-ordinating people's efforts. Examples of relationship orientation roles are giving encouragement, being willing to compromise, listening attentively, taking an interest in others, disagreeing in a way that is tolerant of others' feelings.

Group maturity   Leading mature and immature groups is very different. The range of activities that can be done in a mature group, and their quality, is better. A therapist who understands the characteristics of mature and immature groups can guide a group towards its optimum level of functioning.

A mature group can plan its own structure, activities and ground rules, as well as set its own long- and short-term goals. The importance of the group as a unit is recognized. The potential for cohesiveness is greater in mature groups — although maturity and a high level of cohesiveness do not necessarily coincide. Leadership is shared according to people's skills and knowledge and most people are able to take a variety of roles. They will be able to lead, question, suggest ideas and so on. There is a good balance between getting a task done and responding to others' ideas and needs. Improving people's ability to contribute to a mature group is often a goal of therapy. People who can function in a mature group can function in a wide range of work and leisure groups.

Group maturity depends on several factors:
- How recently the group has been formed. Newly formed groups are usually immature and quite formal and, even if the group is capable of mature functioning, the members let the therapist do the leading. There is a limited emphasis on listening to others and on concern about the group as a unit. Compromise is infrequent and there is limited cooperation. However, when a group is made up of people accustomed to working in mature groups the group's progress towards maturity can be very rapid.
- How task-oriented and time-limited the group is. In task-oriented groups the focus is on getting a job done rather than on the relationships within the group.
- Age. Groups need to be more structured and more task-oriented for young people because they have limited group skills and experience.
- Intellectual ability and knowledge. The level of maturity possible for a group is partly dependent on each member's intelligence, skills and knowledge relevant to the goals of the group.
- Nearness to the end of the group as a unit. When a group is drawing to an end and is in the process of separating, it becomes less mature.
- Psychiatric or physical condition. Chronic psychiatric patients or people who are preoccupied with a new physical disability may be unable to take the overview necessary for functioning in a mature group.

With an immature group the therapist organizes activities, plans sessions in detail, regulates behaviour if necessary and sets a tone and climate that will work. He or she role models desirable attitudes towards people in the group and towards the activities.

The therapist must be directive and, because the group has limited skills, sessions and activities need to be structured. Both the relationship and task aspects of the group can be structured.

Structure helps people know what is going on. Even in mature groups, it is important to have some structure so people know who is doing what, when and where. On the other hand, when there is too much structure it is difficult for a group to become more mature. Limited scope for creativity can also lead to disruptive behaviour.

When people are capable of functioning at a mature level and the goals of the group are obvious to them, they will be able to move from a situation where most of the interaction is suggested by the therapist, to one where they cooperatively share all the tasks of the group.

Growth in maturity also depends on what the therapist emphasizes. Wherever possible, encourage people to take new roles and decrease structure and encourage autonomy. Ways to encourage less dependence on the therapist include throwing questions back to the group, 'I'd like to hear what someone else has to say about that', or waiting for people in the group to answer. A useful ploy is to avoid eye contact with any one person.

Therapist participation As therapist how much can you participate? If the activity is very structured you may not be able to join in because of the amount of help people need, however, as long as leadership responsibilities and therapeutic roles are maintained you can be part of the group. In mature groups, especially insight-oriented groups, therapists usually take part in activities in order to experience them first-hand with the group.

In mature groups goals are more likely to be open-ended. The therapist is often a group member and resource person with particular skills to offer and a few responsibilities as the designated leader. Such responsibilities may include negotiating with other staff members or agencies, monitoring therapeutic goals and ensuring that someone takes the initiative when problem solving is needed. Maintaining at least a minimum structure or established format is important even with mature groups.

Therapists with a personal need to remain dominant limit the potential maturity of the groups they lead. Like group members, therapists can have personal needs. Know yourself as a leader – 'stand back' from your role occasionally and assess what needs the group is meeting for you. Recognize the difficulties of being needed less as the group matures.

The Stages of a Group Session

The warm up

A warm up gets everyone acquainted, in tune with each other, aware of their common goals and committed to the session. It generates a sense of momentum. (See p. 42 and p. 54 for more information on the purpose of warm ups and for activity ideas.)

- Recognize the variety of moods people are likely to be in when they arrive. People who have just come from a stimulating discussion, a large lunch or the hassles of parking in the rain will be in quite different frames of mind.
- Greet people by name and begin with welcomes and introductions. Introductions can be handled in many ways; the therapist can introduce each person or get everyone to say their own name and perhaps a bit about themselves. One advantage of people saying their own names is that they experience speaking in the group and, as a result, are more likely to speak up again later. Name tags or an activity can also help people introduce themselves.
- What do people need to know or be reminded of at the begining of the session? Deal with any questions and check people's preconceptions about the group.
- Sometimes it is important to check if people have any unfinished or future tasks which will take their minds off the session. If the length of a session is not fixed, establish how much time people can spend or expect to spend at the session.
- Plan how much you will say about yourself, your background and your role in the group when you introduce yourself.

- When you introduce yourself clarify the way you plan to run the session and what you expect of the group. Making brief eye contact with each person helps people feel included and so does a personal word at some stage during the session.
- Check whether people are comfortable and whether they can see and hear adequately.
- Establish or review the broad goals of the group and the specific goals for the session. With a mature group this discussion can be comprehensive. With a dependent, immature group it is usually better to keep the orientation to the session brief.
- In subsequent sessions, link one session with another by reminding people what they did or learnt in previous sessions and how this relates to plans for the current session.
- Establish some sort of timetable.
- Explain methods of working and the use of tools and materials.
- When people know one another and the activity is familiar, the warm up can often be reduced to greetings and the practicalities of getting started.

The body of the session

Some activities have very obvious natural stages (arts, crafts). With others (drama, discussion) plan for breaks in the session. Plan a number of linked activities which form a varied, balanced whole.

- Explain activities and concepts using short sentences and simple words. Leaving out the niceties of polite conversation ('Would everyone like to . . .') will make instructions clearer. Start with verbs ('Go to the . . .', 'Sit by . . .', 'Ask . . .').
- Give concrete, specific information. Say 'We're cooking chops and potatoes' rather than 'We're going to cook' and change 'We'll role play' to 'We'll act out John's job interview'.
- Encourage questions and comments but try to start on the activity without too much delay. If people are stalling ask yourself why. Explain the value of the activity briefly and confidently, expect everyone to give it a go and judge it afterwards. A tentative request invites refusal; when you lead activities and role plays be definite and direct – keep the activity moving. (There are limits to this of course – sometimes there will be a problem with the activity, or within the group, that you are unaware of or have overlooked.)
- One easy way to create a break in a session is to get people to collect their own equipment. It mobilizes people and is an act of participation.
- In insight-oriented groups 'go round' the group at intervals and get each person to give their ideas or opinion. Start at a different point in the circle each time, use open-ended questions and decide how pressing you will be if people want to 'pass'. Brief questions of the 'Do you agree?' type are useful when people are likely to have difficulty elaborating or there is little time. Give people non-verbal encouragement to speak (a nod, smile, expectant look).
- Pose questions at random so that people stay alert.

Potential problems and how to avoid them

Anticipation is the key to avoiding problems. If problems are major (inappropriate referrals, an inadequate venue, lack of support from other staff or faulty equipment) it may be necessary to consider whether the group or session is viable at all.

- Sound assessment is essential; will everyone benefit from the session? Will they be able to do the activity? Will they participate?
- How much warm-up time is needed? Too little and people will not be really in tune with the session, too much and they will begin to feel impatient or bored.
- Do you have enough time, assistance, space, materials, tools? Alternative material or activities to fall back on?
- Establish ground rules about confidentiality and explain how difficulties will be handled.
- Observe people's body language so that you are alert and sensitive to early signs of frustration, changes of mood or individual problems.
- People can have difficulty understanding information or doing an activity for many reasons; lack of perception of relevance, lack of skill or confidence or because of the painful feelings the activity generates. Acknowledge people's feelings. In practical activities, offer help to get people started or limit choices. Be aware of your options throughout the session and have alternatives ready if the session is not working.
- Groups can be overactive. Some groups can tolerate less stimulation than others (people with schizophrenia, children). In such cases, increase the structure of the session.
- The reverse, under-stimulation, leads to boredom. The signs are obvious – wriggling, sitting back from the group, sighing, talking. Try to increase active involvement with questions, or by changing from a whole group format to pairs or small group work or by introducing a physical activity. Check people's perceptions of the relevance of the material and activities. There must be enough variety to keep people interested, but not so much that the session becomes disorganized and confusing. Plan a balance of active/quiet, hard/easy, familiar/new elements. Again, increase the amount of structure overall but offer more alternatives within the different stages of the session.
- If someone asks a 'Why' question in an insight-oriented group ask them for their views on the subject. 'Why' questions are often a sign that the person wants to put their view, not that they want to hear reasons.
- In practical activities make sure people can manage the task and judge their willingness to attempt it. (For written activities check that everyone can read and write). Plan an activity for people who finish the task early.
- People's contributions in a group can be very uneven. Observe the group's participation patterns – who speaks to who and how often? What can you do to include those who are on the fringe of the group

and to make sure that those who contribute most actively do not dominate?

If someone does dominate indicate as early as possible in the session that you plan to make sure everyone has an equal turn. Look at the person and raise your hand just a few centimetres – or a finger to the lips as a reminder of this rule. With a very quiet group member, make eye contact and ask him or her a simple question that requires only a yes or no answer. This gives the person an easy opportunity to contribute.

- Set clear ground rules the first time the group meets or at the beginning of the session. Issues which therapists often make rules about (that is, clarify their expectations about) are talking, smoking, the time plan, cleaning up, confidentiality, materials, tools, punctuality, attendance and participation.
- Role model the attitudes and behaviours you want.
- If people do not keep to the rules restate them in general terms so that offenders do not feel 'picked on'. Say how the problem affects you using 'I' rather than 'You' at the beginning of your statement. Be matter-of-fact and definite about what needs to happen to put matters right. Do it straightaway. You might say 'What we need to do now is . . . ' 'We could do . . . or . . . Which would be easier?'
- If arguments arise, be goal directed. (Say, for example, 'We're here to do . . . We need to move on . . . ' or 'We'll discuss that later. Right now we'll . . .'.) Options include breaking into sub-groups, physically regrouping people or helping the person to express his or her ideas more positively.

  If one person verbally attacks another interrupt firmly.

- When people refuse to do an activity, simply do not do it, do a token amount or act in ways that are unhelpful (clown around, make critical remarks) you have a number of options:
  a. Confront the person directly about his or her behaviour. Say what you feel (that it is inappropriate, prevents others doing the activity etc).
  b. Ask the group how they feel about the behaviour and if possible get them to comment on it in turn.
  c. If the whole group is reluctant, stop the activity and do something else.
  d. Get another staff member to work with the person who is causing the problem.
  e. Ask the person to leave the group and arrange to see him or her at another time.
  f. Ask the person if he or she is willing to try again.
  g. Ask the person if there are any simple changes that could be made to make it easier for them to participate, or ask 'What help do you need?'
  h. Restate the purpose and ground rules of the group.

Reinforce attitudes and actions that are positive for the group. Do not persist if the problem is major.

- Sometimes it is appropriate to ask the group for suggestions when difficulties arise. The way a group is asked can make a difference to the answers. When you are interrupted, for example, you might ask 'Is there a way we can go on with this?', rather than the less optimistic 'Do you think we'll have to abandon this?'

- When there are other staff members or visitors in the group who have not been involved in the planning stage, give a very brief outline of the purpose, and perhaps history, of the group. A sentence or two is usually enough. Clarify the role you would like them to take. Do you want them to observe, participate, assist, co-lead or what? Try to establish a relationship that will be useful to you and them.

- With any problem an approach that often helps is to describe what you see out loud, then say what you think about it. This helps you (and the group) clarify what you are thinking. For example, 'No one is contributing and I don't know why'. 'You all seem angry about . . . and I'm worrying about how little time we have to resolve the issue.'

- Violence: if violence is a potential problem be constantly observant. Avoid a build up of frustration. Be aware of likely triggers to strong emotion and keep people who are antagonistic to each other apart as much as possible. Include everyone in discussions so that overly suspicious people are well informed. Be aware too, of potential weapons in the setting. Avoid being in a position where it is physically difficult to get to the door or a phone. Arrange to have a co-therapist or some system of support available.

  Deal with early signs of aggression by restating rules in a definite, matter-of-fact way. Reassure and offer support without invading the person's need to keep a distance. People who are aggressive are often feeling vulnerable.

Ending a session

At the end of a session link what has happened together and round the session off. Sometimes the conclusion only needs to be brief, especially if there is a natural end to the activity. A little while before the end remind people how much time is left so that they have time to finish what they are doing.

It is difficult to end a session well if people finish at different times. One way of dealing with this is to say at the beginning, 'Everyone will finish at different times so I'll remind you now about . . . (cleaning up, future plans).' Suggest something people might do if they finish before others.

If there is an end product to the activity it may be important for people to compare and discuss their results.

For the last part of a session have the whole group together if possible. An ending activity, like the warm up, should be something that is likely to be easy and successful so that the session finishes on a positive note.

Ideally, the ending should involve everyone, summarise what has been done, indicate future activities, pull people's ideas together and generate a sense of cohesiveness.

Resolve any issues or problems. If anyone has been upset, check how they feel and offer, or plan, support if it is needed.

Plan what you want to discuss at the end of the session but be ready to use what comes up too. Review the goals of the session. Were they achieved? What comes next?

Allow time for questions and feedback. If time is very limited and you want everyone to contribute invite people to 'Say one word to sum up how you feel about the session/activity.'

In insight-oriented activities discuss the personal relevance of the session to each individual. How can what was learnt be used? How can learning be reinforced? Are there any tasks which could build on what was learnt and prepare people for the next session?

If there is a silence avoid speaking too quickly – let people have time to frame what they want to say.

When you comment on how you experienced the session begin with statements concerning your own feelings rather than speaking up for the group. Use 'I' instead of 'We'. You can never be sure the group felt as you did, even when it seems likely. Describe the accomplishments of the session as you see them and let others speak for themselves.

Endings should be brief. If they are too long they form part of the session. Stand up and move towards the door or start putting things away if it is difficult to get people to stop.

Remind people when and where they will meet again and deal with any transport problems. If relevant, remind people about what they are going to do next and of any tasks you or they have agreed to accomplish by that time.

If necessary sort, clean or return equipment. Label end products and file them. Review the session with a co-therapist and write record notes.

Issues and Relationships

Feedback for therapists To develop their skills therapists need to hear how others experience their sessions.

The timing and the way feedback is asked for makes a difference to people's responses. Of course people sometimes tell all regardless but, to limit the amount of feedback and to ensure that it is positive, a therapist might ask 'What did you enjoy most in this session?' or 'What was the most useful part of that activity?'

'What did you get out of that?' still invites positive feedback but is more open-ended.

'If I was to change one thing about this activity what should I alter?' invites a limited amount of constructive criticism.

'Can you think of variations on that activity?' and 'Is it worth repeating?' may also be relevant questions.

Decide what you can cope with before you ask!

When a normal social situation is being replicated, for example, a dance, feedback at the time is inappropriate.

Feedback and praise   The feedback you give to others should follow some well tried ground rules if it is to be useful. Effective feedback needs to come soon after the event. It should be simple, easily understood and generally brief. It should also be consciously non-judgmental. This is usually achieved by stating your own feelings — beginning with 'I' rather than 'You'. Decide on the amount of feedback the person or group is able to hear and cope with. Make it specific rather than global and about things that can be changed. It should be about an event or concrete result rather than personality. Often it should include checking the accuracy of your perception with the person or group. Overall, it must have the obvious intention of being helpful and show caring and concern. It should be sensitive to the goals of the person or group.

Therapists give praise to encourage people. To be effective, praise, like feedback, should be of efforts and accomplishments rather than personality. It should be given promptly and be obviously sincere. As with feedback, it should be as specific as possible so that the person knows exactly what you liked. Praise allows people to make positive inferences about themselves and their abilities.

It is important to recognize that the feedback people get naturally from what they do is also very powerful.

Learning new roles   Group membership skills can be taught. Suggest people take a more active role, talk directly to others, be interested in and curious about others and express their ideas spontaneously. Give people leadership tasks or other definite new roles which give them opportunities to expand their skills.

To evaluate a group and its members' participation skills make a record of interaction patterns in the group, that is, note who speaks to who over a set period. Aspects of the quality of the interaction can be recorded too. Note how many comments were connected with the maintenance of the group and how many with the task of the group. Set the group a task and observe how the group accomplishes it.

Ideas for discussion directed towards group processes are: 'Cohesiveness and disruption in groups', 'Sabotage and support', 'Leadership styles and their short- and long-term effects'.

Emotional Issues

How do you control the emotional impact of activities? With practical activities this is rarely an issue but with insight-oriented activities the depth, or level of personal significance of activities should be considered. While a therapist cannot know for certain what people are thinking, it is possible to control the emotional impact of discussion/activities to a considerable extent.

If there is limited trust in a group increase the structure of the session to give people a greater sense of security. When people feel secure the therapist is able to make more use of material that arises in the session.

Depth of topics   Lightweight topics are ones with limited emotional impact. In-depth topics focus on people's values and goals, the things that are important to them.

Questions asking for factual information or checking the accuracy of information are generally lightweight, although they do encourage people to go on talking and share more. If you want to keep the level 'light' and someone in the group brings up an emotionally complex topic you might say, 'That's important but I'd rather talk to you about it after the group'. Or be matter-of-fact and accept what the person says but reply, 'That would take too long to explore here. It's important, but in this group we will keep to . . .'

Questions can be used to increase the degree of emotional significance of a dialogue. Leading questions invite people to examine a particular point in greater depth. Therapists choose the potential direction of discussion through the questions they put. Questions may be about facts or feelings or a combination of both.

Evocative questions, such as 'How did you feel about that?' or 'You seem happy about that?' draw out the personal significance of an event for the person. 'Why?' questions go further and ask for explanations of feelings or discrepancies in information in a way that is confronting. They challenge people's beliefs and values. 'You say . . . but you look as though you feel . . . ?' Therapists have a responsibility for the emotional security and comfort of each person but they also have a responsibility for the person's growth. Unless insight-oriented activities prompt active exploration of what people say and do they will be of little use. Confrontation involves stating what you see and what you think it means — and repeating the statement if necessary. It should have a matter-of-fact tone and the obvious intention of clarifying actions and feelings.

Feedback: guidelines for group members   Guidelines about the type of comment and feedback that are useful can be worth discussing with the group. Outline the effects of 'I', 'You' and 'We' statements and the principles of feedback and praise. The overriding concern is to make the comments helpful. Built into this concern, in insight-oriented groups, is an assumption that everyone has the inner strength and the resources to solve his or her own problems.

Another basic assumption is that people usually judge themselves more harshly than is realistic, so they need support for their strengths rather than criticism of their weaknesses. Focus on what is going well — this provides a foundation to build on.

Giving support   There are a number of ways to provide support for people who become distressed in a group session, and it is usually helpful if the group can share in offering it.

Some statements help people acknowledge that what they feel is part of our common humanity. For example, 'Anyone would feel... if that happened to them', or 'It's really ... when ... happens.'

Or the therapist, by stating his or her own feelings, can role model a type of comment others can add to. 'I'm concerned about...' 'That really upsets me. I feel... What do you feel Jim? Anne?'

If people in the group offer advice, 'She should ...' or make judgmental statements of the 'You've only got yourself to blame' type the therapist can say, 'Tell her what you feel. "I'm" ...' (look expectantly at speaker) or, interpret the statement, 'You're saying you feel sad (upset, angry) because ... ?'

The aim is to help people express their feelings constructively rather than to speak for them. Both the person making the comment and the person it is directed to are likely to appreciate this assistance.

After strong feelings have been expressed it is sometimes useful to speak on behalf of the group by asking something like, 'Can you accept our help (comfort, assurance)', 'Is there someone in the group you would like to help you?', or, 'Is there someone you would like to spend some time with you?'

At other times it is more realistic to acknowledge how people are feeling in a matter-of-fact way, then help them and the group move on. You could say: 'Do you feel able to carry on with the activity or would you like some time out?', or 'We'll carry on. Join in again when you feel ready', or 'That's important (upsetting, alarming), but I'd rather talk about it after the group.'

Role reversal is another possibility. Ask, 'What advice would you give yourself now if you were your own good friend?'

Physical contact can help. Put your arm round someone who is upset if you judge that he or she will accept this type of comfort. This conveys a willingness to 'be with' the person (a pat on the arm or shoulder is more likely to seem placating or imply limited caring). The contact can come from someone else in the group but you should monitor its appropriateness.

When you restart on material/the activities of the session, remind everyone where they were up to.

Self-disclosure   Self-disclosure is something novice therapists can find difficult. They may find themselves saying things about their personal lives which, in retrospect, they would have preferred to keep to themselves. To guard against this, keep disclosures general. For example, 'I felt... when someone close to me was angry with me too.' Avoid giving details of the event and the people involved.

Occasionally a personal incident is worth telling but it is a mistake to do this if it amounts to a request for help or takes the focus off the people the group is designed to serve. It is important to be aware of your feelings and to only share personal experiences when they can help the group. Such disclosures may help the group understand why you think or act in a particular way. After a personal comment make sure the focus of attention goes back to the group; direct a question to them or invite comments that generalize from your specific example. For example, 'Has anyone else experienced a situation like that?'

In summary, relax and offer yourself as a human being with feelings and good sense. Observe your group and see what they have to teach you.

2 | *Practical Planning*

Careful planning enables you to get the most out of an activity.

The setting or environment   The setting for a session makes a difference to the way people respond. In the widest sense, the tone of a setting includes the physical nature of the setting, the furnishings, the materials and equipment available, and the people, their attitudes and relationships. A rundown, uncared-for room can suggest that the activities which happen in it are not really important. A radio playing may be a distraction. Such details influence people's expectations of the session and their feelings about its significance.

If people have to work in a room that is too small they will feel cramped and cooped up. On the other hand, a room that is too large will not give a sense of privacy and security and the group will be less likely to develop cohesiveness. The need for privacy (physical or psychological) varies with individuals or groups and the type of session. (For example, in drama activities people will feel happier to 'let their hair down' if no one's looking through the window. In social skills groups a phone is an intrusion.) A 'comfortable' environment means that there is a good match between the activity and the setting people have to do it in.

People also need a secure place to put their belongings so that they will not worry about their bags and coats or what happens to things they make.

Seating arrangements   Seating arrangements can make a critical difference to both group and individual activities and it is usually something that the therapist has control over. Get to your venue in time to arrange things the way you want them — or make this the first task for the group. Consider the space, the people and the activity and make the combination work as well as possible for the group.

For most group work a close circle is good because everyone can see and talk to everyone else and there is no status position. (Avoid sitting where the teacher would sit if the room were a classroom.) For talks, a close semi-circle with those taking the lead in the centre is probably the best arrangement. When rows of seats are needed, try to angle them so that each row faces towards the centre, thus giving a feeling of focus. How

How does seating affect a group?

easy is it going to be for people to see? Get in and out of the seating?

As therapist do you want to sit as one of group? Stand? Sit separately? Sit on a high stool? Each choice creates a different kind of relationship with the group.

In one-to-one situations look at the effects of sitting opposite the other person, at an angle, or side by side. What facilities will you be sharing? A desk? A coffee table? A counter top? Make them useful to you rather than a barrier. (Occasionally, when working with people who are aggressive and disturbed, a barrier may be an advantage.) How can you make best use of a window? Generally, it is more comfortable to sit one either side of it than have one person with their back to the light and the other facing it.

Sometimes you may prefer to have a group sit close together round one table rather than spread out over two. Make definite decisions about your arrangement — they should only be left to chance when the arrangements will make no difference.

Materials   The materials you offer should be of reasonable quality. This does not mean to say that there is no place for practice materials or for being economical in activities where the process of the activity is more important than the end product. However, carefully cut newsprint is better than roughly torn paper, large-sized crayons are better than stubs and strong coloured paints that can be mixed for tones are better than muddy or insipid colours.

Time   Time is an important consideration in planning activities. It includes deciding how long is needed to complete an activity satisfactorily and how to break a long session into sections to suit people's concentration span. When an activity is in progress watch for restlessness and arrange some kind of break when it occurs.

Many kinds of devices and opportunities can be used to introduce variety into an over-long session. Possibilities are breaks for a drink or stretch and getting people to move about and collect their own materials rather than passing them out. Blocks of information-giving can be divided into short units and interspersed between activities, role plays and so on.

Other considerations   As well as the above, location, access, facilities, storage, lighting, heating and kitchen and bathroom facilities should all be checked for suitability.

3 | *Teaching and Learning*

The roles of therapist and teacher overlap. In general, therapy aims to alter people's state of health while teaching aims to impart skills and information. Both are concerned with changing attitudes and, in the longer term, behaviour.

Occupational therapists make extensive use of activities. They are used both for their intrinsic value and as a method of teaching and illustrating concepts.

Assessing Values and Existing Knowledge

A teacher must know the people he or she is teaching. What do they value? What knowledge and skills do they have already? Values, knowledge and skills are the foundations on which new learning is built. They are also a potential resource for a group.

How do you find out what people know and value? Usually through discussion, observation and assessment tests. Sometimes, values-oriented awareness activities or games will clarify people's previous experiences and interests.

What to Teach

- Start with something familiar, then add new material to stimulate curiosity.
- Explore new ideas one at a time, breaking information into logical chunks.
- Link new ideas to existing knowledge. This linking is especially important with adults. It speeds learning and people find it easier to reason and question when they see the similarities and differences between 'old' and 'new' information.
- Teach whatever will be most useful first. If two things overlap, start with what is more common or simple. There is a problem with teaching closely related information — people get similar ideas muddled and the 'learning burden' is higher than when the information is given at separate times.

Barriers to Learning

Attitudes People's attitudes can be a problem. Are they used to learning new skills? Are they worried about working with strangers or unfamiliar materials, coping with disability, lack of time or resources, a classroom situation? Time spent assessing problems and giving people support as they start is well worthwhile. Ideally, each person should feel that what they are being offered is relevant to them, and that it is within their ability to learn it. Once people have made a start the best motivator is a sense of getting somewhere, of making progress.

Emotional and socio-cultural attitudes People's backgrounds can inhibit learning. Examples of inhibiting attitudes are, 'I can't do this', 'Men shouldn't have to do this' or 'They're better than me'. Similarly, socio-cultural perceptions like, 'Our people do it differently' or a sense of not belonging in a group can make it less likely that learning will take place. Mild anxiety stimulates learning but too much will prevent people from thinking clearly; people learn best when they feel at ease. (See *WORKING IN GROUPS, Potential problems and how to avoid them* p. 214.)

Competition Competition is a poor motivator unless it is against time or oneself. However, competition can have a place within a group as long as the teacher is able to make people feel that by competing everyone has learned more and done well.

Good conditions for learning Good physical conditions make a difference. Avoid an environment with distractions (noise, other activities nearby) and make sure people can see and hear. Things like hard chairs and cold or over-hot rooms are also potential sources of distraction, as well as being physically uncomfortable. Avoid a schoolroom atmosphere with adult learners.

The environment helps form people's expectations of the session. As a teacher, think about how the people you are teaching are likely to react to a traditional classroom atmosphere, a workshop setting, a circle of chairs, floor cushions for a discussion, an outdoor activity and so on.

How to Involve the Learner

People are motivated to learn when they know they need particular skills or information. Timing is the key — people learn best when they are ready to learn and the skills seem attainable.

When people set their own learning goals they are usually more committed to reaching them. Plan with the learner a logical succession of sub-goals so that they have a sense of achievement as each is mastered.

Encourage people to try things out, ask questions and experiment with ideas, physically and verbally. People are then more likely to remember what they have learnt. They are also more likely to act on solutions which they have generated themselves.

Learning depends on the time the learner puts in and the effort he or she makes to retain ideas. These two factors — time spent and effort made — are the best predictors of successful learning.

Do not assume that people learn by osmosis, that is, by simply 'picking up' information. Concepts should be made explicit and learners actively encouraged to test new ideas. Promote 'deep processing' of information, that is, real thought and effort. Activities in which people put the information to use are good for this. Having to show or tell others what they have learnt also forces people to actively get to grips with the subject and think about it. Written assignments have the same effect.

Novelty, surprise, success, rewards, good visual materials and vivid examples all make learning easier.

Planning and Presentation

How much should you cover at one time? What rate of learning is it reasonable to expect? Teachers assess a person's capacity to learn on the basis of abilities. Assessment should enable you to set realistic goals. What will people know or be able to do after each session? To what standard? Under what circumstances and conditions?

Good teaching, whether it is five minutes on how to scramble eggs or sixty minutes on preparing a resume, begins with an explanation of the broad aims of the session and an overview of what is to follow. It may describe how this activity/topic relates to what is already familiar.

Aim to get basic principles and methods across accurately from the beginning. If people miss an early point, or misunderstand it, it can be difficult to correct wrong assumptions or habits later; anticipating problems is the best way to avoid them. Clarify any terms that are likely to be new and if possible write them up somewhere so that people can see how they are spelled and refer back to them if necessary.

A teaching session should cover just two to four main points or physical techniques. Facts need to be up-to-date, relevant and described in language the learner will understand. Skills must be demonstrated clearly.

Aim to keep people working hard for limited periods only. Twenty minutes is the maximum for full concentration and in a therapeutic situation somewhere between three and ten minutes is often preferable. Three short sessions are better than one long one. Let people move at their own pace, as slowly or as rapidly as they need to, but push them supportively forward if you think they could attempt more. Factual information should be interspersed with other kinds of learning experiences.

Offering people too little leads to boredom but in treatment settings the problem is often the reverse. The therapist, acutely aware that people need to be discharged as quickly as possible, attempts to cover too much in a very short time.

There are at least three good reasons for teaching only a few ideas/skills at one time.

- First, it is much better for people to understand a few ideas well than many at a superficial level. Information that is only partly understood is likely to lead to incorrect assumptions. (How many trainee health professionals self-diagnose imaginary diseases early in their education?)
- Second, when people are pushed to learn too much too quickly, they are made acutely aware of their limitations. The amount still to be learnt then seems more daunting.
- And third, people who are coping with disability or change are often grieving or depressed. Their ability to learn is reduced. Keep the focus on their strengths and the progress they are making rather than on gaps in knowledge or skills.

The teacher can check if the amount of new learning is reasonable by asking people if they are happy about what they are being offered or by asking them questions that will indicate how well they understand the ideas. Read their body language and listen to the level and content of their questions.

Repetition and Reinforcement

At the end of the session concepts should be summarized so that people have an overview of what was covered and how the parts fitted together. Link the information to people's lives, to previously taught information and to practical skills.

Integrating new information takes time. People need opportunities to make use of an idea or to repeat skills in different but related situations. Practice is an essential part of learning — if people 'over-learn' they are more likely to remember.

At the end of a session discuss problems and accomplishments. Were the goals met? What comes next? Reinforce learning by getting people to carry out a task before the next session. This can also prepare them for the next session.

Variety in Teaching Methods

Repeat information in as many ways as possible; visual, written and spoken. Reinforce ideas through trial runs, simulations and role play. Use as many senses as possible — the more ways in which information is presented, the more likely it is to 'reach' the learner. It will also make it easier to use the new skills/knowledge in a variety of situations.

In the body of the session, factual information should be interspersed with demonstration, activities, role play, examples, discussion and visual aids. These techniques bring teaching to life. In order of effectiveness, the best ways to get information across are: real experience, contrived experiences and activities (including role play), demonstrations, exhibitions, films/

videos, samples/pictures, examples, the written word and the spoken word.

If a group or individual looks tired or unresponsive, make your explanation time as brief as possible and move on to activities.

Role play   In role play people try out interactions and practise explaining what they think. It helps them see their alternatives and understand other people's reactions. As well as being a verbal rehearsal, a role play can be a trial run of an activity, such as giving a talk. In other activities, it can be worthwhile having a 'dry run' or 'walking through' the activity before using the real materials or equipment. (See *DRAMA, Role play* p. 48.)

Examples   Use examples that learners can relate to and understand. Make them brief, appropriate and memorable.

Visual aids   As people learn more through sight than any other sense, visual material should be part of any teaching situation. Any visual prop on which to base thinking makes remembering concepts easier.

Visual aids are anything pictorial or diagrammatic. They can be simple line drawings on a handout sheet, drawings on a blackboard, pictures pasted on card, posters, bulletin boards or photographs. Visual aids used to put across a particular point should be clearly relevant, not just decorative. A caption or title may be needed.

With overhead transparencies and charts the 'rule of sevens' is useful. It suggests, 'Seven lines of script with seven words per line, seven millimetres high' for each overhead. A bold, one-word or wholly pictorial transparency

Overhead transparencies

can also be effective. Use lined paper under the transparency so that the lines of script are level and the lettering consistent. (With computer-generated transparencies this is not a problem!) Give the transparency an explanatory heading and aim for simple, accurate wording. Avoid cluttered layouts.

If you lack confidence in your ability to draw, decorate your transparencies with ruled lines, perhaps in a different colour to the text. Check how well the colours show on the overhead screen. 'Collect' effective techniques you see on others' transparencies.

Other visual aids are resource books, films, slides and videotapes. Preview films and videos to avoid showing something inappropriate.

Written handouts   These should be brief, clear and to the point, well laid out and illustrated if possible. (See DRAMA, Role play p. 48 and VERBAL ACTIVITIES, Discussion in teaching and learning p. 139.)

Choosing a Teaching Approach

The traditional lesson and student-teacher relationship probably works best with groups which have some of the skills of students (note-taking, questioning skills, willingness to read round topics). In this kind of situation learners need to be well-motivated, recognize the teacher's expertise and prefer the information to be presented as a lesson. Such an approach is best suited to information giving. It can complement written material, practical skills or attitudinal learning.

Attitudes in teachers   Some teachers focus primarily on the content of what they are teaching. While content is important, a learner-centred attitude — a willingness to be flexible and respond to the learner's needs — is generally better. Learner-centred teachers adapt to the learner's needs — they slow down, speed up, change from theory to activity and so on, as the situation demands.

In a group a teacher is a role model and resource. He or she encourages, cajoles, limits, refocuses, challenges and offers choices.

Two well-known formulae which can help teachers make realistic plans are the traditional ACME formula, aims, content, method and evaluation, and dividing material into 'must know, should know, could know' to establish an order of priority.

4 | *Assessment*

Confidence as a therapist depends on planning — and planning starts with assessment. Assessments identify problems, issues, constraints and resources. They should also indicate which types of intervention, teaching and activities people will find relevant and enjoyable. As well, they provide a baseline for measuring progress.

Assessment starts from what is already known about the person's needs and abilities and what you are able offer in terms of time, resources and approach. The therapeutic model likely to be used is relevant to the choice of assessment.

Assessments can focus on the routine activities of daily life: work, self-care, leisure and education. Or, they can focus on a combination of abilities, attitudes and practical constraints:

- Physical, sensory and intellectual capacities and limitations.
- Relationship skills and group participation skills.
- Practical and intellectual skills and education.
- Values, attitudes, motivation, habits, self-esteem and self-concept.
- Roles, family situation, lifestyle, social networks, living arrangements, financial constraints/situation, means of transport.

What important skills has the person never acquired or what skills have they lost or stopped using? In what ways are they unable to meet their own needs or solve their own problems? As well as giving a full picture of problems and needs, assessment should describe the person's strengths, assets and resources.

Information from existing medical records is often a starting point for assessment or can be used to supplement it. Existing records are likely to contain information about the reasons for a person being in a healthcare setting, and other health professionals' expectations and plans for them. They may indicate contraindications and precautions which need to be observed. Medical prognosis and the environment the patient is expected to return to are usually significant for interpreting assessment data.

People can be assessed in many ways. Each assessment method or test gives different types of information and requires different skills of the therapist. The following are the three most common assessment methods.

Observation Plan what you will look for. Main points are: general appearance, medical signs and symptoms, posture, speech, expression, memory, concentration span and attitudes.

Observation is not just what can be seen or heard directly. Useful information can be gathered in various ways. This is a continuous process and every new encounter with the person will add to the assessment data. Setting up specific tasks or situations to observe people's skills and abilities can be done on an informal basis or using a published assessment test. Tasks can be as simple as having a cup of tea with others or they can examine very specific skills.

There are two parts to observation: the objective things that were seen heard, smelt or felt and the interpretation of these observations. Interpretation is based on knowledge and experience. Conclusions can and often should be checked with the person, their family and friends, other health professionals and so on.

Observation is also a basic skill in activities-based therapy — it tells you what is working and what should be changed.

Informal and formal interviews Interviews are useful for getting the patient's view of their situation (their problems, needs and goals) and information about their motivation, interests and expectations.

Interviews are a means of both giving and getting information. As well as acquiring information expect to explain what you are able to offer and the limits of your service.

Assessment tests Which test is likely to give the most useful information? A good test enables the therapist to explore a specific area in depth. Choose tests which relate to what is already known about the person — it is only possible to carry out a certain number.

Activity configurations can provide useful information for planning activities.

Assessment of groups Therapists need to be able to assess groups. They can be assessed in a number of ways: the level the group operates at, the balance between group relationships and task skills, the patterns of interaction, age range, norms, goals and expectations.

Outcome evaluation Measuring the outcomes of therapy is an important part of professional accountability. When outcome evaluation is based on sound initial and ongoing assessment its meaning and relevance will be clear.

Activities help define progress and clarify further goals.

5 | *Recording Information*

After a session, it is important to record information so that you can remember what happened and assess outcomes. Recorded information enables someone else to work with a group or individual more easily. It is an invaluable resource when a report must be written. Records are useful for training sessions and research. They allow professionals to monitor the quality of their service and claim reimbursement. In most institutions keeping records is a legal requirement.

A record entry should be in language suited to its readers, well organized, physically easy to read, precise and factual. Headings and subheadings help the reader find key information quickly. Any record should be dated and signed.

A list of items which it may be appropriate to record after a group activity follows. For more formal report writing it is important to be familiar with standardized terminology and systems of reporting.

Basic data The type of group, the date, the number present and their names, the age range, the length of the session, a breakdown of how the time was spent, the equipment and resources used, the location and its relevant characteristics.

Goals and aims The long- and short-term goals/aims of the session (physical, intellectual, sensory, social/emotional).

Content Skills or information taught, description of any end product, description or list of specific activities.

Relationships The mood of the group, the depth of interactions, individual responses (significant statements and non-verbal communication). The style of the group: social, educational, supportive, energetic and so on.

Leadership The leadership style used and the roles taken by therapist and co-therapist, the main methods and procedures used, the contribution of a visiting speaker, any unfinished business.

Reports on individuals To what extent were therapeutic goals met? Should goals be reviewed? Information that adds to or updates assessment data.

Problems and potential problems The nature of the problem, its causes, how it was solved. Precautions observed. Ways in which the activity was graded or adapted. Limitations of the activity.

Plans Follow-up? Things that should be changed if the session were repeated.

Practical matters Transport arrangements, materials used, sources of bought or borrowed equipment, books and samples used.

Signature and date

Bibliography

Key

AAA — *Activities, Adaptation and Aging*, The Howarth Press, New York.

AOTJ — *Australian Occupational Therapy Journal*, Australian Occupational Therapy Association

AJOT — *American Journal of Occupational Therapy*, The American Occupational Therapy Association, Rockville.

BJOT — *British Journal of Occupational Therapy*, The British Occupational Therapy Association, London.

CJOT — *Canadian Journal of Occupational Therapy*, (*Revue Canadienne d'Ergotherapie*), The Canadian Occupational Therapy Association, Toronto.

OTMH — *Occupational Therapy in Mental Health*, The Howarth Press, New York.

OTHC — *Occupational Therapy in Health Care*, The Howarth Press, New York.

Part I — The Activities

1. Activities as Therapy

Early, M. B. *Mental Health Concepts and Techniques for the Occupational Therapy Assistant*, Raven Press, New York, 1987

Hopkins, H. L. Smith, H. D. *Willard and Spackman's Occupational Therapy*, 7th ed, Lippincott, Philadelphia, 1988

Jennings, S. (ed.) *Creative Therapy*, 2nd ed. Kemple Press, Banbury, 1983

Kielhofner, G. *Health Through Occupation, Theory and Practice In Occupational Therapy*, F. A. Davie Co., Philadelphia, 1983

Kielhofner, G. (ed.) *A Model of Human Occupation: Theory and Application*, Williams and Wilkins, Baltimore, 1985

Mosey, A. C. *Psychosocial Components of Occupational Therapy*, New York, Raven Press, 1986

Purtilo, R. *Health Professional/Patient Interaction*, 3rd ed. W. B. Saunders, Philadelphia, 1984

2. Self-awareness Activities

Barrow, I. *Know Your Strengths and Be Confident*, Auckland, Heinemann Books, 1983

Bolles, R. N. *The Three Boxes of Life and How to Get out of Them: An Introduction to Life/Work Planning*, Ten Speed Press, California, 1981

Brandes, D. *The Gamester's Handbook Two: Another Collection of Games for Teachers and Group Workers*, Hutchinson, London, 1984

Forbess-Greene, S. *The Encyclopedia of Icebreakers*, University Associates Inc., 1983

Gawain, S. *The Creative Visualization Workbook*, Whatever Publishing, Mill Valley, California, 1982

Hendricks, S. Wills, R. *The Second Centring Book, Awareness Activities for Children, Parents and Teachers*, Prentice-Hall, New Jersey, 1975

Howe, M. A. *Imagining*, Spiral, Victoria, Australia, 1986

Pfeiffer, J. W. Jones, J. E. (eds) *A Handbook of Structured Experiences for Human Relations Training*, University Associates Publisher and Consultants, California, 1974–85

Posthuma, B. W. *Small Groups in Therapy Settings: Process and Leadership*, Little Brown, Boston, 1989

Remocker, A. J. Storch, E. T. *Action Speaks Louder: A Handbook of Non-verbal Group Techniques*, 4th ed, Churchill Livingstone, Edinburgh, 1987

Rider, B. B. Gramblin, J. T. *The Activity Card File*, Michigan, Fred Sammons, Illinois, 1981

Satir, V. *The New People Making*, Science and Behaviour Books, California, 1988

Simon, S. B. Howe, L. W. Kirschbaum, H. *Values Clarification, A Handbook of Practical Strategies for Teachers and Students*, Dodd, Mead Co., New York, 1972

Stevens, J. O. *Awareness: Exploring, Experimenting*, Bantam Books, New York, 1973

Weiss, J. C. *Expressive Therapy with Elders and the Disabled: Touching the Heart of Life*, The Howarth Press, New York, 1984

3. The Creative Arts

Feder, E. Feder, B. *The Expressive Arts Therapies: Art, Music and Dance as Psychotherapy*, Prentice Hall, Englewood Cliffs, New Jersey, 1981

Jennings, S. (ed.) *Creative Therapy*, 2nd ed., Kemble Press, Banbury, 1983

Lord, G. (ed.) *The Arts and the Disabilities*, McDonald, Edinburgh, 1981

Warren, B. (ed.) *Using the Creative Arts in Therapy*, Croom Helm, London, 1984

Drama

Bailey, C. H. 'Soul Clap Hands and Sing' Living History Theatre as a Process of Creativity, *AAA*, 9:4, 1–43

Blatner, H. A. *Acting-in. Practical Applications of Psychodramatic Methods*, Springfield Publishing, New York, 1973

Corsini, R. J. *Role-Playing in Psychotherapy*, Adline Pubs, Chicago, 1966

Jennings, S. (ed.) *Dramatherapy Theory and Practice for Teachers and Clinicians*, Croom Helm, London, 1986

Johnstone, K. *Impro: Improvisation and the Theatre*, Methuen, London, 1979

Langley, D. M. Langley, G. E. *Dramatherapy and Psychiatry*, Croom Helm, London, 1983

Lee, A. *A Handbook of Creative Dance and Drama: Ideas for Teachers*, Longman Cheshire, Melbourne, 1985

Shaw, M. E. Corsini, R. J. Blake, R. R. Mouton, J. S. *Role Playing: A Practical Manual for Group Facilitators*, California, University Associates, 1980

Art

Dalley, T. (ed.) *Art as Therapy: An Introduction to the Use of Art as a Therapeutic Technique*, Tavistock Pubs, London/New York, 1984

Edwards, B. *Drawing on the Right Side of the Brain*, Fontana Collins, London, 1979

Hughes, J. Art in Psychosocial Occupational Therapy: Guidelines for Use and an Art Exercises Battery, *AOTJ*, 36:1, 14–23

Keightly, M. *Investigating Art, A Practical Guide For Young People*, The Garden City Press, London, 1976

Leibmann, M. F. *Art Therapy for Groups; A Handbook of Themes*, Croom Helm, London, 1986

Rhyne, J. *The Gestalt Art Experience*, Brooks/Cole, California, 1973

Robertson, E. The Role of the Occupational Therapist in a Psychotherapeutic Setting, *BJOT*, 84:3, 106–110

Dance

Lee, A. *A Handbook of Creative Dance and Drama: Ideas for Teachers*, Longman Cheshire, Melbourne, 1985

Wilks, J. *Better Contemporary Dance*, Kaye & Ward, London, 1981

Music

Bennett, S. L. Maas, F. The Effect of Music-Based Life Review on the Life Satisfaction and Ego Integrity of Elderly People, *BJOT*, 51:12, 433–436

Ben-Tovim, A. *Children and Music*, A&C Black, London, 1979

Bright, R. *Music in Geriatric Care*, Angus and Robertson, Sydney, 1972

Gaston, E. (ed.) *Music in Therapy*, Macmillan, New York, 1968

Karris, B. Music and Reminiscence for Groups and Individuals, *AAA*, 10:1/2, 79–96

McCloskey, L. J. Music and the Frail Elderly, *AAA*, 7:2, 73–75

Munro, S. *Music Therapy in Palliative/Hospice Care*, Magnamusic-Baton, St Louis, 1974

Sacks, O. *The Man Who Mistook His Wife for a Hat*, Summit Books, New York, 1986

Schulberg, C. H. *The Music Therapy Source Book*, Human Sciences Press, New York, 1981

Creative Writing

Coberly, L. M. McCormick, J. Updike, K. *Writers Have No Age: Creative Writing With Older Adults*, Howarth Press, New York, 1984

Dynes, R. Using Creative Writing, *BJOT*, 52:4, 151

Foster, L. Writer's Workshop, the Word Processor and the Psychiatric Patient, *BJOT*, 51:6, 191–192

Moss, G. *Getting Your Ideas Across: A Handbook to Improve Your Listening, Speaking and Meeting Skills*, Moss Associates, Wellington, 1988

Peck, C. F. From Deep Within: Poetry Workshops in Nursing Homes, *AAA*, 13:3

Strunk, W. White, E. B. *The Elements of Style*, Macmillan, New York, 1979

Verbal Activities

Holmes, T. H. Rahe, R. H. Stress Rating Scale, *Journal of Psychiatric Research*, 11, 1967

Klippel, F. *Keep Talking: Communicative Fluency Activities for Language Teachers*, Cambridge University Press, United Kingdom, 1983

Martin, J. M. Expanding Reminiscence Therapy with Elderly Mentally Infirm Patients, *BJOT*, 52:11, 435

Michael, N. *How to Say What You Mean: A Guide to Effective Communication for People at Work*, Reed/Methuen, Auckland, 1988

Milburn, J. D. *Handbook for Public Speakers*, Price Milburn, Wellington, 1976

Moss, G. *Ways With Words*, Government Printer, New Zealand, 1976

Moss, G. *Getting Your Ideas Across: A Handbook to Improve Your Listening, Speaking and Meeting Skills*, Moss Associates, Wellington, 1988

Pinder, T. H. Effective Speaking for All Occasions: (1) The 'What' and 'How' of Speaking, *BJOT*, 2, 57–58; (2) The 'Eyes' Have It!, *BJOT*, 3, 95; (3) How to Run Successful Meetings, *BJOT*, 5, 162

Stock, G. *The Book of Questions*, Workman, New York, 1987

Ur, P. *Discussions that Work*, Cambridge University Press, United Kingdom, 1981

4. Communication Skills

Argyle, M. Trower, P. *Person to Person: Ways of Communicating*, Harper and Row, New York, 1979

Bolton, R. *People Skills*, Prentice Hall, New Jersey, 1979

Bower, S. Bower, G. *Asserting Yourself, A Practical Guide for Positive Change*, Addison-Wesley, Massachussetts, 1975

Manthie, M. *Positively Me: An Assertive Training Guide*, Methuen, Wellington, 1979

Peck, C. Hong, C. S. *Living Skills for Mentally Handicapped People*, Croom Helm, London, 1988

Posthuma, B. W. *Small Groups in Therapy Settings: Process and Leadership*, Little Brown, Boston, 1989

Scott, D. W. Katz, N. *Occupational Therapy in Mental Health: Perspectives in Psychiatry*, Taylor Francis, London, 1988

Trower, P. Bryant, B. Argyle, M. *Social Skills and Mental Health*, Methuen, London, 1978

Zelik, L. L. The Use of Assertiveness Training with Chronic Pain Patients, *OTHC*, 1:3

5. Relaxation and Massage

Benson, H. *The Relaxation Response*, William Morrow, USA, 1975

Bright, R. *Music in Geriatric Care*, Angus and Robertson, Sydney, 1972

Brown, B.B. *Stress and the Art of Biofeedback*, 1st ed, Harper and Row, New York, 1977

Coleman, J. C. Life Stress and Maladaptive Behaviour, *AJOT*, 27:4, 169–180

Davis, M. McKay, M. Eshelman, E. R. *The Relaxation and Stress Reduction Workbook*, 2nd ed., New Harbinger Publications, Oakland, California, 1983

Downing, G. *The Massage Book*, Wildwood House Ltd, London, 1973

Giles, G. M. Allen, M. E. Occupational Therapy in the Treatment of the Patient with Chronic Pain, *BJOT*, 49:1, 4–9

Hewitt, J. *The Complete Relaxation Book: A Manual of Eastern and Western Techniques*, Rider, London, 1986

Lidell, L. et al. *The Book of Massage: The Complete Step-by-Step Guide to Eastern and Western Techniques*, Ebury Press, United Kingdom, 1985

Mitchell, L. *Simple Relaxation*, John Murray, Pitman Press, London, 1983

Tubesing, D. A. *Kicking Your Stress Habits — A Do-It-Yourself Guide For Coping With Stress*, Signet Books, New York, 1981

Part II — The Group Setting

1. Working in Groups

Ginott, H. *Between Parent and Child*, Macmillan, New York, 1965

Johnson, D. W. Johnson, F. P. *Reaching Out: Interpersonal Effectiveness and Self-actualization*, 3rd ed, Prentice Hall, New York, 1972

Johnson, D. W. Johnson, F. P. *Joining Together: Group Theory and Group Skills*, Prentice Hall, New Jersey, 1982

Kaplan, K. The Directive Group: Short-Term Treatment for Psychiatric Patients with Minimal Level of Functioning, *AJOT*, 40:7, 474–481

Langley, D. M. Langley, G. E. *Dramatherapy and Psychiatry*, Croom Helm, London, 1983

Mosey, A. C. The Concept and Use of Developmental Groups, *AJOT*, 24:4, 272–275

Posthuma, B. W. *Small Groups in Therapy Settings: Process and Leadership*, Little Brown, London, 1989

Remocker, A. J. Storch, E. T. *Action Speaks Louder: A Handbook of Non-verbal Group Techniques*, 4th ed., Churchill Livingstone, Edinburgh, 1987

Yalom, I.D. *The Theory and Practice of Group Psychotherapy*, Tavistock, London, 1976

2. Practical Planning

Early, M.B. *Mental Health Concepts and Techniques for the Occupational Therapy Assistant*, Raven Press, New York, 1987

Kielhofner, G. (ed.) *A Model of Human Occupation: Theory and Application*, Williams and Wilkins, Baltimore, 1985

3. Teaching and Learning

Braunstein, S. *Motivating Your Patients*, Unpublished Workbook, Central Institute of Technology, Wellington, 1985

Mosey, A. C. *Activities Therapy*, Raven Press, New York, 1973

Moss, G. *The Trainer's Handbook for Managers and Trainers*, Moss Associates, Wellington, 1987

Moss, G. *Getting Your Ideas Across: A Handbook to Improve Your Listening, Speaking and Meeting Skills*, Moss Associates, Wellington, 1988

Zepke, N. Nugent, D. *The Teacher Self-Help Book*, Tutor Publications, Wellington, 1988

4. Assessment

5. Recording Information

Gleave, G. M. Medical Records and Reports in Occupational Therapy, *AJOT*, 14:4, 180–182

Hemphill, B. J. Mental Health Evaluations Used in Occupational Therapy, *AJOT*, 34:11, 721–726

Hemphill, B. J. (ed.) *The Evaluative Process in Psychiatric Occupational Therapy*, Charles B Slack, New Jersey, 1982

Index

Numbers in bold indicate chapters.
An index of activities follows the main index.

Activities Index

244